OUTLOOK: GRIM

The Dead Nasties

OUTLOOK:GRIM

Volume One: The Dead Nasties

written and illustrated by
Black Olive

edited by
John "eagle eyes" Palmer

outlook:grim logo by
Robbie "sweet cheeks" Bolick

guest artist pin-ups by
Jennifer Feinberg
Christopher
Elizabeth Watasin
Logan Hicks
FSc
AttaBoy

Published by SLG Publishing

PRESIDENT & PUBLISHER
Dan Vado

EDITOR-IN-CHIEF
Jennifer de Guzman

DIRECTOR OF SALES
Deb Moskyok

PRODUCTION ASSISTANT
Eleanor Lawson

OPERATIONS
Joe "Big Bopper" Nakamura

SLG Publishing
577 South Market St.,
San Jose, CA 95113

Office: (408) 971-8929
Orders Only: 1-800-866-8929

Outlook:Grim Volume One:
The Dead Nasties collects
issues 1-6 of the SLG
Publishing series *Outlook:Grim*

Special Thx to

   Mom, Dad, Dani, Robbie,
The Ericksons, The Bolicks, Biggie,
 John P, Kim, Joey, Daryll, Rosie,
Jack, Tina, Jim, Chey, Manuel, Sue,
 Torrey, Adam, Marie, Christopher, Melissa,
Ron, Devon D, Woodrow, Logan, Heather,
 Jennifer F, Todd, Elizabeth W, Attaboy, FSc,
 the entire Slave Labor family, Rob at Comickaze,
 Chloe at Reading Frenzy, Kevin at Zanadu II, Dark Delicacies,
 Joe at Atlantis Fantasyworld, Mimi and Al at Night Flight,
Bill at Golden Apple, Hijinx Comics, Ralph at Alternate Reality,
John and Gail at Metropolis, all the hard core O:G fans & all
their hard cores, & everyone who came out to chill with us
                 on The Beastly Book Tour.

Mad Props to

Dan Vado for supporting me & my vision so much ya
put it all in print. Thx times a gazillion.

Jennifer de Guzman for believing in the O:G & pushing
for me. And for kicking serious ass.

Deb Moskyok for keepin' it real homemade cookie-style.

Robbie for all your love, support & inspiration.

John for the countless times you've helped me & for
being such a great pal.

Dear Friends Living and Dead,

Despite what we keep trying to tell ourselves, the world is on the fast track to becoming a terrifying place, and not just because of things that go bump in the night. While this regression is apparent on many levels (global, political, cultural, etc.), we keep hoping and working (and necessarily so) to build the delirious vision of slaphappy goodness crafted in our childhood imaginations. If we deferred more frequently – as children do – to our imaginations, in all their naive and limitless glory, we might live to see truly revolutionary times. For now, we may have to depend on comics.

I realize this might seem like a lofty introduction to the feel-good, spooky humor of Outlook: Grim, but trust me, comrades – it is a dangerous time to be living outside the mainstream as you and I and Wren and Chloe do.

Although comic book artists and fans have always been proudly separate from the masses, we have only recently begun to embrace diversity and alternative voices in our own "comics world." Even still, we have a looooong way to go. So while our first instinct may be – in these post-feminist, post-modern, post-politically-correct times – to think that a female artist making a hilarious book about ghosts starring two spunky, intelligent gals who aren't being sexually exploited is no big whoop, it is! It truly is. I'm impressed, as I hope you are, and I give mad props to Black Olive and Slave Labor for making it happen and to you for reading. And in case you missed it, folks, B.O. wrote, drew, and inked every single panel you are about to read, all by her lonesome. (Well, a ghoul or two may have helped scare her awake under deadlines, but I assure you that no goblin sweatshops were used in the making of this book.)

I've known B. O. since she was a wee olive, her pit barely the size of a rabbit poo (and let me just say – the flashback depiction of young Chloe in her Morrissey t-shirt looks awfully familiar). I always knew she'd go on to do awesome things, but I had no idea it would be in the fantastic art form we all know and love as the comic book.

A beautifully drawn book about supernatural activity featuring razor-sharp wit and nary a whiff of gothic seriousness is pretty damn cool. Throw in our trusty ghostbusters Wren and Chloe, and you're approaching bliss. Wren and Chloe are everyday anti-heroines in many ways. While they're confident and sassy, they're dorky and fearful at the same time. They're the type of gals who can't help but always be themselves, in all their freak-ish glory. This, of course, is a beautiful thing and makes them all the more irresistible. Wren has a frickin' paranormal panty drawer, for crying out loud! How cool is that?! ICE COLD!!

Rest assured that, back in the day, these girls were 100% Grade A geeks and outcasts. They probably weren't the absolute bottom of the barrel, but I'm quite confident that they weren't the first, second, or third ones picked as teammates in P.E. But look at them now! Who wouldn't give their right button nip to be as with it as Wren and Chloe are through an infestation of slimy spirits?

This is a glorious example, and an accurate one. The un-popular folk of yore always grow up to become the coolest cats in town (and I'm not talking about any friends of Mr. Winkles!). Meanwhile, the jocks and cheerleaders always fall out – marry young, gain weight, make vile babies, and become alcoholic EZ-Mart employees faster than you can say, "Go Team!" [Important note for readers who might still be in the nasty throes of the K-12 school system: It gets better! It really does! You too might find Chinese food-munching ghosts oozing out of your underwear drawer one day!!]

Best of all, Wren and Chloe are truly great friends and – like all good friends – rely on each other in order to get through the day (whether Wren would admit it or not). To them, the most important thing is looking out for each other and their loved ones (snails and snot-nosed sisters alike). And, as we each fight our own battles against the ghosties under our beds (and the even scarier ones in the living world), I can't think of anything more revolutionary than that.

With Love,
John Palmer

John Palmer is a Los Angeles based filmmaker, editor, badass, and coconspirator.

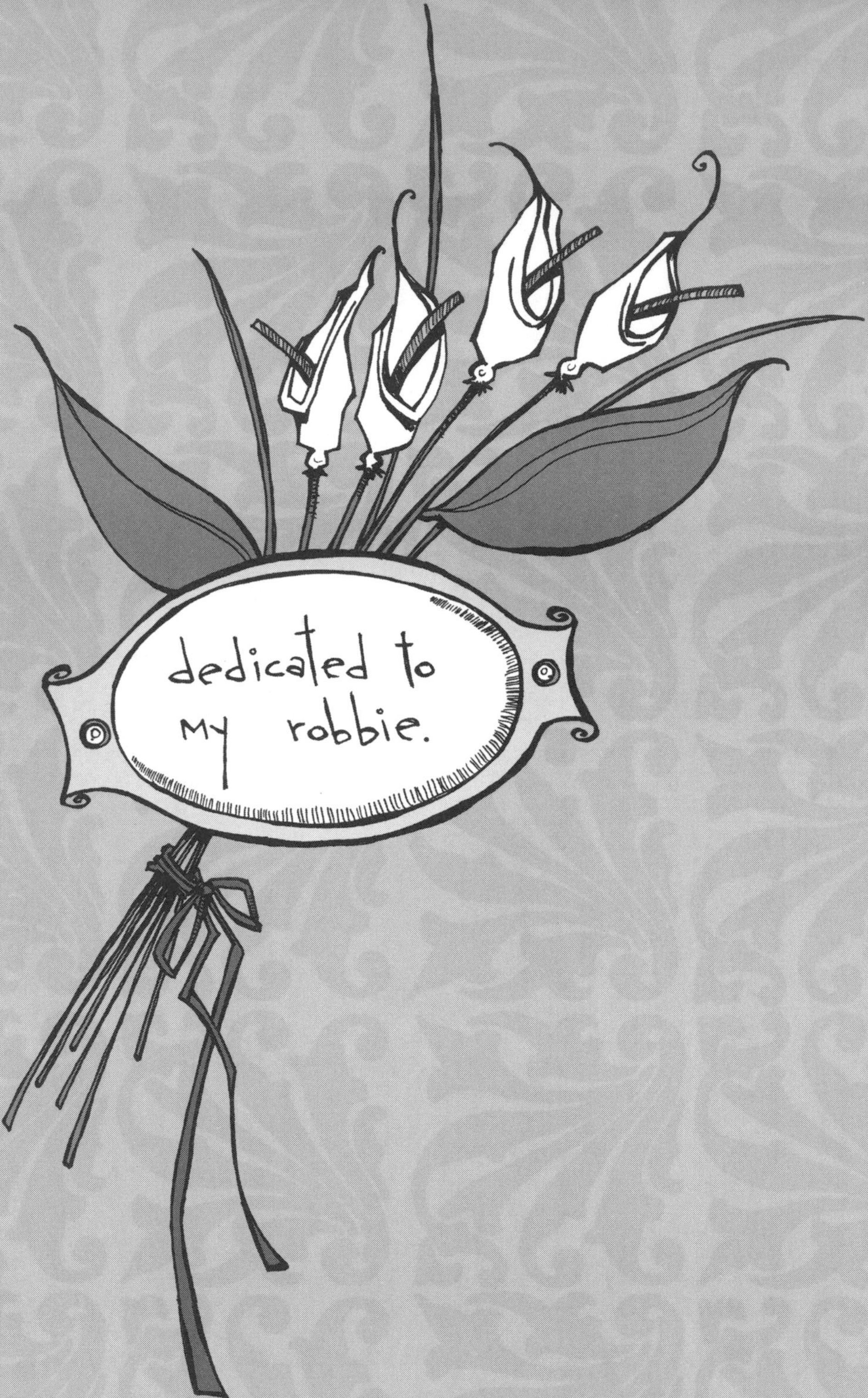
dedicated to
my robbie.

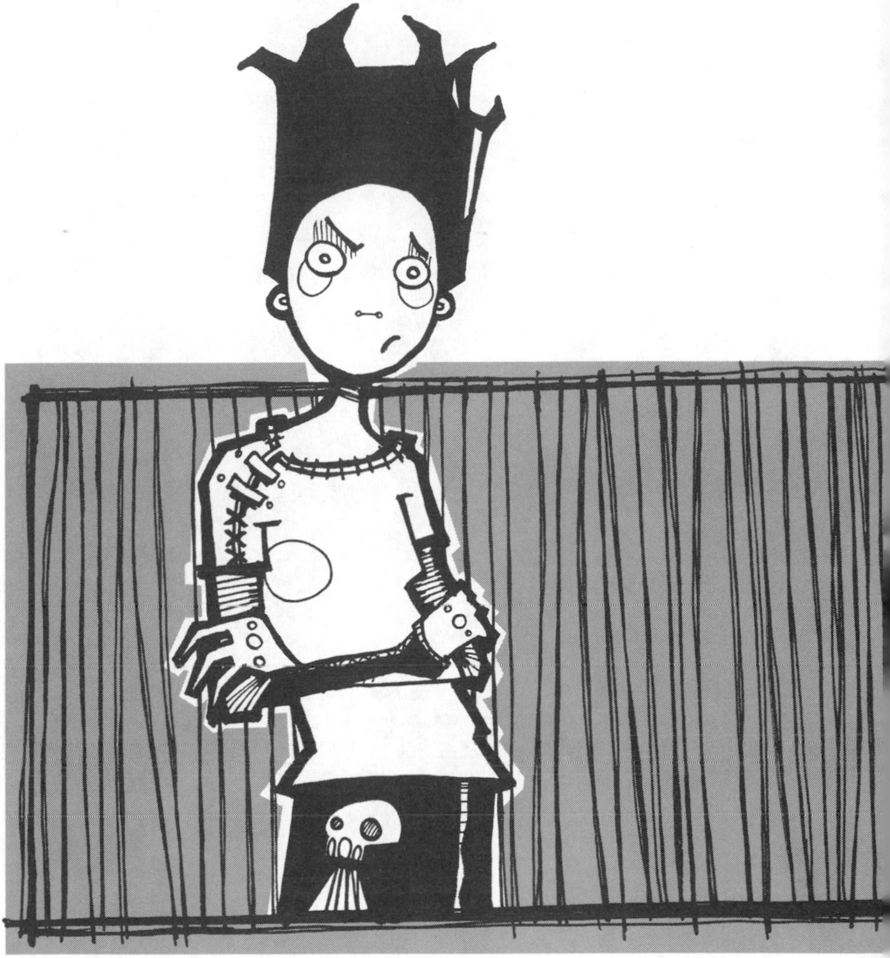

chapter one.

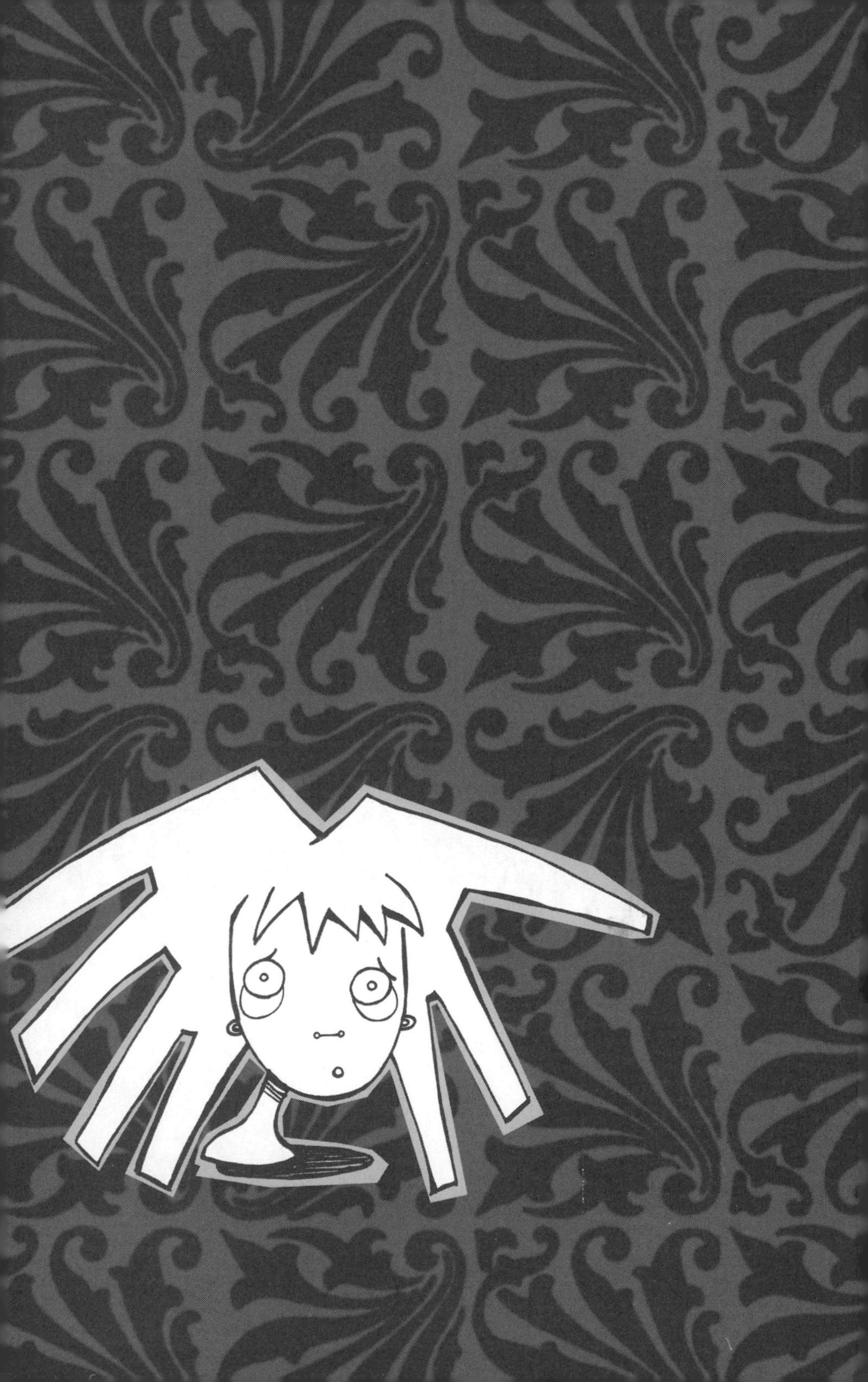

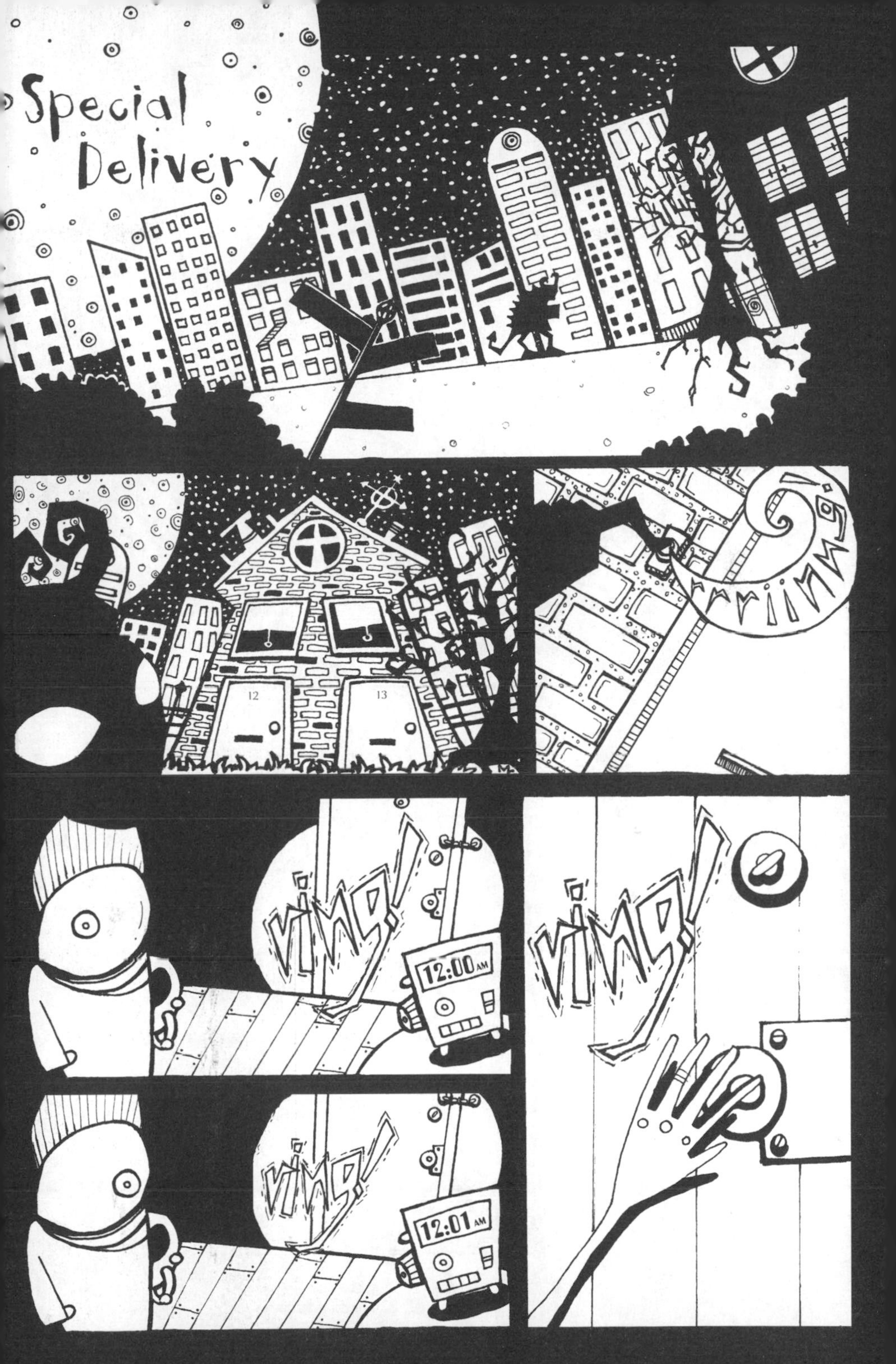

Special Delivery
12
13
rrriinng!
ving!
12:00 AM
ving!
ving!
12:01 AM

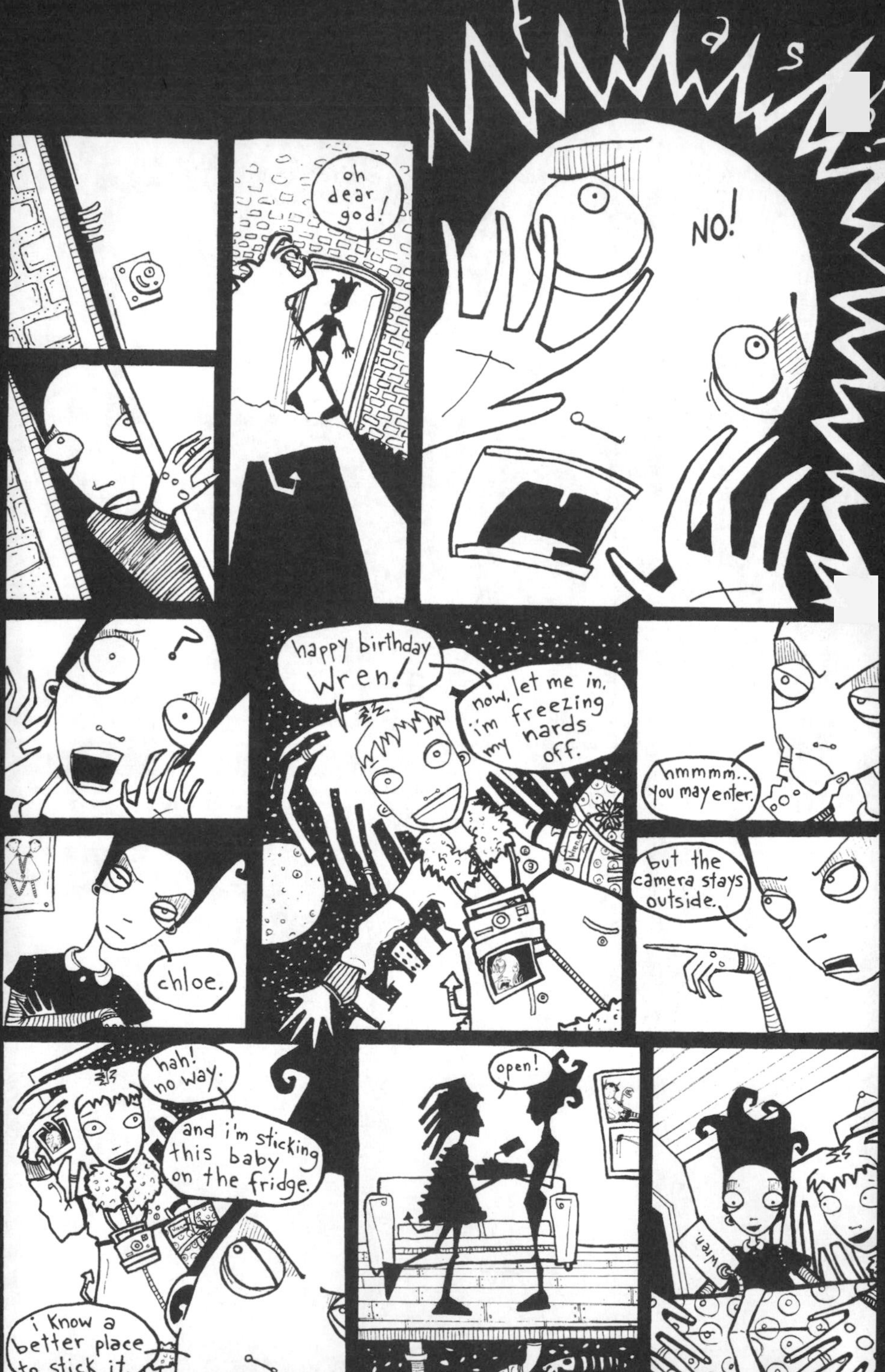
t l a s
oh dear god!
NO!
happy birthday Wren!
now, let me in, i'm freezing my nards off.
hmmmm... you may enter.
chloe.
but the camera stays outside.
hah! no way.
and i'm sticking this baby on the fridge.
i know a better place to stick it.
open!
wren.

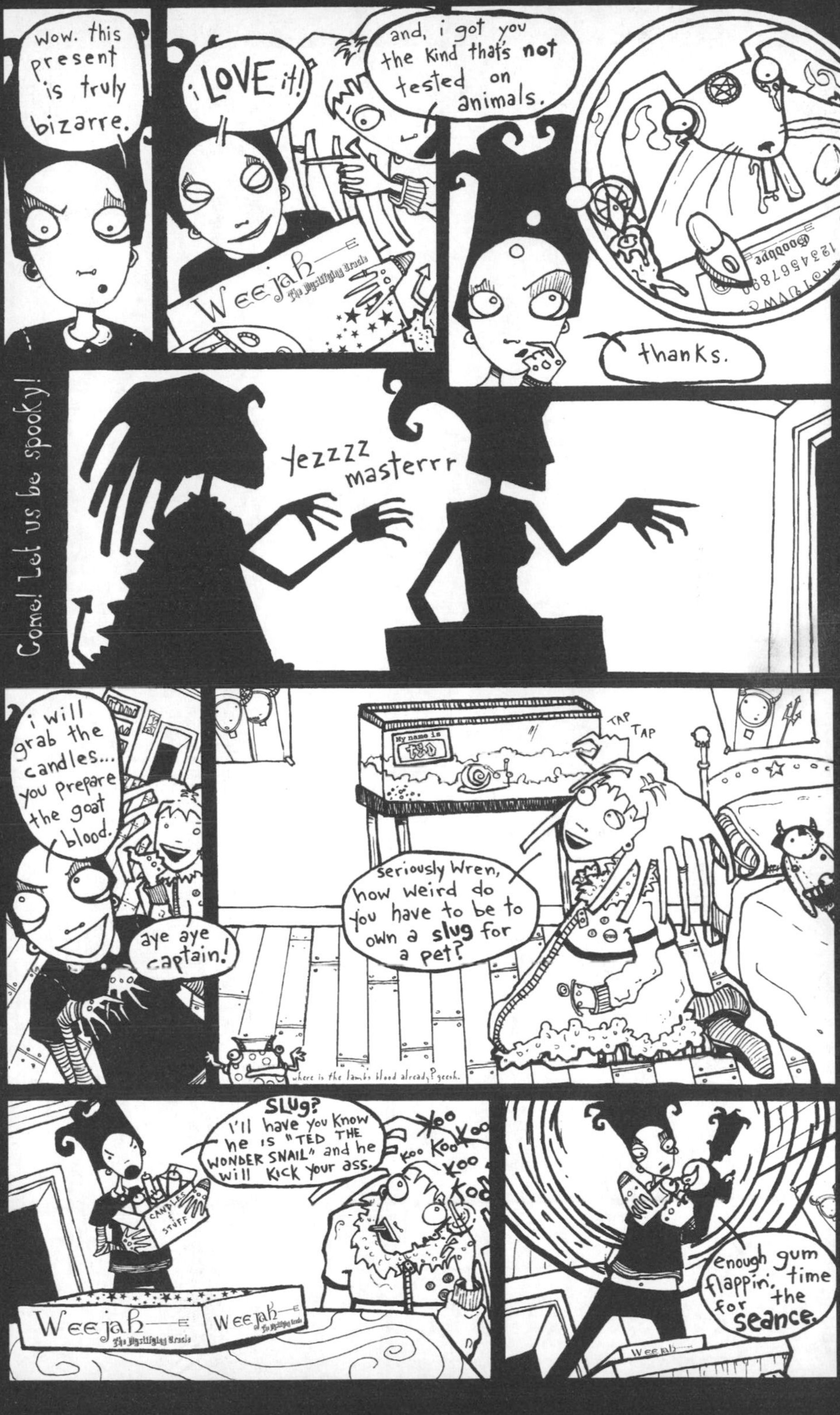
wow. this present is truly bizarre.
¡ LOVE it!
and, i got you the kind that's not tested on animals.
Weejah The Mystifying Oracle
thanks.
Come! Let us be spooky!
yezzzz masterrr
i will grab the candles... you prepare the goat blood.
aye aye captain!
My name is TED
TAP TAP
seriously Wren, how weird do you have to be to own a slug for a pet?
where is the lamb's blood already? geesh.
SLUG? I'll have you know he is "TED THE WONDER SNAIL" and he will kick your ass.
KOO KOO KOO KOO KOO
CANDLES & STUFF
Weejah The Mystifying Oracle
Weejah The Mystifying Oracle
enough gum flappin', time for the seance.

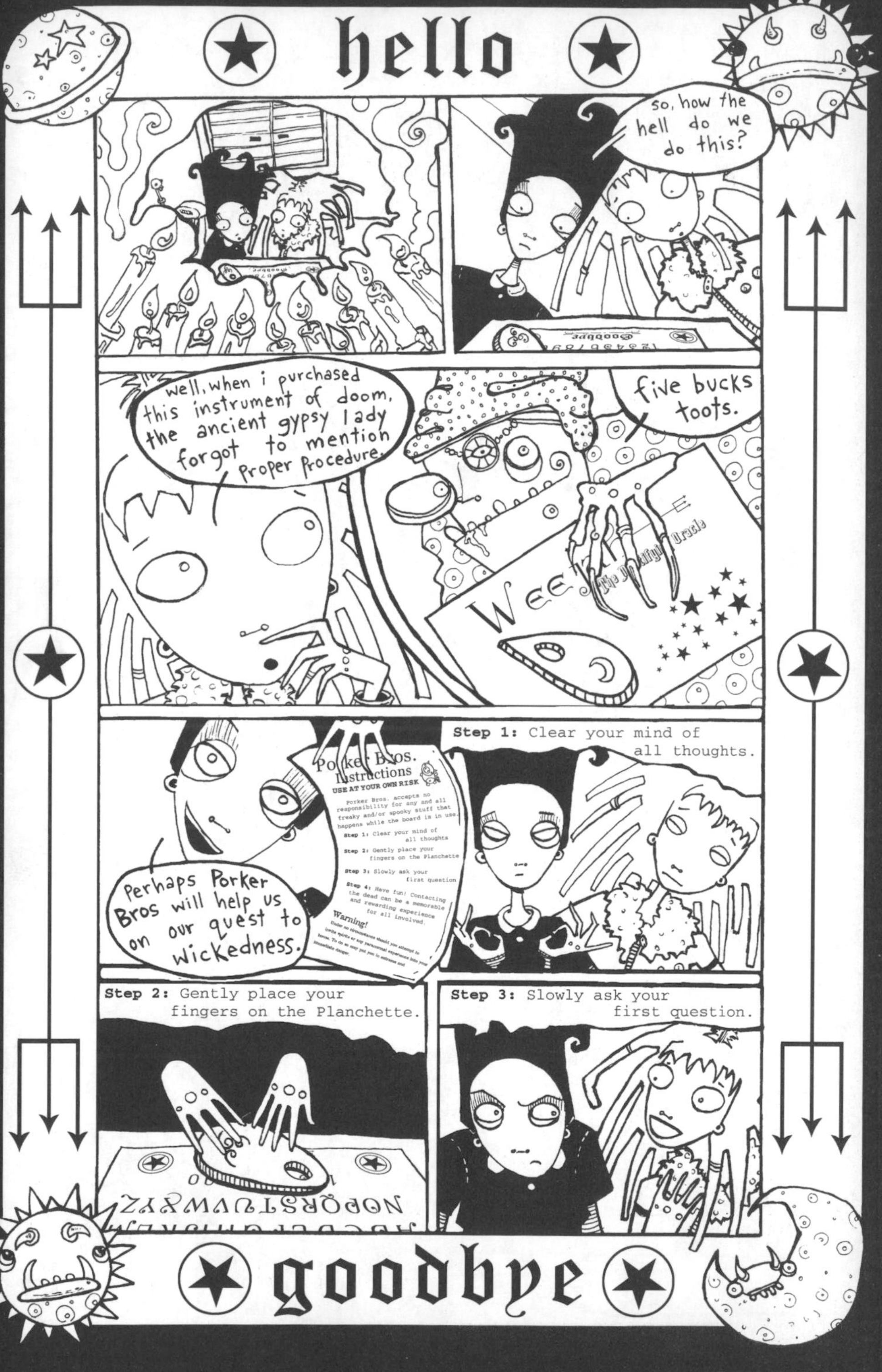
hello
so, how the hell do we do this?
well, when i purchased this instrument of doom, the ancient gypsy lady forgot to mention proper procedure.
five bucks toots.
Porker Bros. Instructions
USE AT YOUR OWN RISK
Porker Bros. accepts no responsibility for any and all freaky and/or spooky stuff that happens while the board is in use.
Step 1: Clear your mind of all thoughts
Step 2: Gently place your fingers on the Planchette
Step 3: Slowly ask your first question
Step 4: Have fun! Contacting the dead can be a memorable and rewarding experience for all involved.
Warning!
Perhaps Porker Bros will help us on our quest to wickedness.
Step 1: Clear your mind of all thoughts.
Step 2: Gently place your fingers on the Planchette.
Step 3: Slowly ask your first question.
goodbye

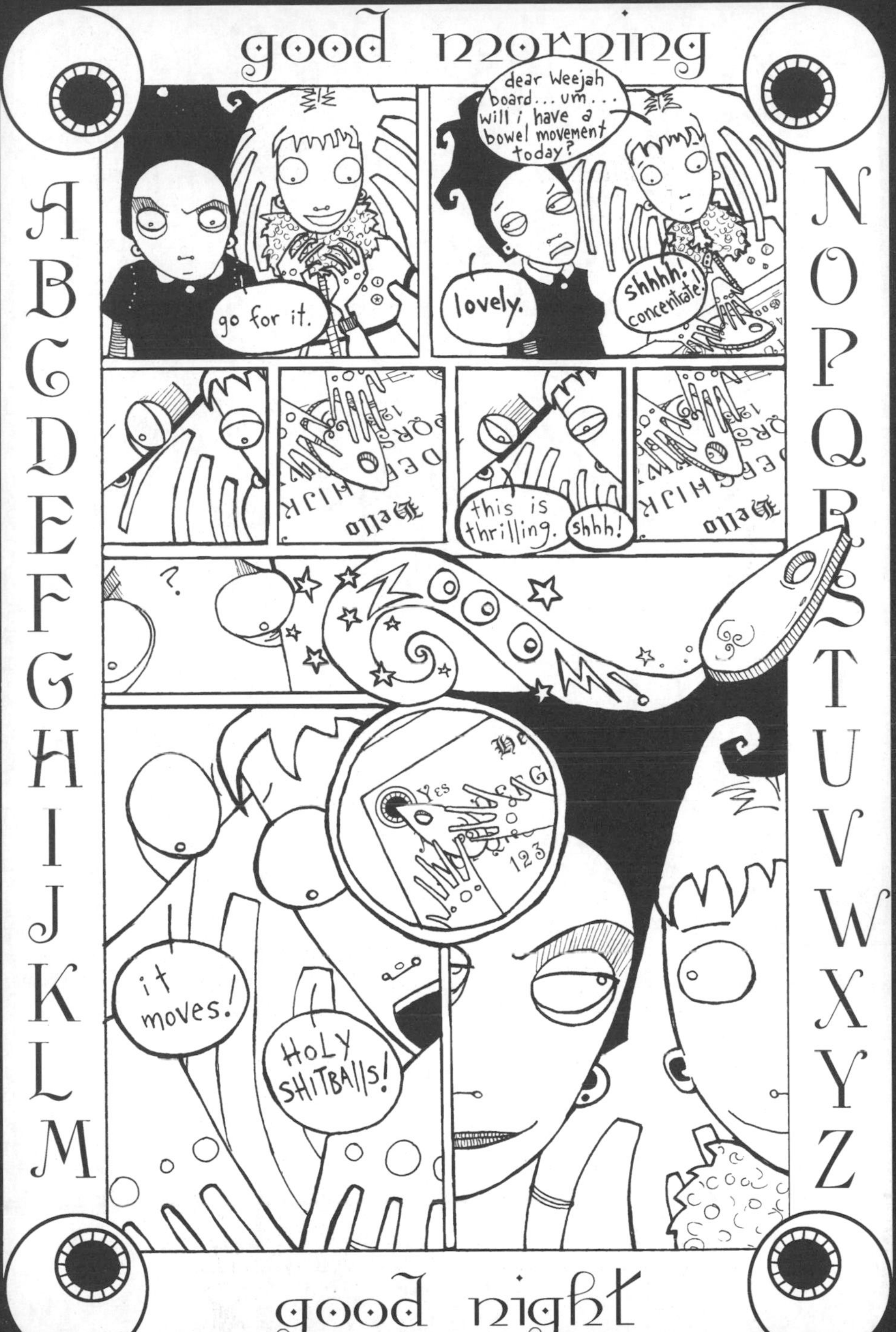
good morning
A B C D E F G H I J K L M
N O P Q R S T U V W X Y Z
go for it.
dear Weejah board... um... will i have a bowel movement today?
lovely.
shhhh! concentrate!
this is thrilling.
shhh!
?
it moves!
HOLY SHITBALLS!
good night

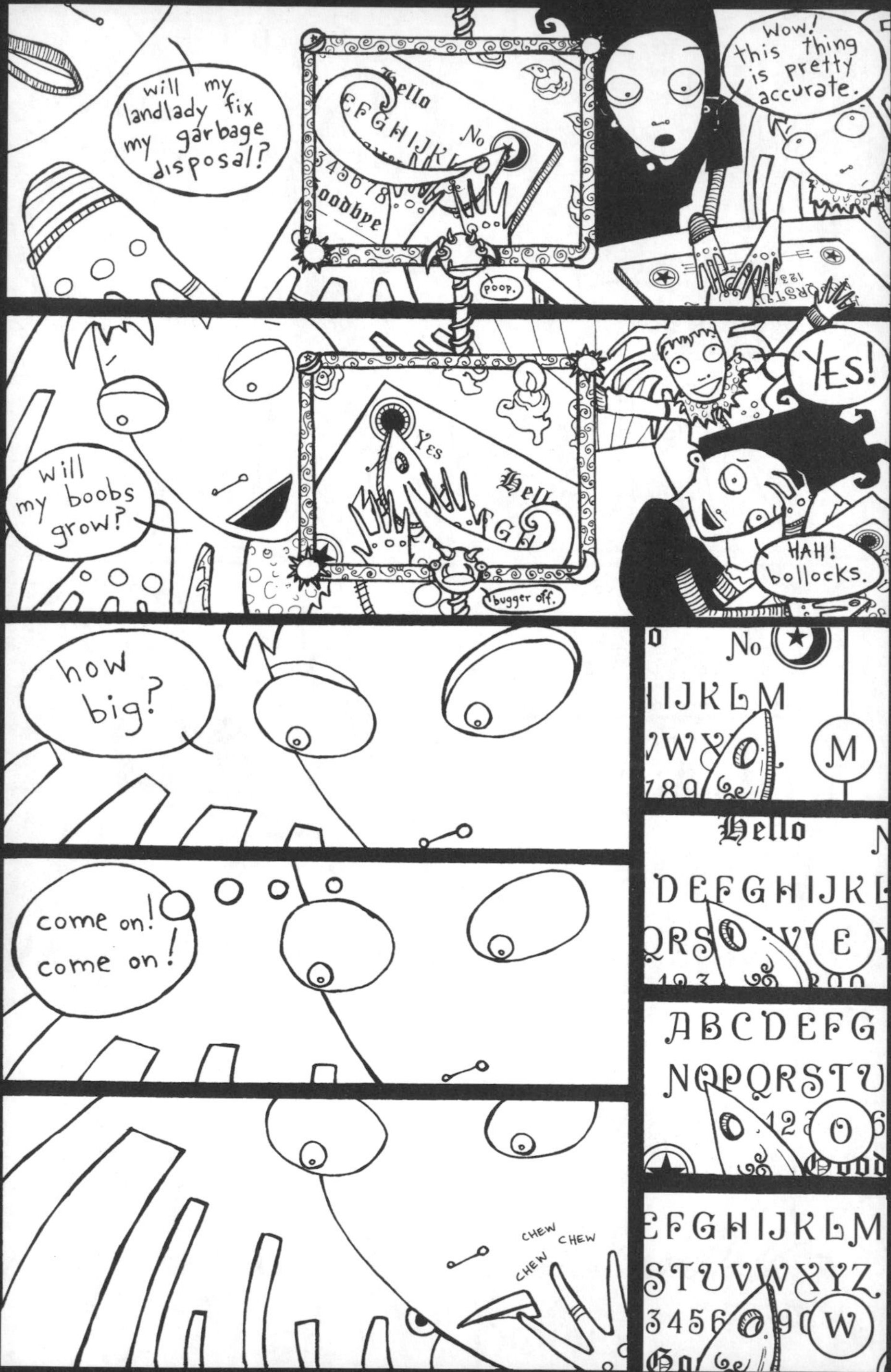

will my landlady fix my garbage disposal?
Hello
No
Goodbye
Wow! this thing is pretty accurate.
poop.
will my boobs grow?
Yes
YES!
HAH! bollocks.
bugger off.
how big?
No
M
Hello
E
come on! come on!
O
CHEW CHEW CHEW
W

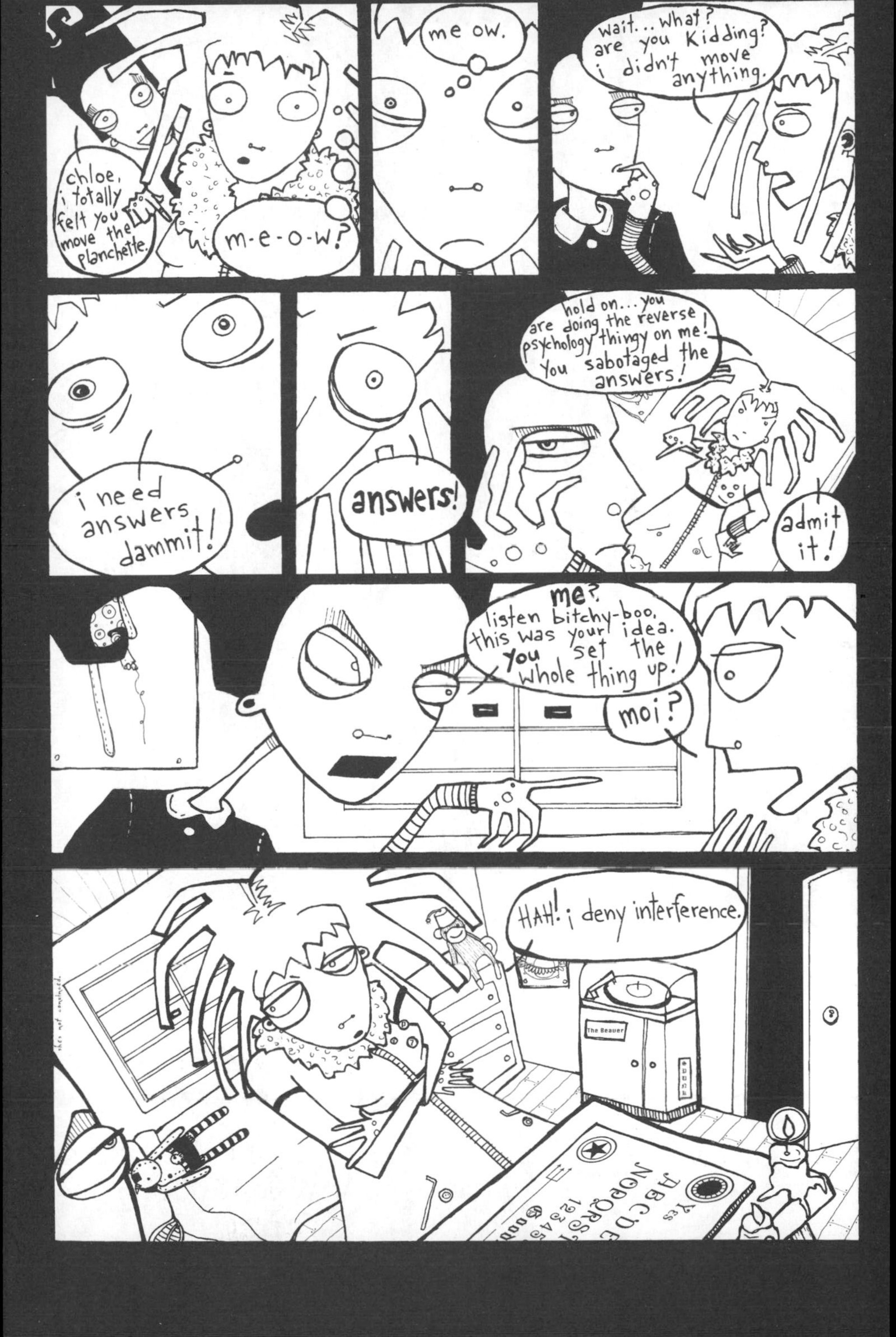
chloe, i totally felt you move the planchette.
m-e-o-w?
me ow.
wait... what? are you Kidding? i didn't move anything.
i need answers dammit!
answers!
hold on... you are doing the reverse psychology thingy on me! You sabotaged the answers!
admit it!
me? listen bitchy-boo, this was your idea. you set the whole thing up!
moi?
HAH! i deny interference.
The Beaver
shes not convinced.
YES
ABCDE
NOPQRS
12345

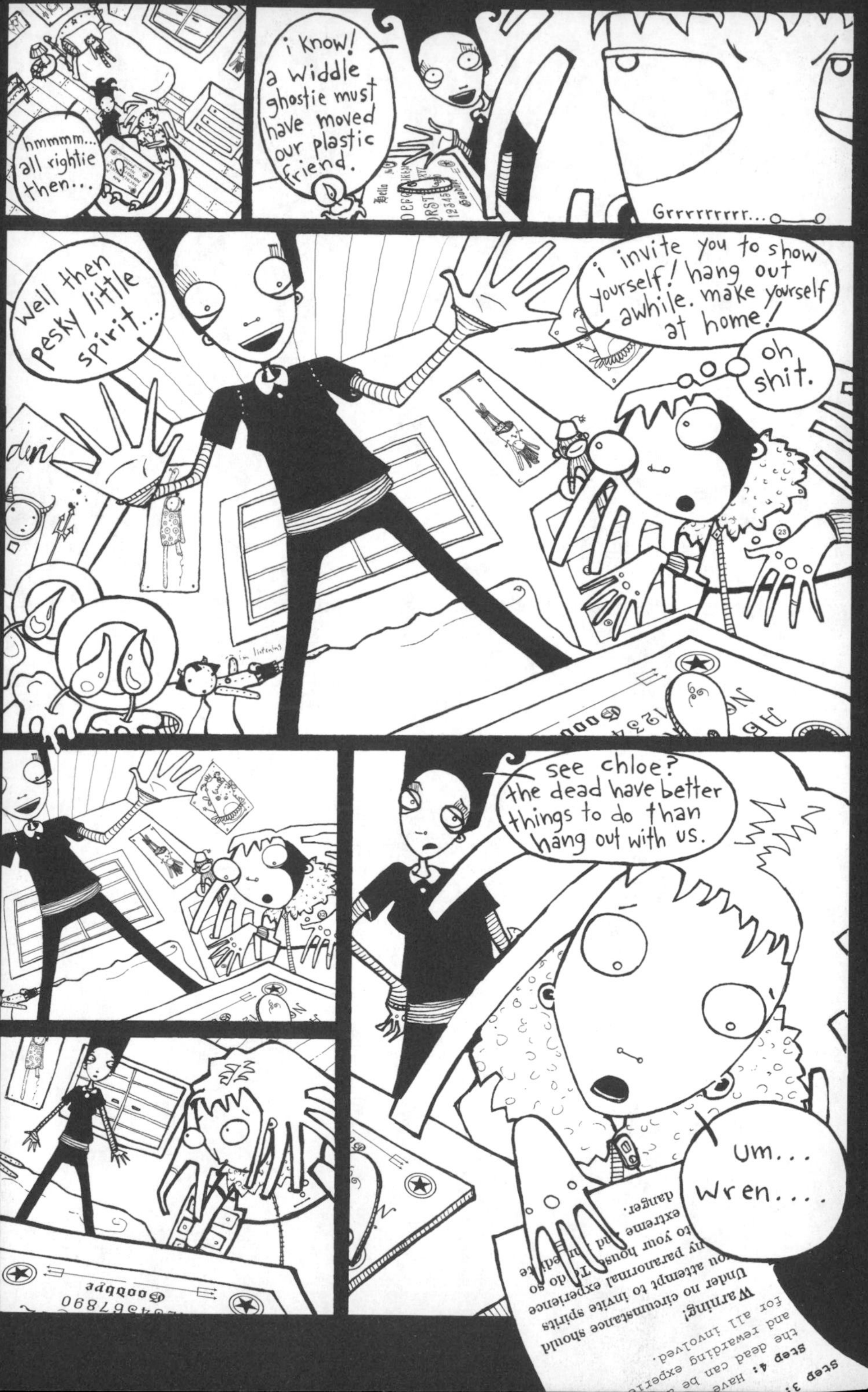
hmmmm... all rightie then...
i know! a widdle ghostie must have moved our plastic friend.
Grrrrrrrrr...
well then pesky little spirit...
i invite you to show yourself! hang out awhile. make yourself at home!
oh shit.
see chloe? the dead have better things to do than hang out with us.
um... wren....
Warning!

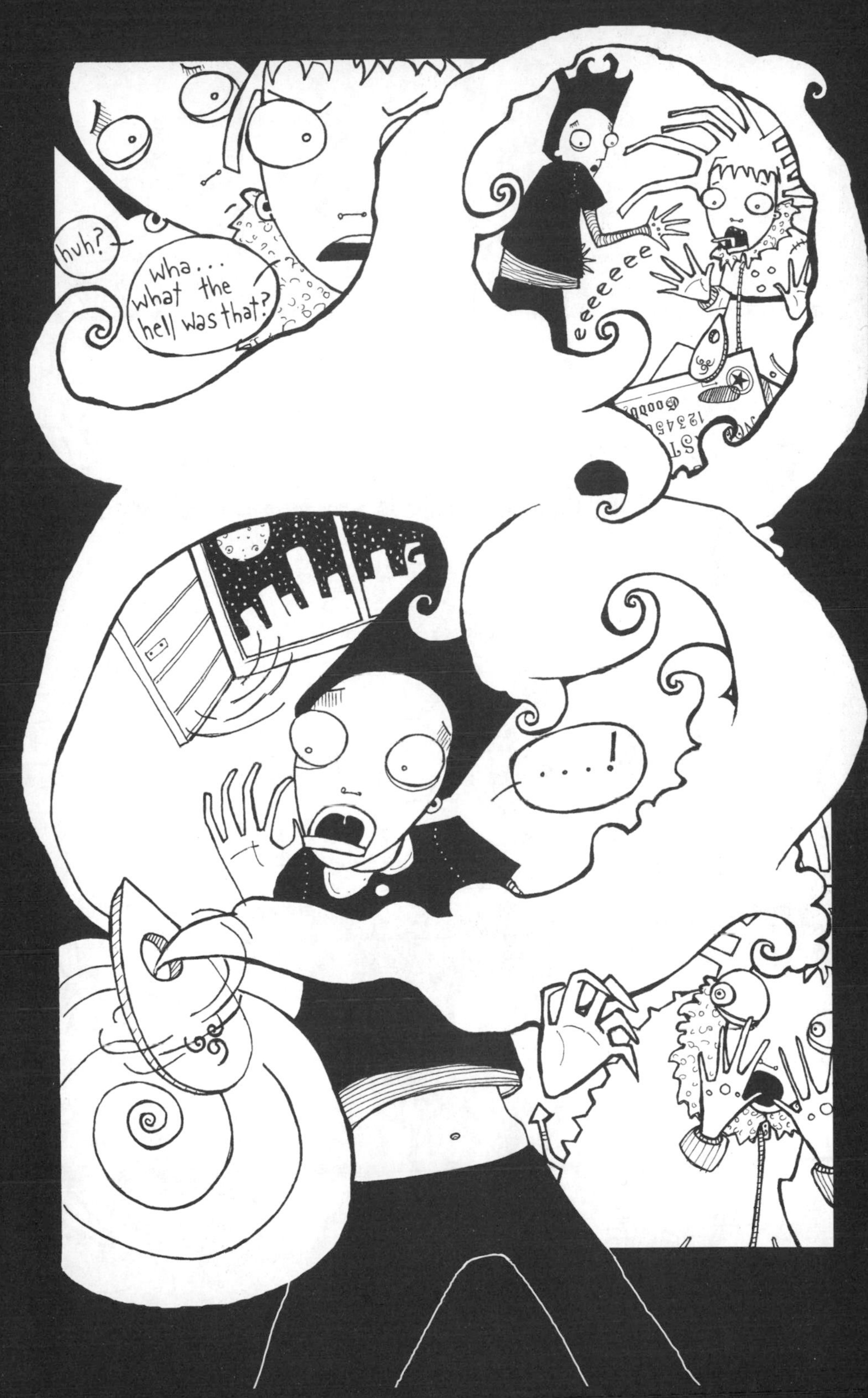
huh?
wha... what the hell was that?
eeeeeee
....!

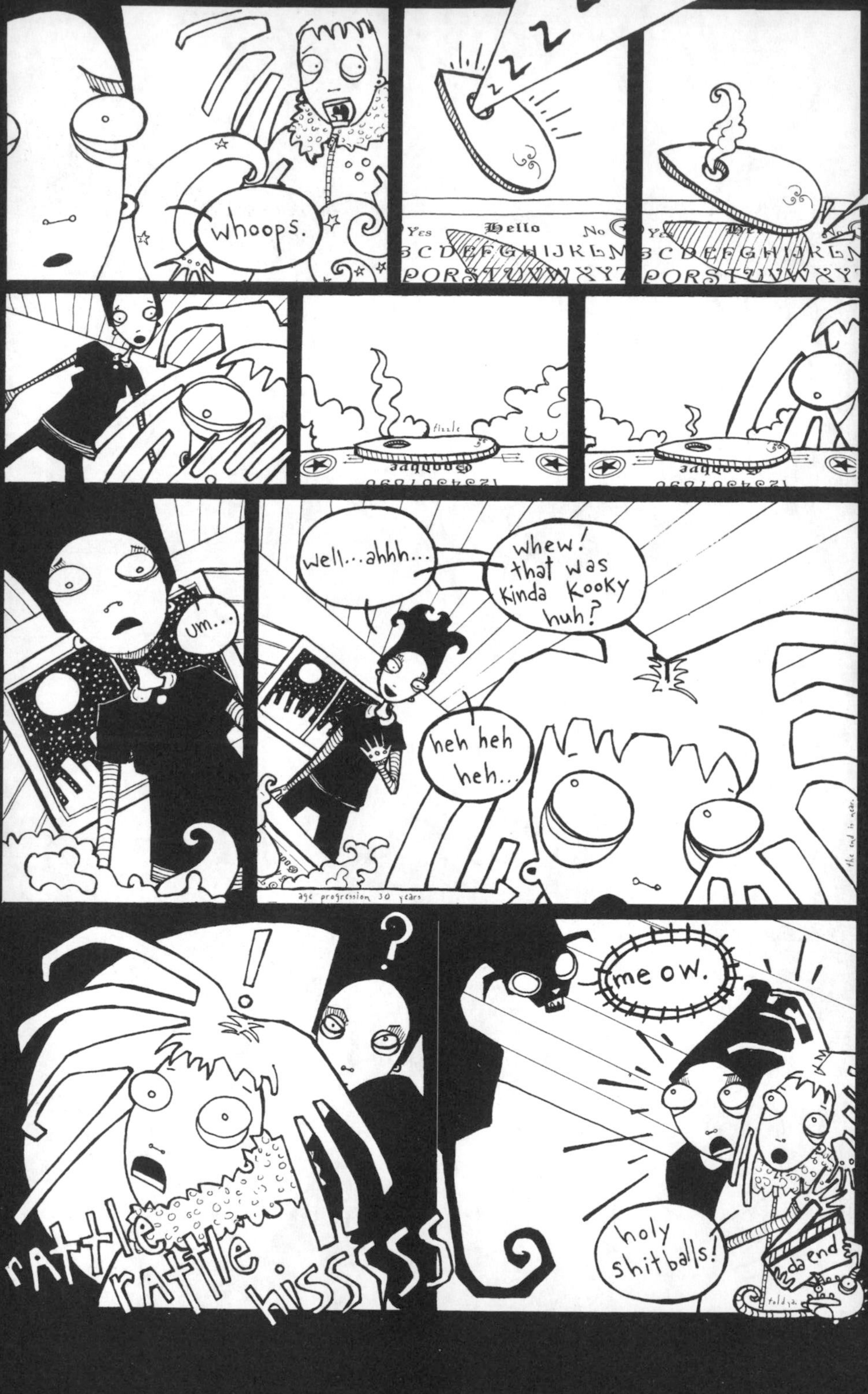

whoops.
um...
well...ahhh...
whew! that was kinda kooky huh?
heh heh heh...
age progression 30 years
the end is near.
!
?
rattle rattle hisssss
meow.
holy shitballs!
da end
told ya.

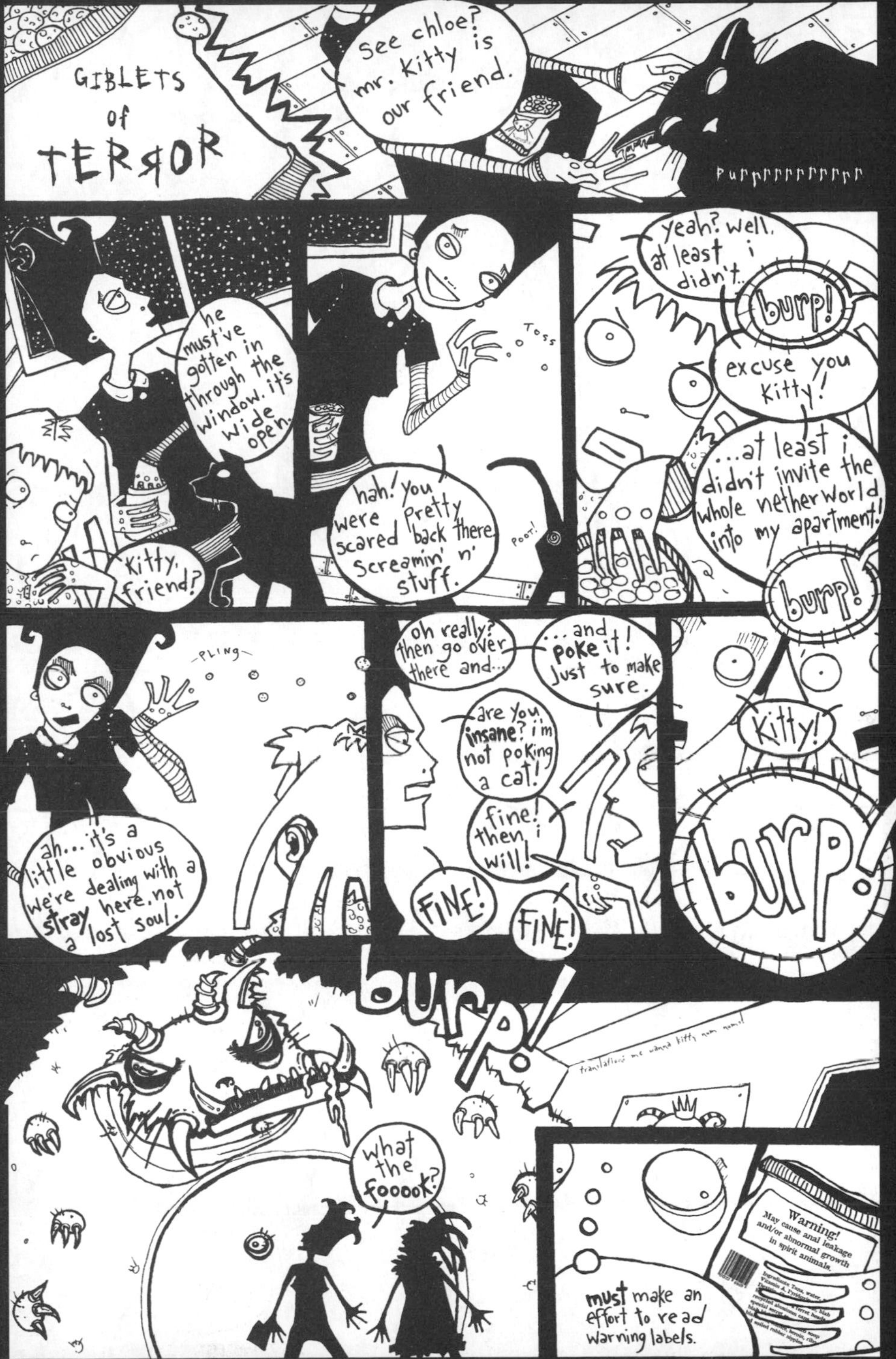
GIBLETS of TERROR
See chloe? mr. kitty is our friend.
Purrrrrrrrrrrr
he must've gotten in through the window. it's wide open.
kitty, friend?
TOSS
hah! you were pretty scared back there. Screamin' n' stuff.
POOT!
yeah? well, at least i didn't..
burp!
excuse you kitty!
...at least i didn't invite the whole netherworld into my apartment!
burp!
-PLING-
ah... it's a little obvious we're dealing with a stray here, not a lost soul.
oh really? then go over there and...
...and poke it! just to make sure.
are you insane? i'm not poking a cat!
fine! then i will!
FINE!
FINE!
kitty!
burp!
burp!
translation: me wanna kitty num nums!
what the fooook?
must make an effort to read warning labels.
Warning! May cause anal leakage and/or abnormal growth in spirit animals.

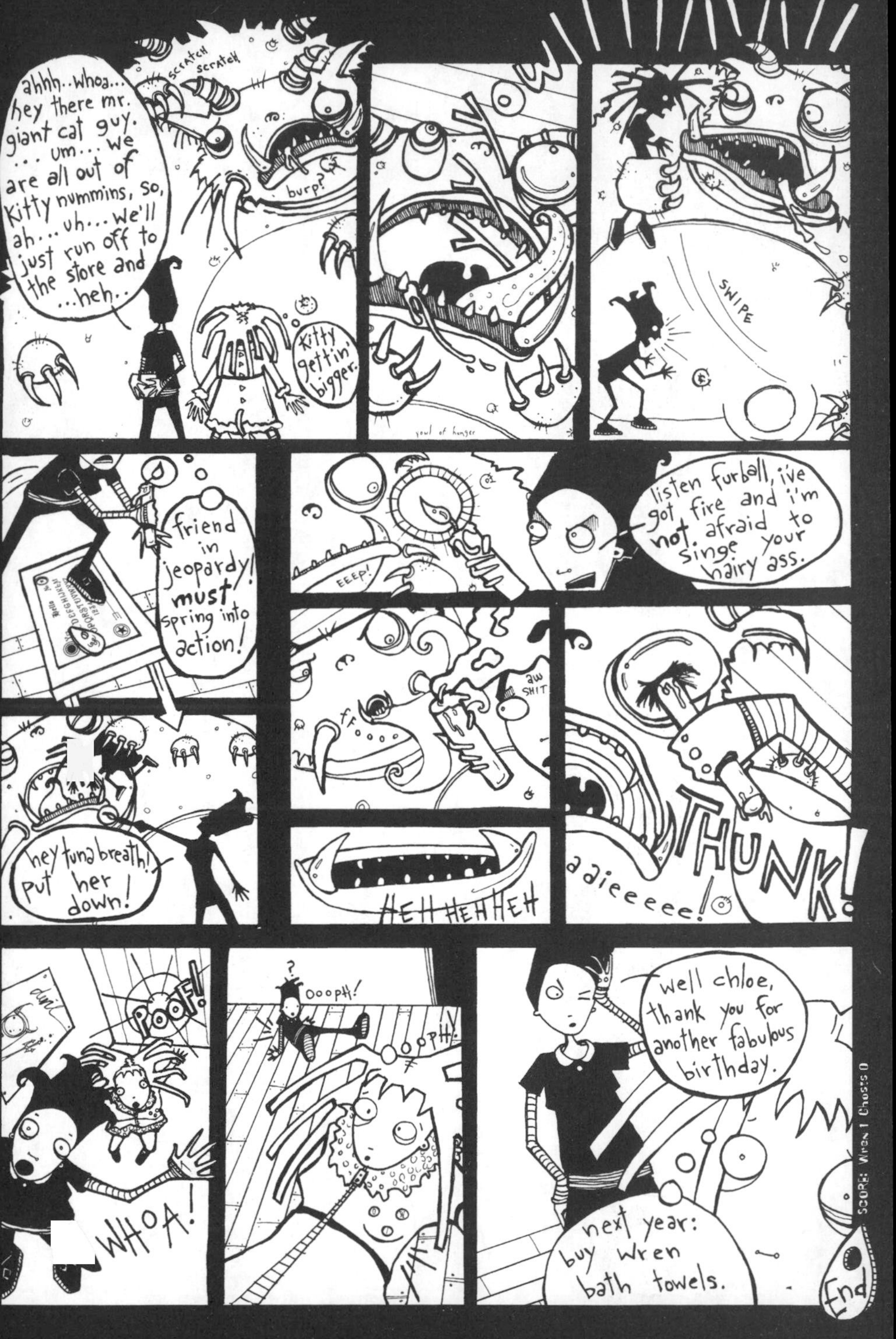

ahhh..whoa... hey there mr. giant cat guy. ...um... we are all out of kitty nummins, so, ah...uh...we'll just run off to the store and ...heh..
SCRATCH SCRATCH
burp?
Kitty gettin' bigger.
WOW
yowl of hunger
SWIPE
friend in jeopardy! must spring into action!
listen furball, i've got fire and i'm not afraid to singe your hairy ass.
EEEP!
hey tuna breath! put her down!
ffoooo
aw SHIT
HEH HEHHEH
THUNK!
aaieeeeee!
POOF!
WHOA!
?
OooPH!
OOPH!
well chloe, thank you for another fabulous birthday.
next year: buy Wren bath towels.
End
SCORE: Wren 1 Ghosts 0

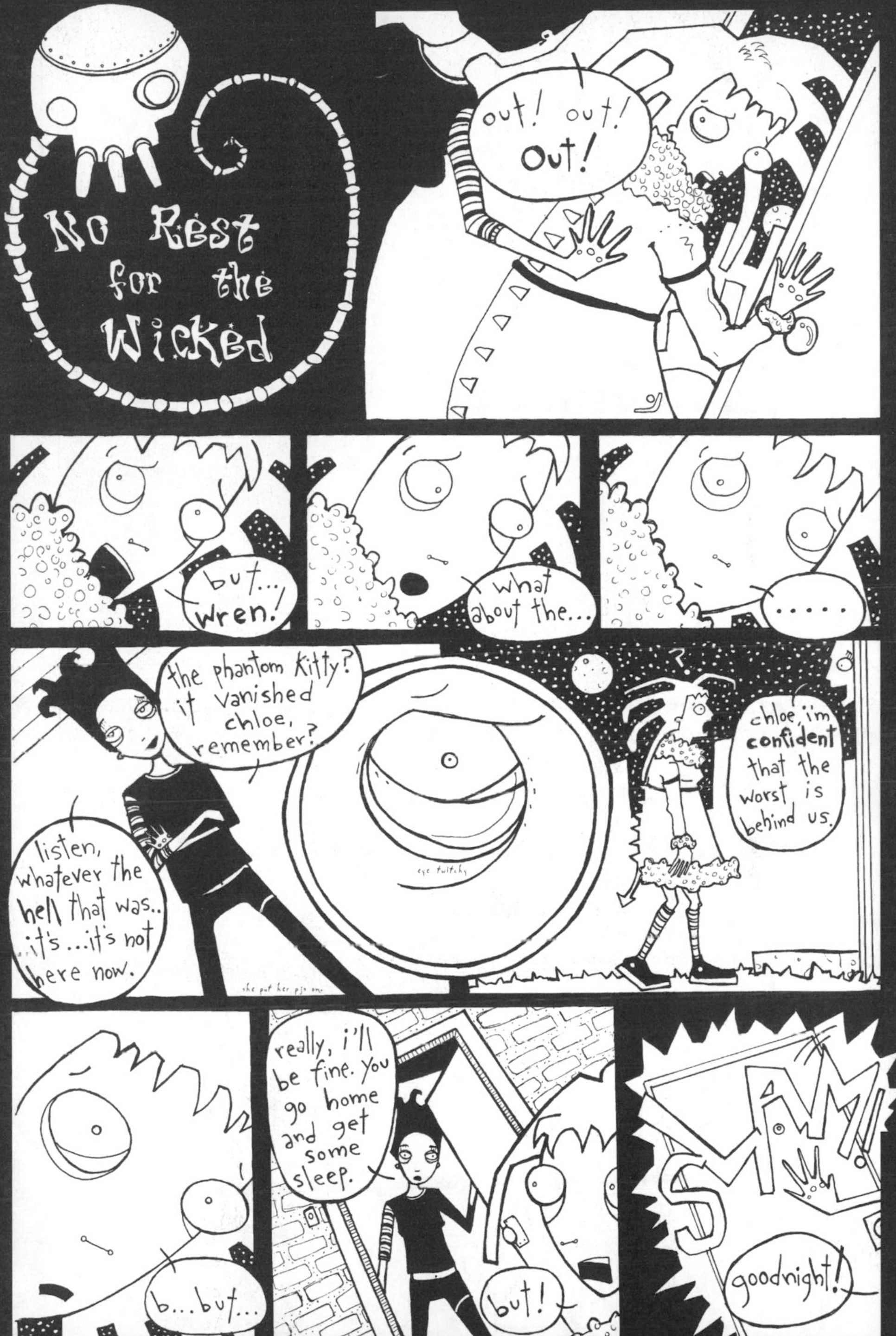
No Rest for the Wicked
out! out! Out!
but... wren.!
what about the...
.....
the phantom kitty? it vanished chloe, remember?
listen, whatever the hell that was.. ..it's ...it's not here now.
eye twitchy
she put her pjs on.
chloe, i'm confident that the worst is behind us.
b...but...
really, i'll be fine. you go home and get some sleep.
but!
SLAM!
goodnight!

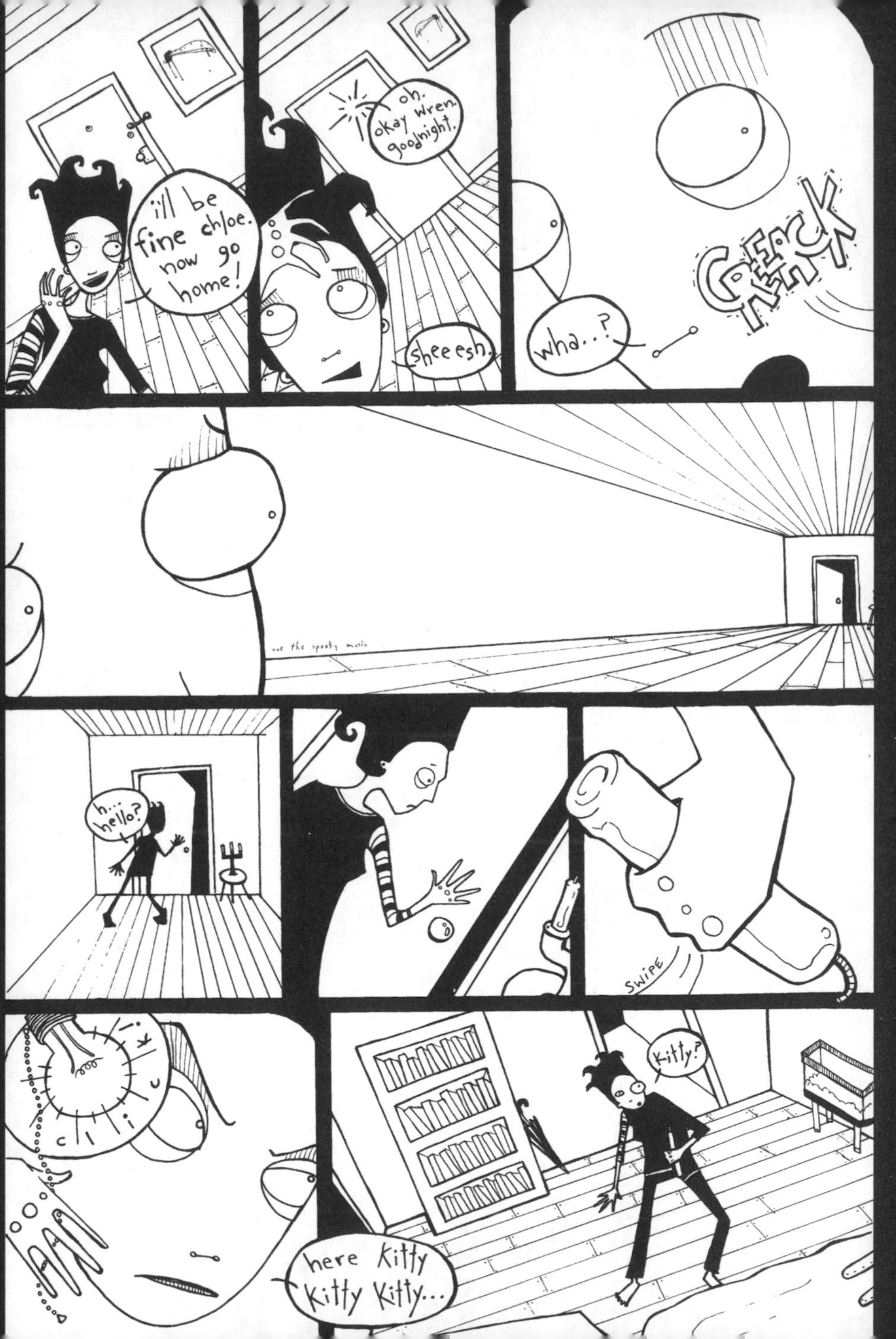
i'll be fine chloe. now go home!
oh. okay wren. goodnight.
sheeesh.
wha..?
CREEACK
cue the spooky music
h... hello?
SWIPE
click
kitty?
here kitty kitty kitty...

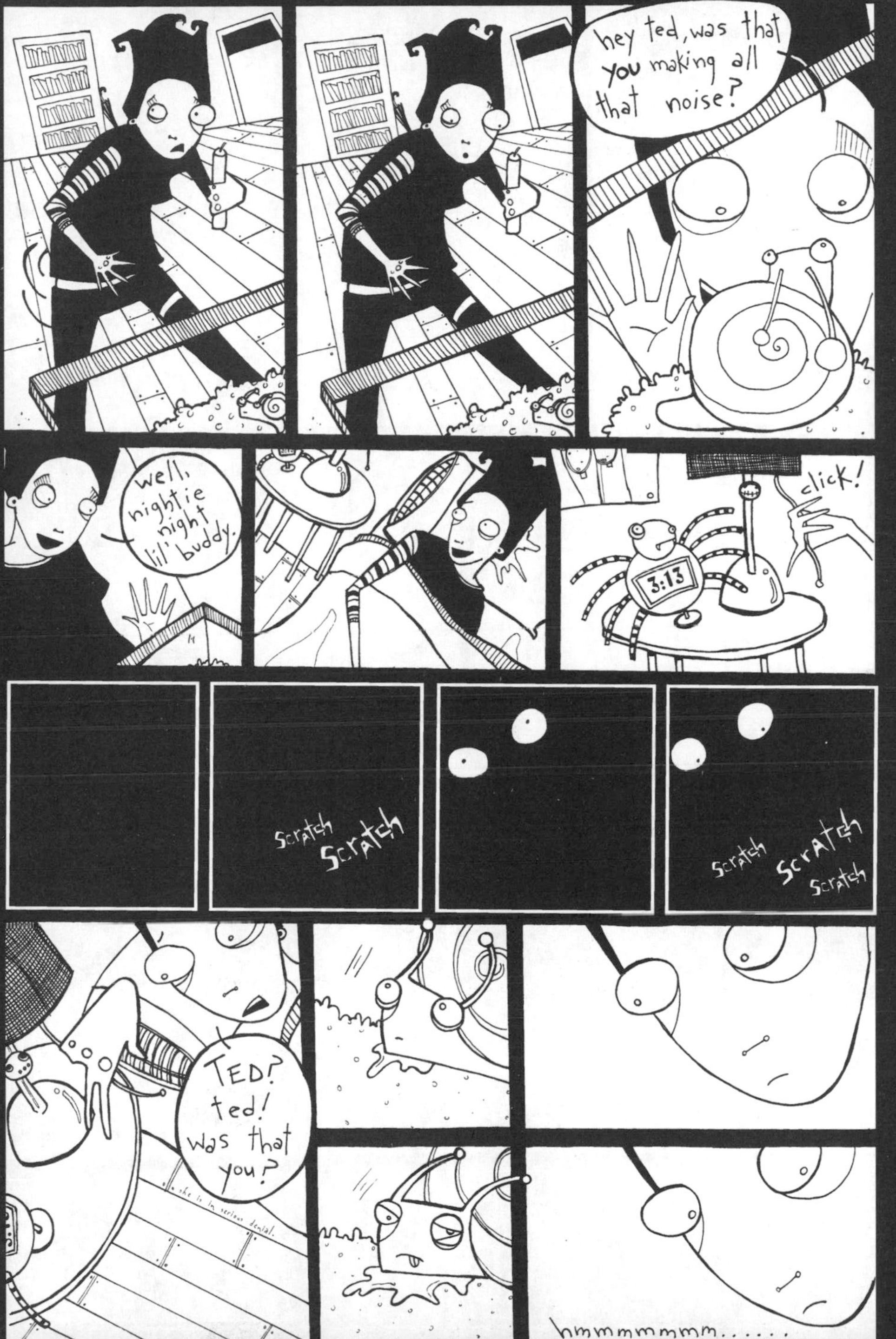
hey ted, was that YOU making all that noise?
well, nightie night lil' buddy.
3:13
click!
scratch scratch
scratch scratch scratch
TED? ted! was that you?
she is in serious denial.
hmmmmmmm.....

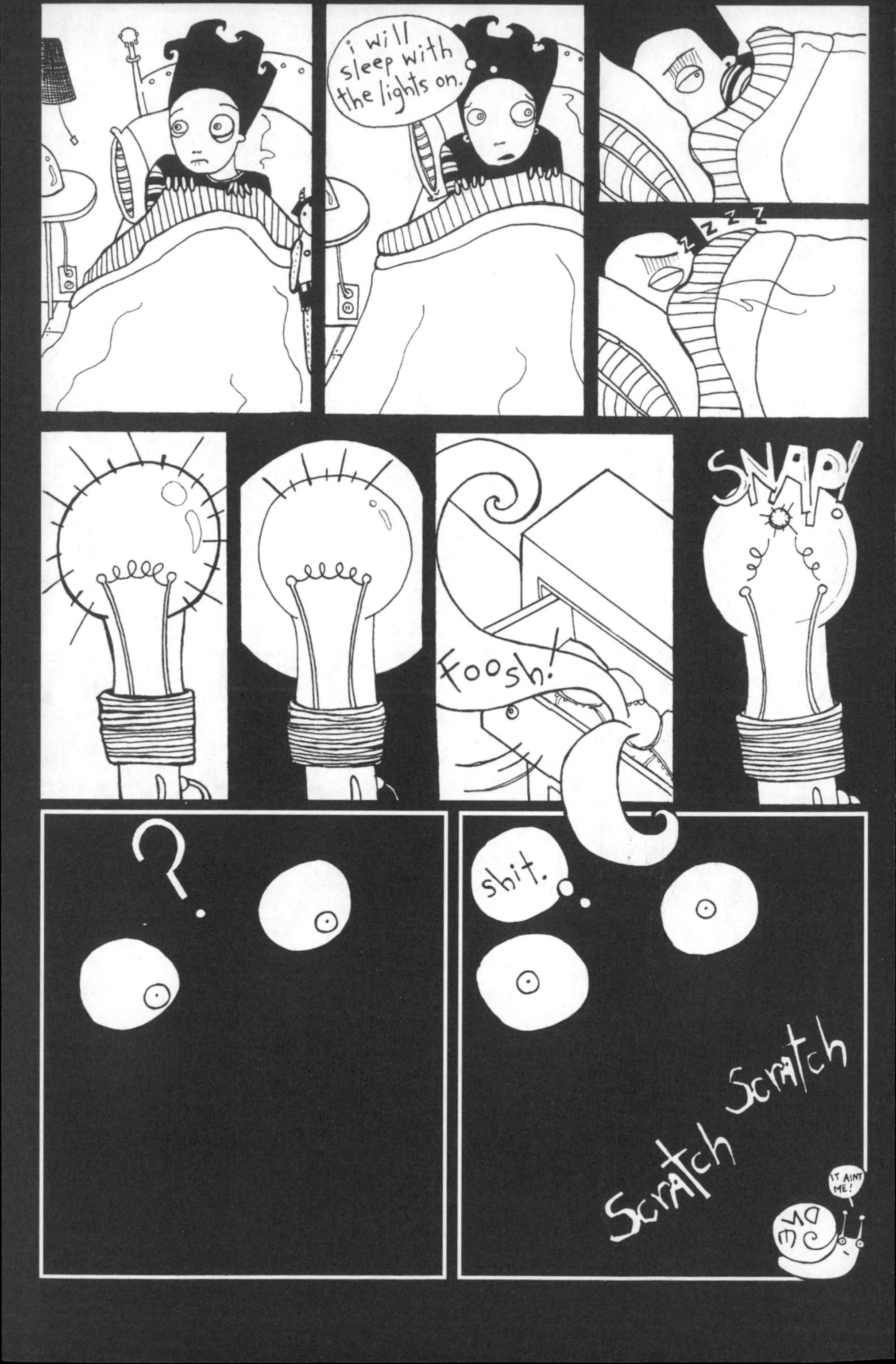
i will sleep with the lights on.
z z z z
SNAP!
Foosh!
?
shit.
Scratch Scratch
IT AINT ME!

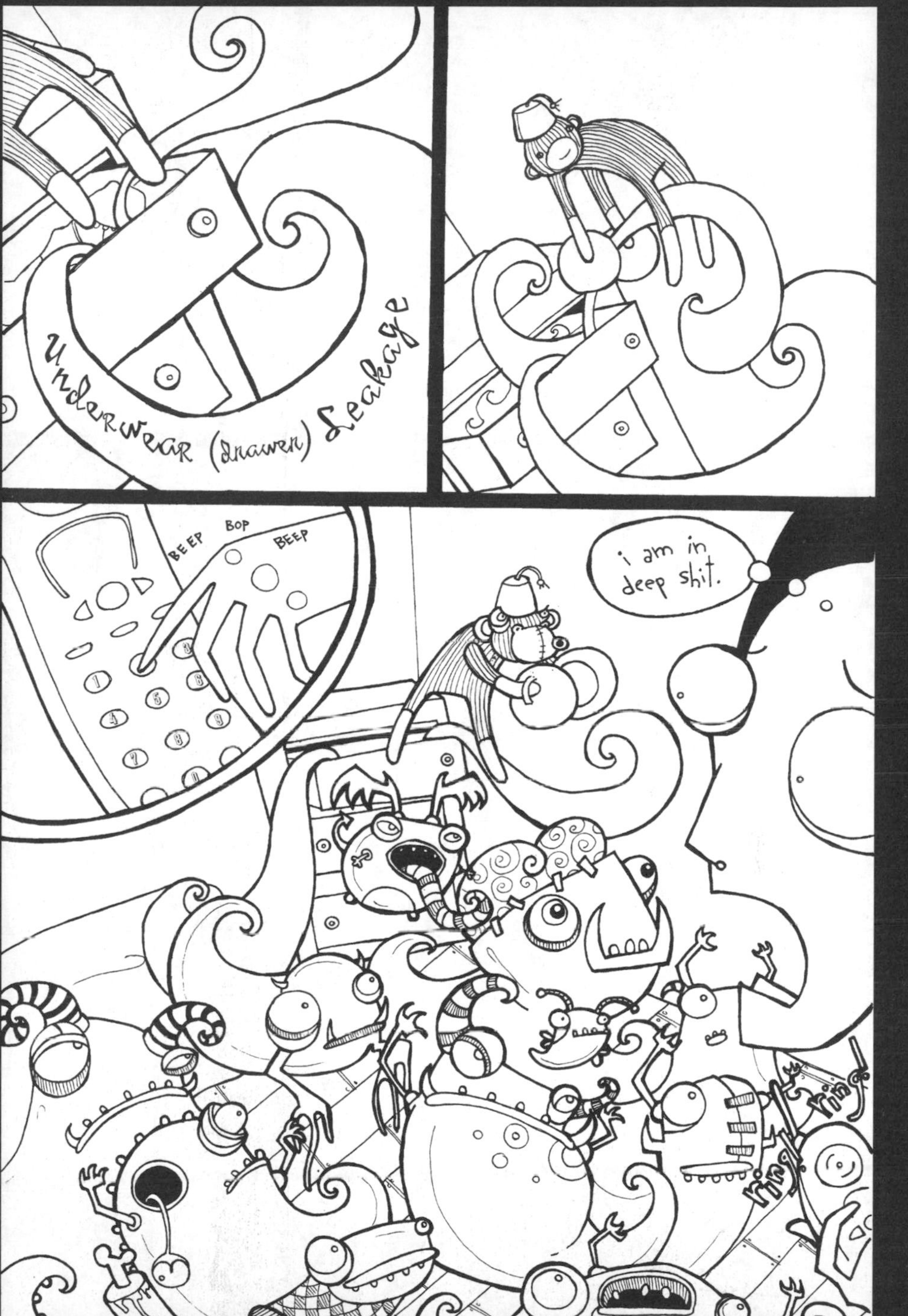
Underwear (drawer) Leakage
BEEP BOP BEEP
i am in deep shit.
ring ring

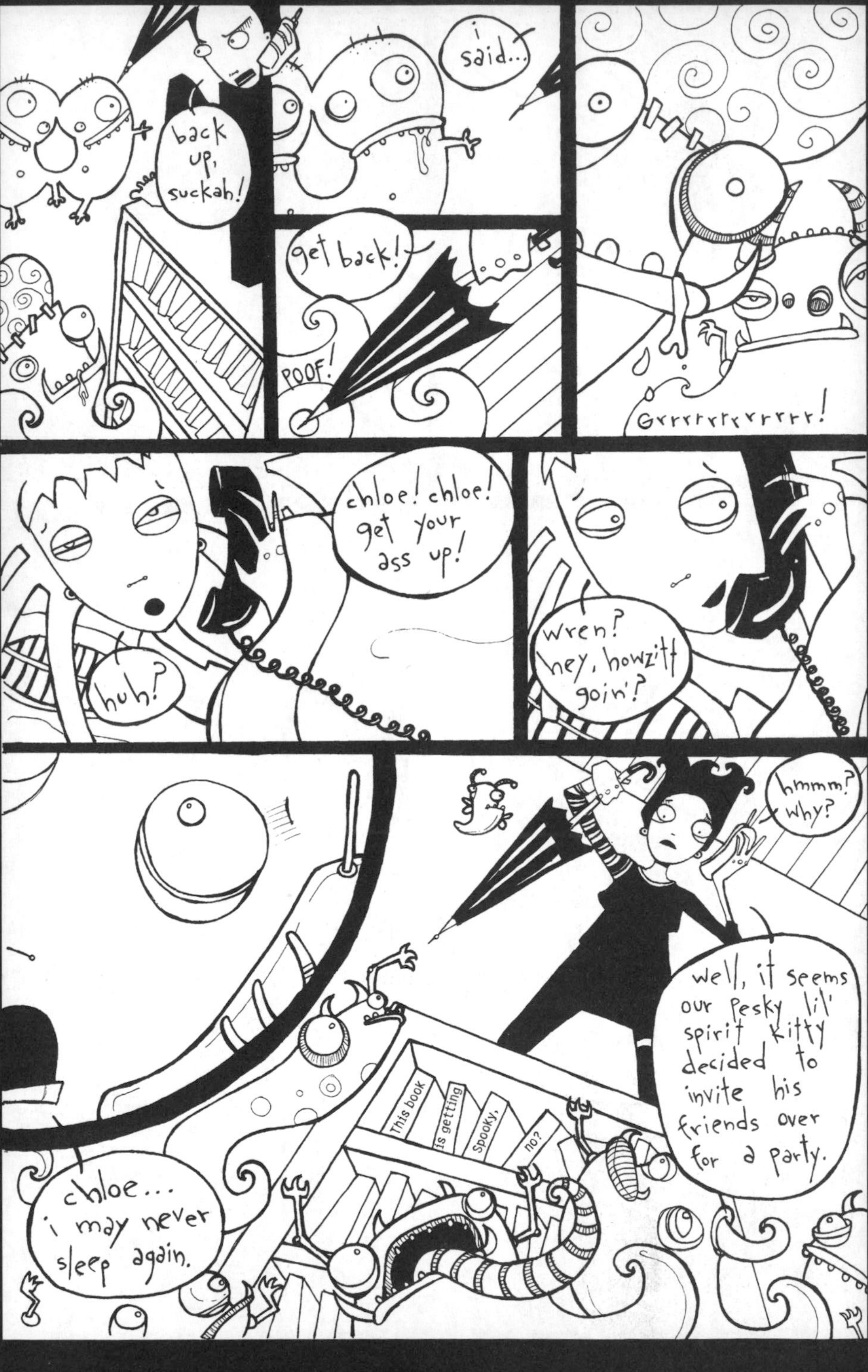
back up, suckah!
i said...
get back!
POOF!
Grrrrrrrrrrrr!
chloe! chloe! get your ass up!
huh?
wren? hey, howz'it goin'?
hmmm? why?
well, it seems our pesky lil' spirit kitty decided to invite his friends over for a party.
This book
is getting
Spooky.
no?
chloe... i may never sleep again.

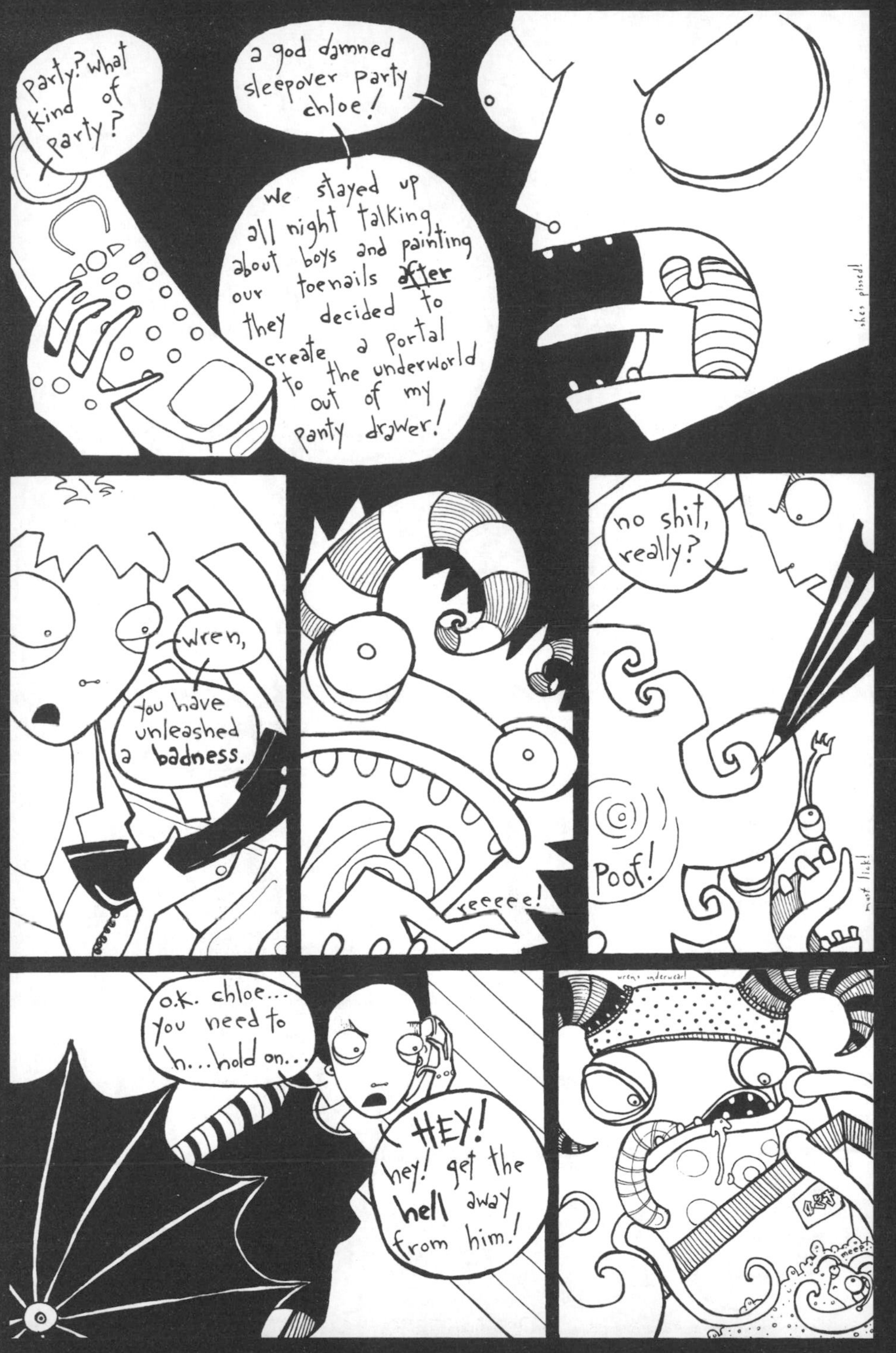
party? what kind of party?
a god damned sleepover party chloe!
we stayed up all night talking about boys and painting our toenails **after** they decided to create a portal to the underworld out of my panty drawer!
she's pissed!
wren,
you have unleashed a **badness**.
reeeee!
no shit, really?
Poof!
must lick!
o.k. chloe... you need to h...hold on...
HEY! hey! get the **hell** away from him!
wren's underwear!
meep!

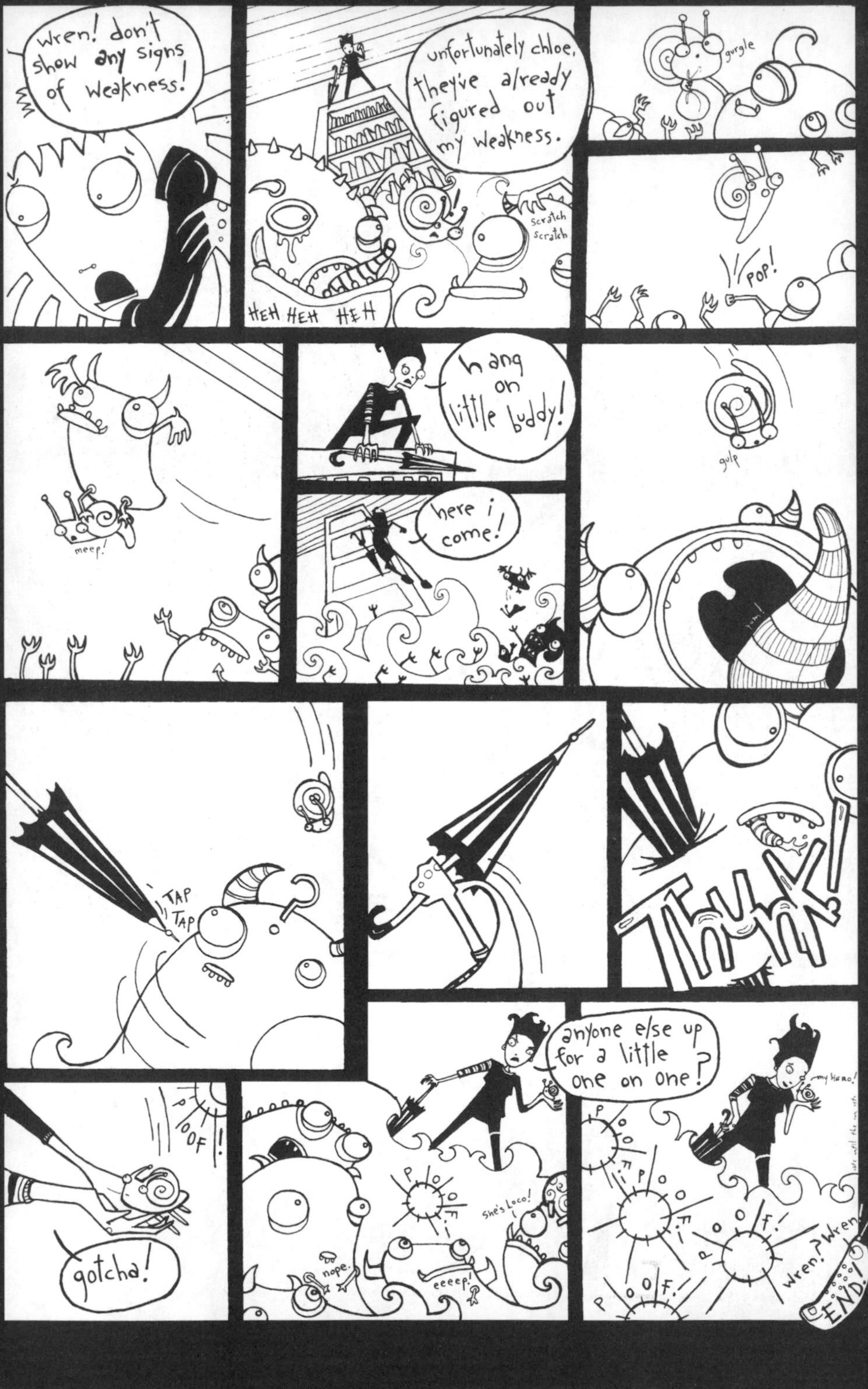
wren! don't show any signs of weakness!
unfortunately chloe, they've already figured out my weakness.
scratch scratch
HEH HEH HEH
gurgle
POP!
meep!
hang on little buddy!
gulp
here i come!
TAP TAP
THUNK!
POOF!
gotcha!
anyone else up for a little one on one?
POOF!
she's loco!
nope.
eeeep!
my HERO!
POOF!
POOF!
POOF!
wren? wren!
END.

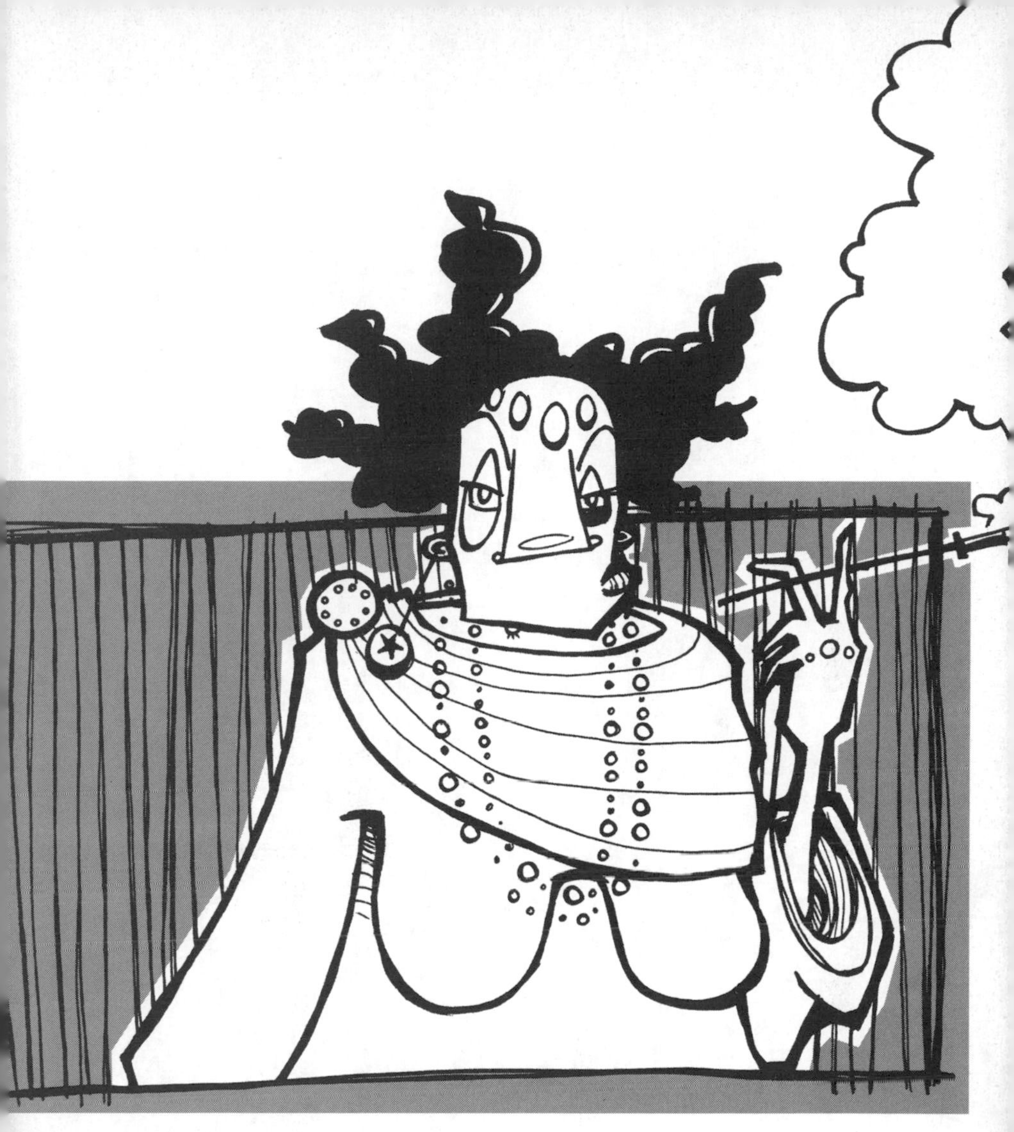

chapter two.

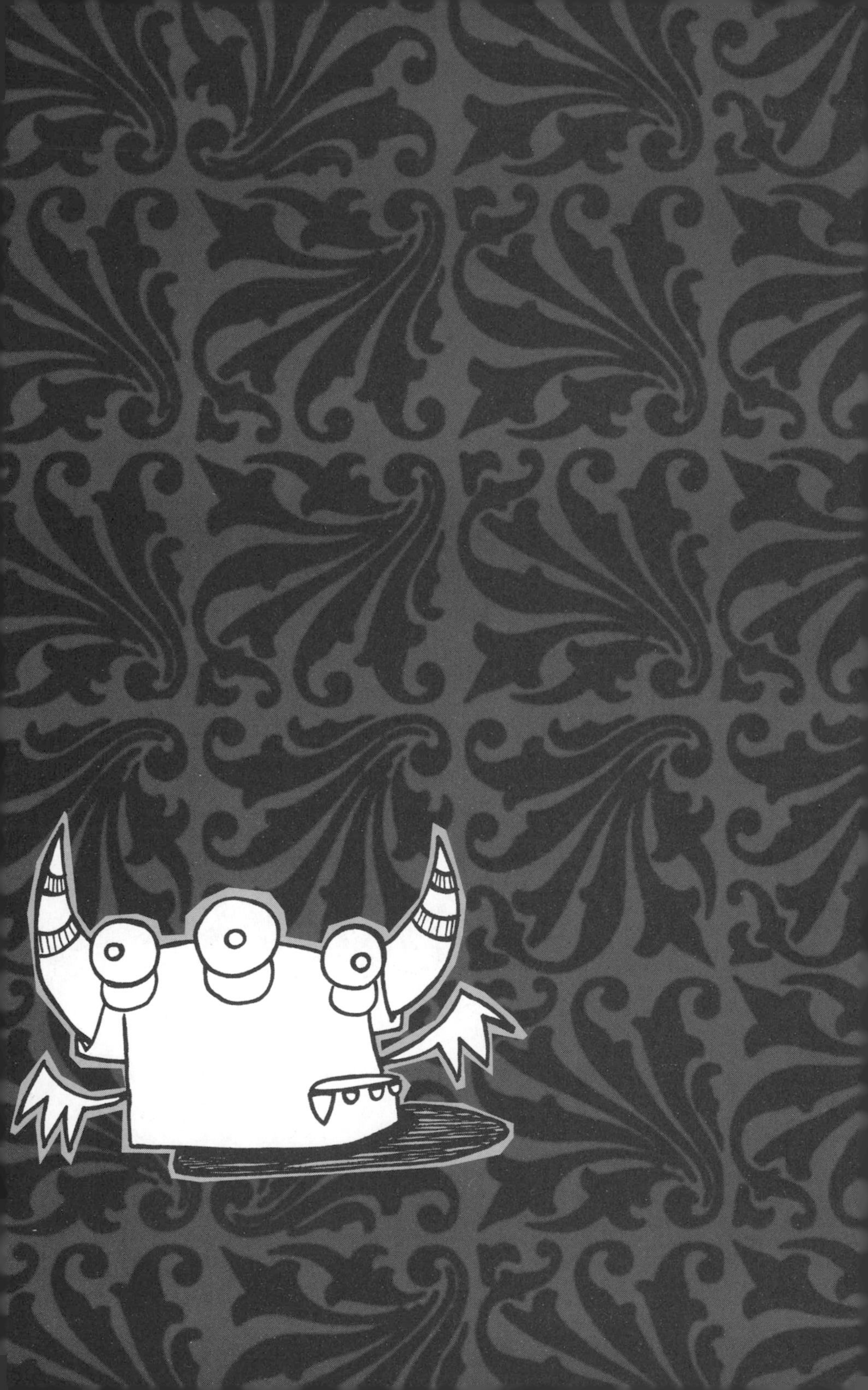

ANNOYED to DEATH

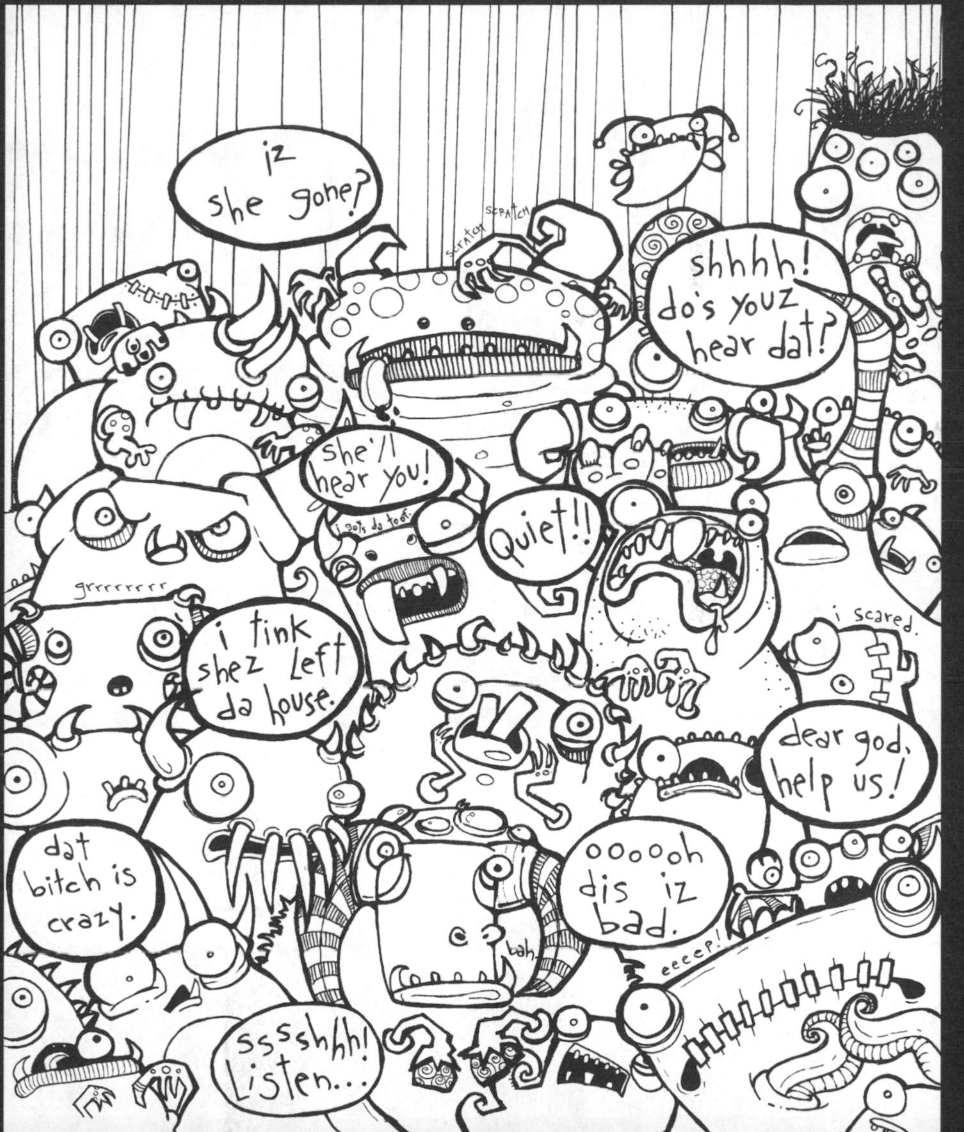
iz she gone?
scratch
SCRATCH
shhhh! do's youz hear dat?
She'll hear you!
i gots da toof.
Quiet!!
grrrrrrrr
i tink shez left da house.
i scared.
dear god, help us!
dat bitch is crazy.
ooooh dis iz bad.
bah.
eeeep!
sssshhh! Listen...

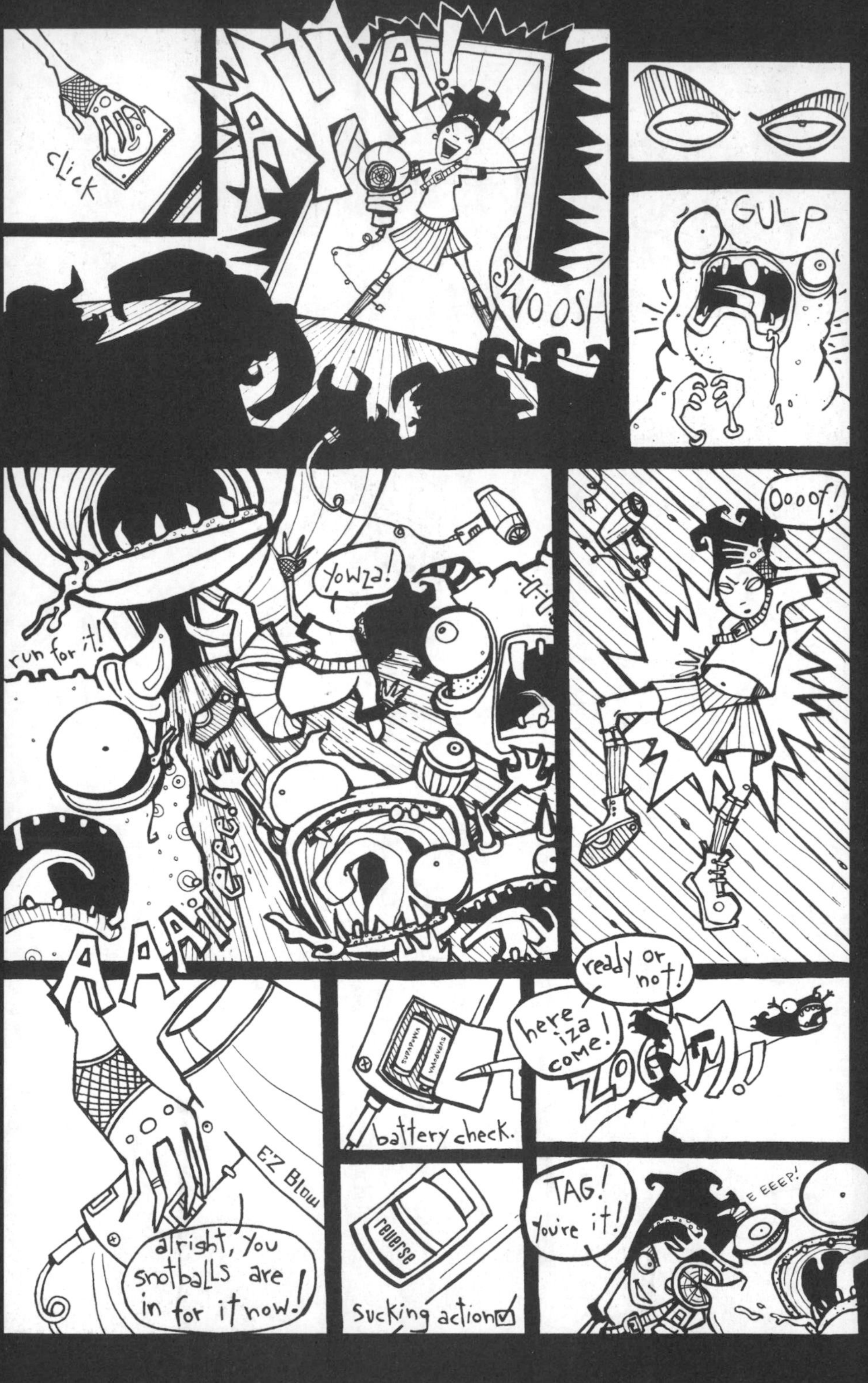

click
AAAA!
SWOOSH
GULP
yowza!
run for it!
AAAiieee!
Ooof!
AA
EZ Blow
alright, you snotballs are in for it now!
battery check.
reverse
sucking action☑
ready or not!
here iza come!
ZOOM!
TAG! You're it!
EEEEP!

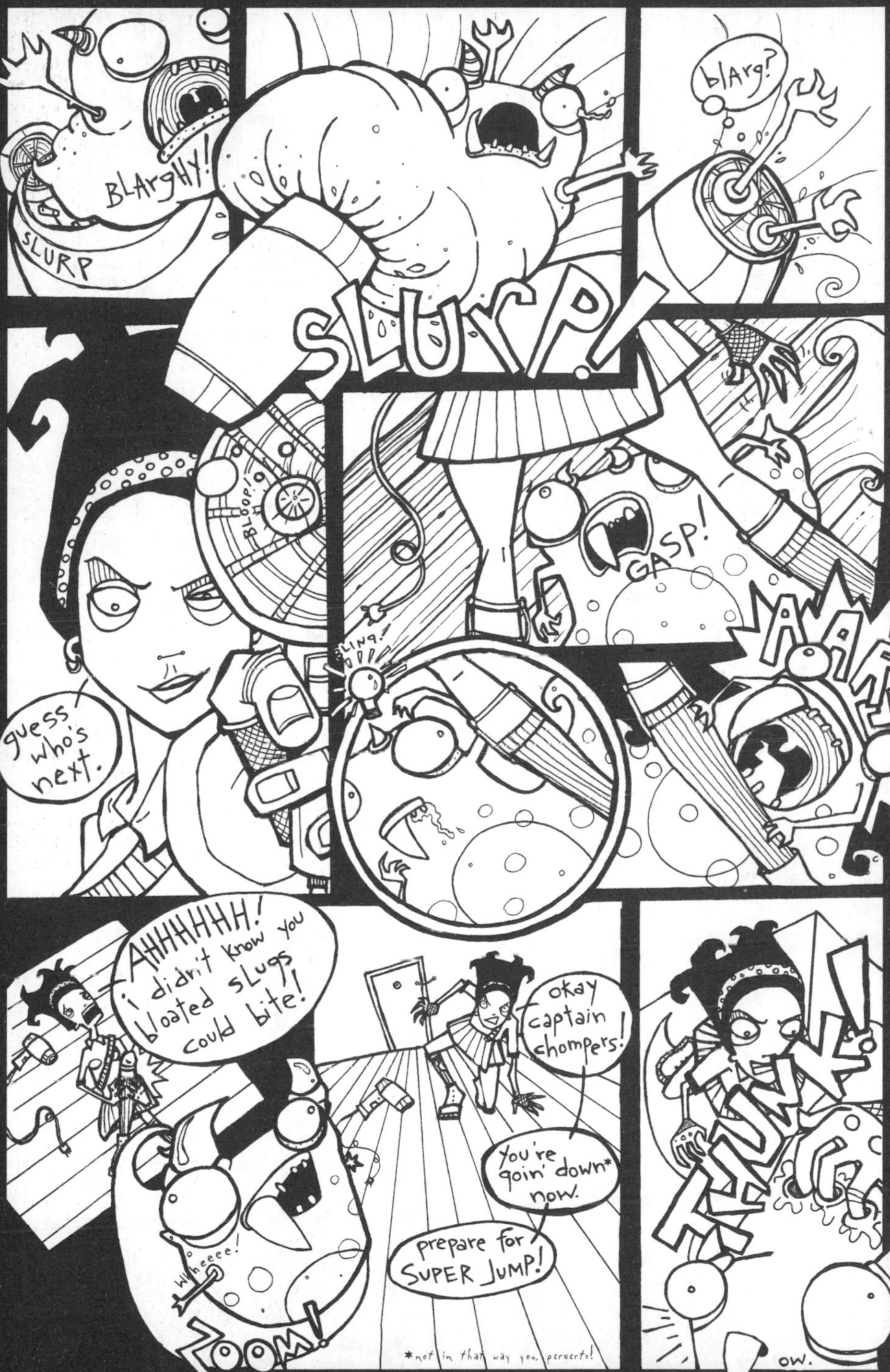
BLARGHY!
SLURP
blarg?
SLURP!
BLOOP!
GASP!
AARG
BLING!
guess who's next.
AHHHHHH! i didn't know you bloated slugs could bite!
okay captain chompers!
you're goin' down* now.
prepare for SUPER JUMP!
wheeee!
ZOOM!
THUNK!
ow.
*not in that way you perverts!

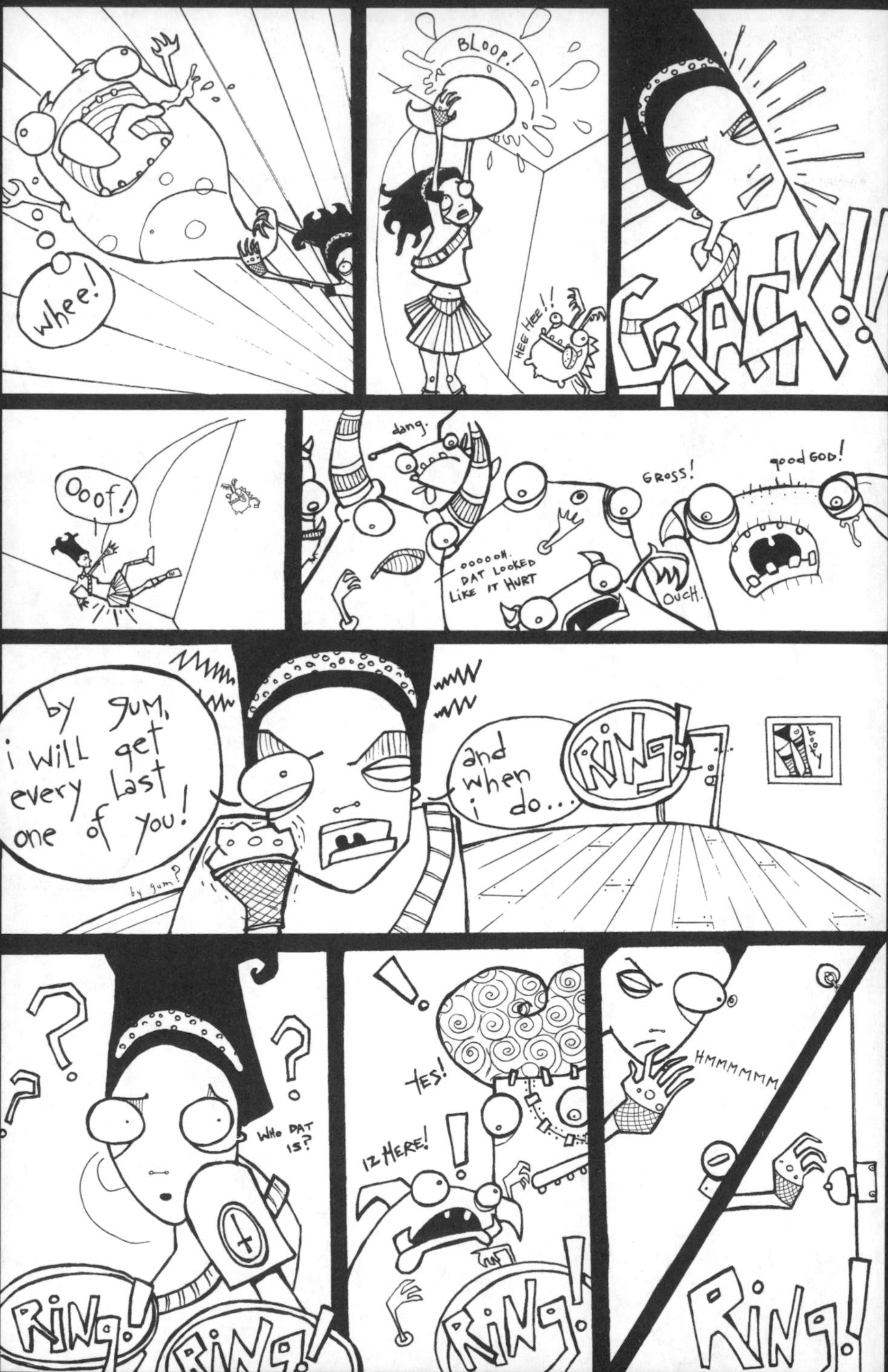
whee!
BLOOP!
HEE HEE!!
CRACK!!!
Ooof!
dang.
GROSS!
good GOD!
oooooH. DAT LOOKED LIKE IT HURT
OUCH.
by gum, i will get every last one of you!
by gum?
and when i do...
RING!
WHO DAT IS?
RING!
RING!
TES!
IZ HERE!
RING!
HMMMMMM
RING!

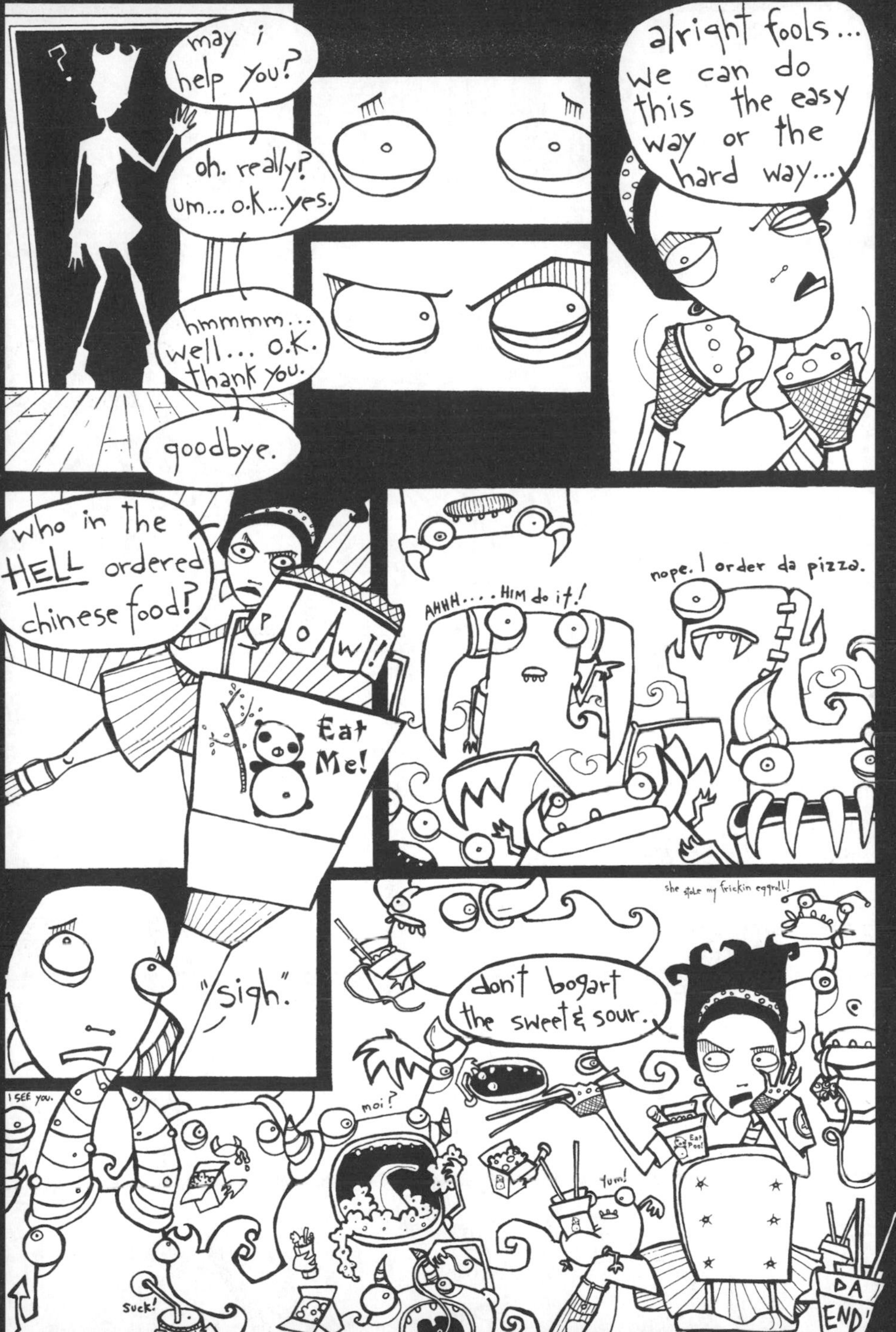
?
may i help you?
oh. really? um... o.k... yes.
hmmmm... well... o.k. thank you.
goodbye.
alright fools... we can do this the easy way or the hard way...
who in the HELL ordered chinese food?
POW!
Eat Me!
AHHH.... HIM do it!
nope. I order da pizza.
"sigh."
she stole my frickin eggroll!
don't bogart the sweet & sour.
I SEE you.
moi?
Eat Poo!
Yum!
suck!
DA END!

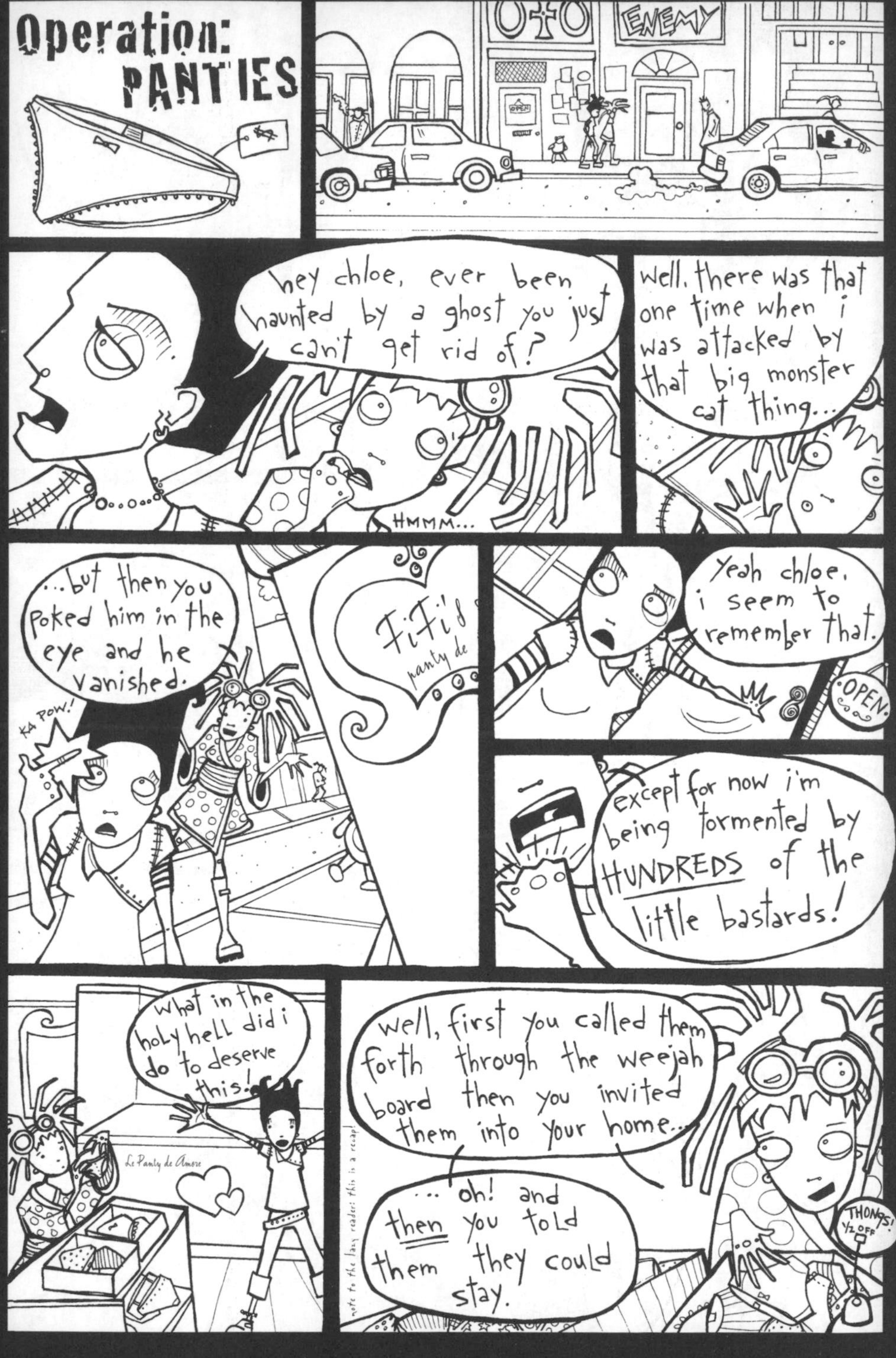
Operation: PANTIES
ENEMY
OPEN
hey chloe, ever been haunted by a ghost you just can't get rid of?
HMMM...
well, there was that one time when i was attacked by that big monster cat thing...
...but then you poked him in the eye and he vanished.
KA POW!
Fifi's panty de
yeah chloe, i seem to remember that.
OPEN
except for now i'm being tormented by HUNDREDS of the little bastards!
what in the holy hell did i do to deserve this!
Le Panty de Amore
note to the lazy reader: this is a recap!
well, first you called them forth through the weejah board then you invited them into your home...
...oh! and then you told them they could stay.
THONGS! 1/2 OFF

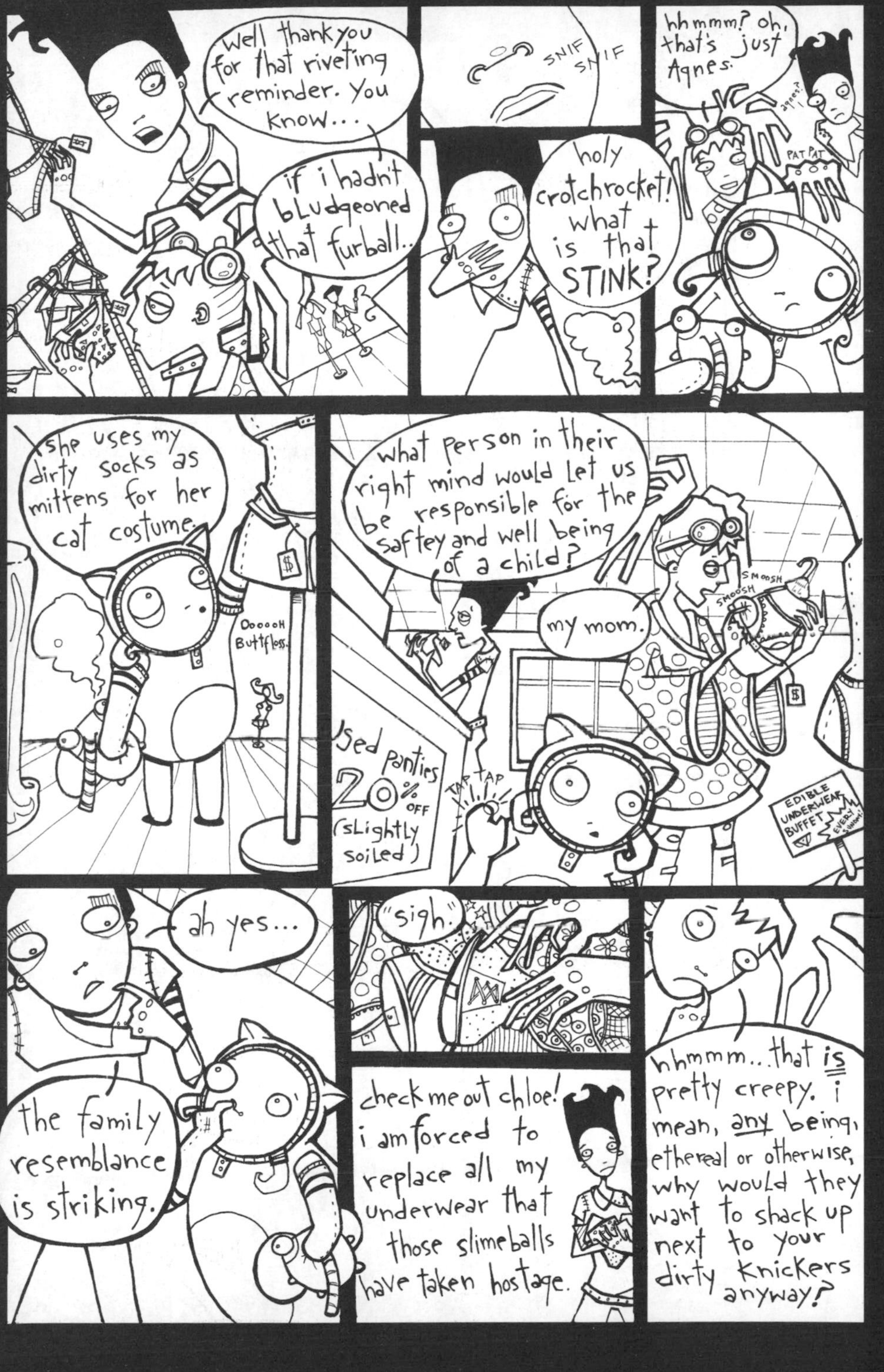
well thank you for that riveting reminder. You know...
if i hadn't bludgeoned that furball..
SNIF SNIF
holy crotchrocket! what is that STINK?
hhmmm? oh, that's just Agnes.
agnes?
PAT PAT
she uses my dirty socks as mittens for her cat costume.
Oooooh Buttfloss.
what person in their right mind would let us be responsible for the saftey and well being of a child?
my mom.
SMOOSH
SMOOSH
Used panties 20% OFF (sLightly soiLed)
TAP TAP
EDIBLE UNDERWEAR BUFFET EVERY SUNDAY!
ah yes...
the family resemblance is striking.
"sigh."
check me out chloe! i am forced to replace all my underwear that those slimeballs have taken hostage.
hhmmm...that is pretty creepy. i mean, any being, ethereal or otherwise, why would they want to shack up next to your dirty knickers anyway?

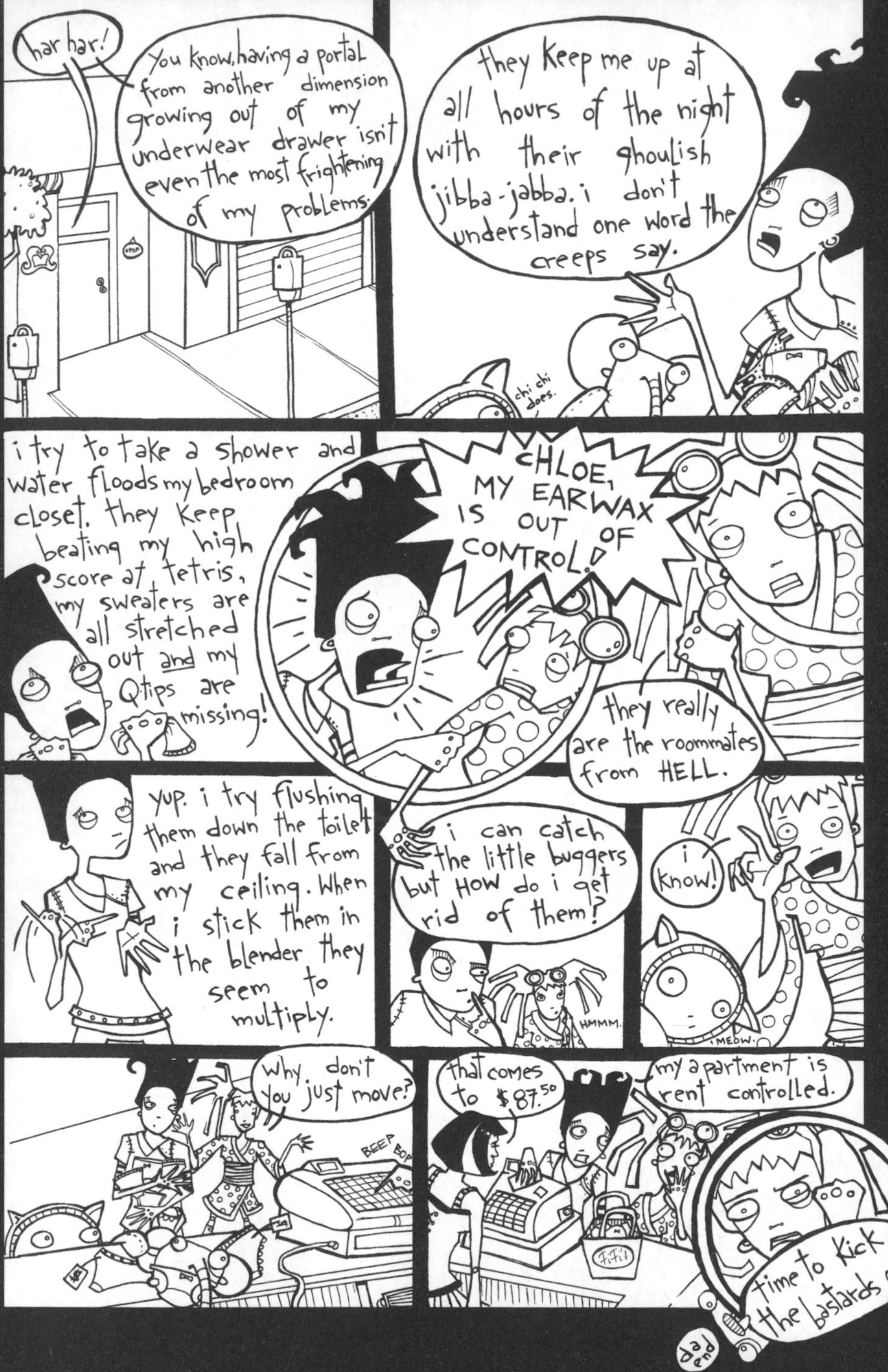
har har!
You know, having a portal from another dimension growing out of my underwear drawer isn't even the most frightening of my problems.
they keep me up at all hours of the night with their ghoulish jibba-jabba. i don't understand one word the creeps say.
chi chi does.
i try to take a shower and water floods my bedroom closet. they keep beating my high score at tetris, my sweaters are all stretched out and my Q-tips are missing!
CHLOE, MY EARWAX IS OUT OF CONTROL!
they really are the roommates from HELL.
yup. i try flushing them down the toilet and they fall from my ceiling. When i stick them in the blender they seem to multiply.
i can catch the little buggers but HOW do i get rid of them?
HMMM.
i know!
MEOW.
why don't you just move?
BEEP BOP
that comes to $87.50
my apartment is rent controlled.
time to kick the bastards out!

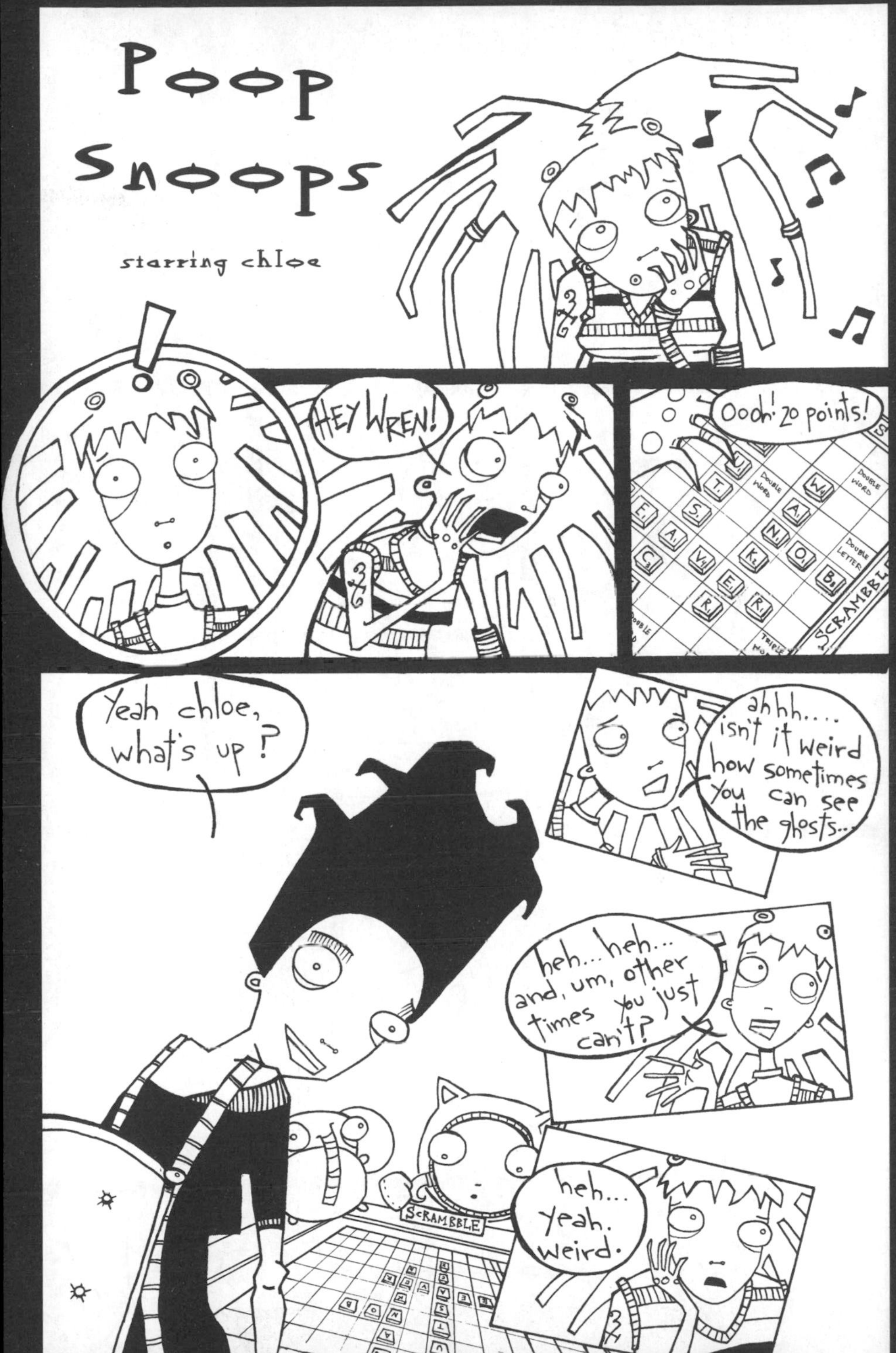
Poop Snoops
starring chloe
HEY WREN!
Oooh! 20 points!
Yeah chloe, what's up?
ahhh.... isn't it weird how sometimes you can see the ghosts...
heh...heh... and, um, other times you just can't?
heh... yeah. weird.
SCRAMBBLE

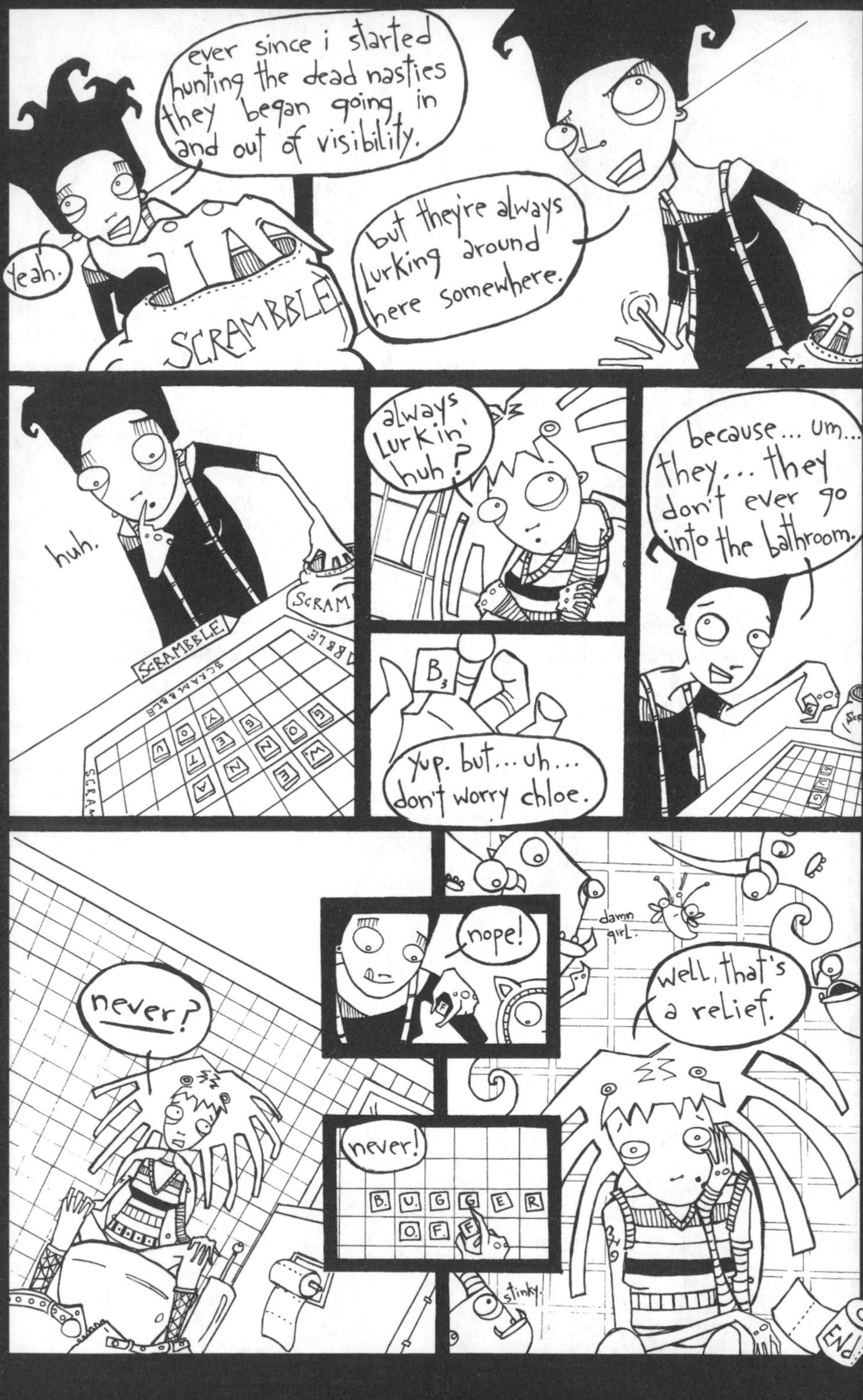
ever since i started hunting the dead nasties they began going in and out of visibility.
yeah.
SCRAMBBLE
but they're always lurking around here somewhere.
huh.
SCRAMBBLE
always lurkin' huh?
because... um... they... they don't ever go into the bathroom.
yup. but... uh... don't worry chloe.
never?
nope!
damn girl.
well, that's a relief.
never!
BUGGER OFF
stinky.
END...

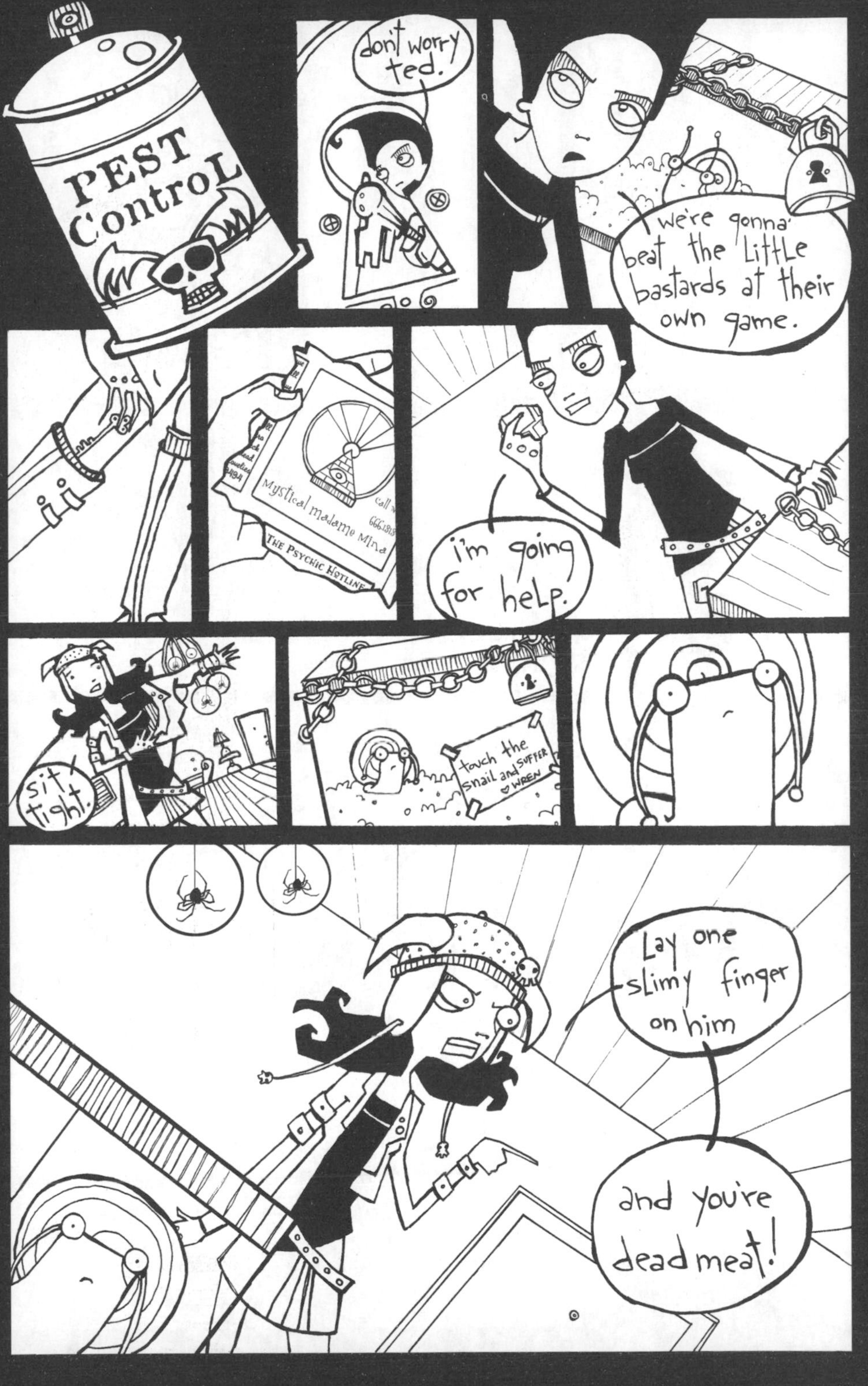
PEST Control
don't worry ted.
we're gonna' beat the Little bastards at their own game.
Mystical madame Mina
The Psychic Hotline
i'm going for heLp.
sit tight.
touch the snail and SUFFER ♥ WREN
Lay one sLimy finger on him
and you're dead meat!

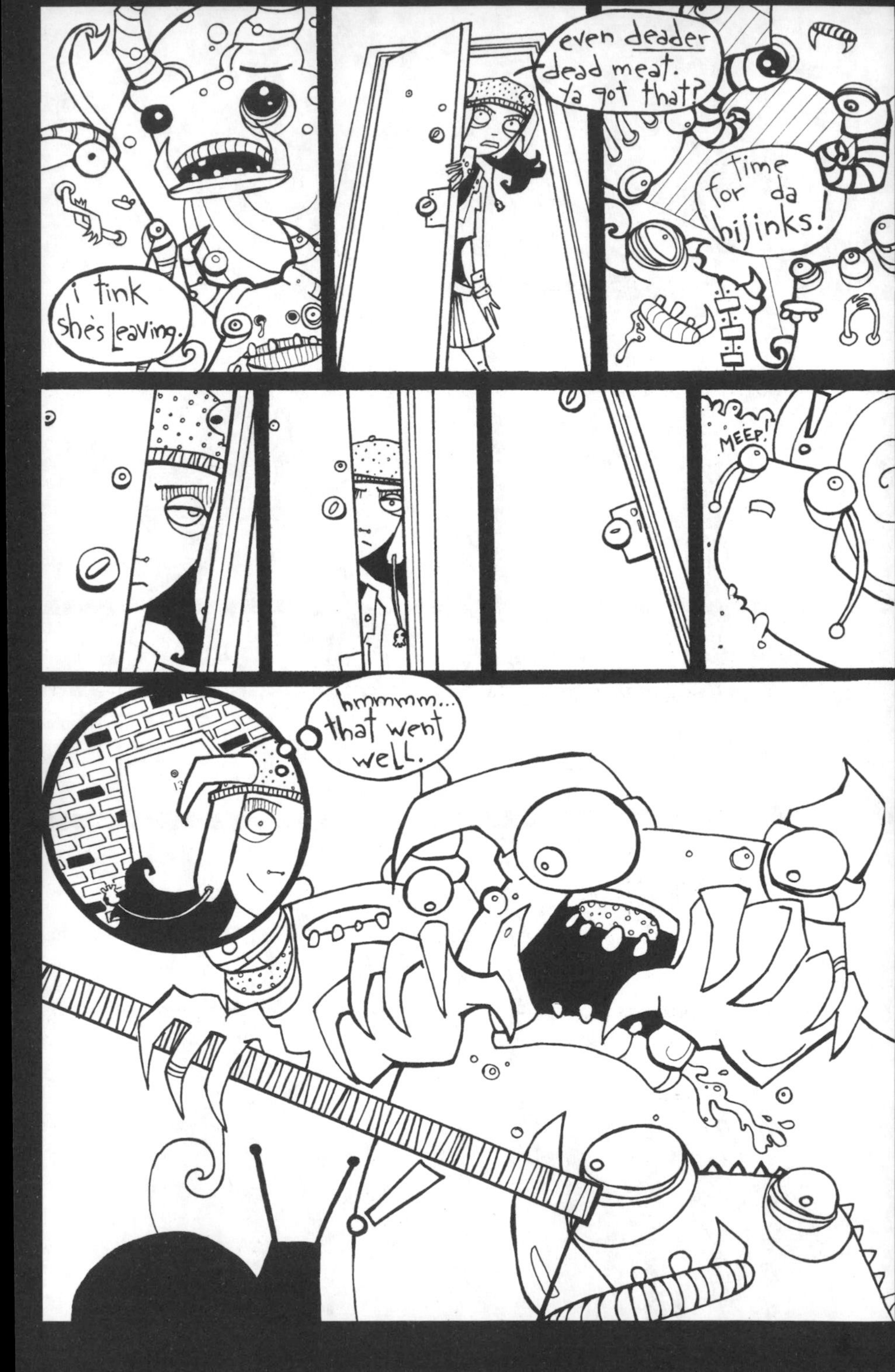
i tink she's Leaving.
even deader dead meat. ya got that?
time for da hijinks!
MEEP!
hmmmm... that went well.
13

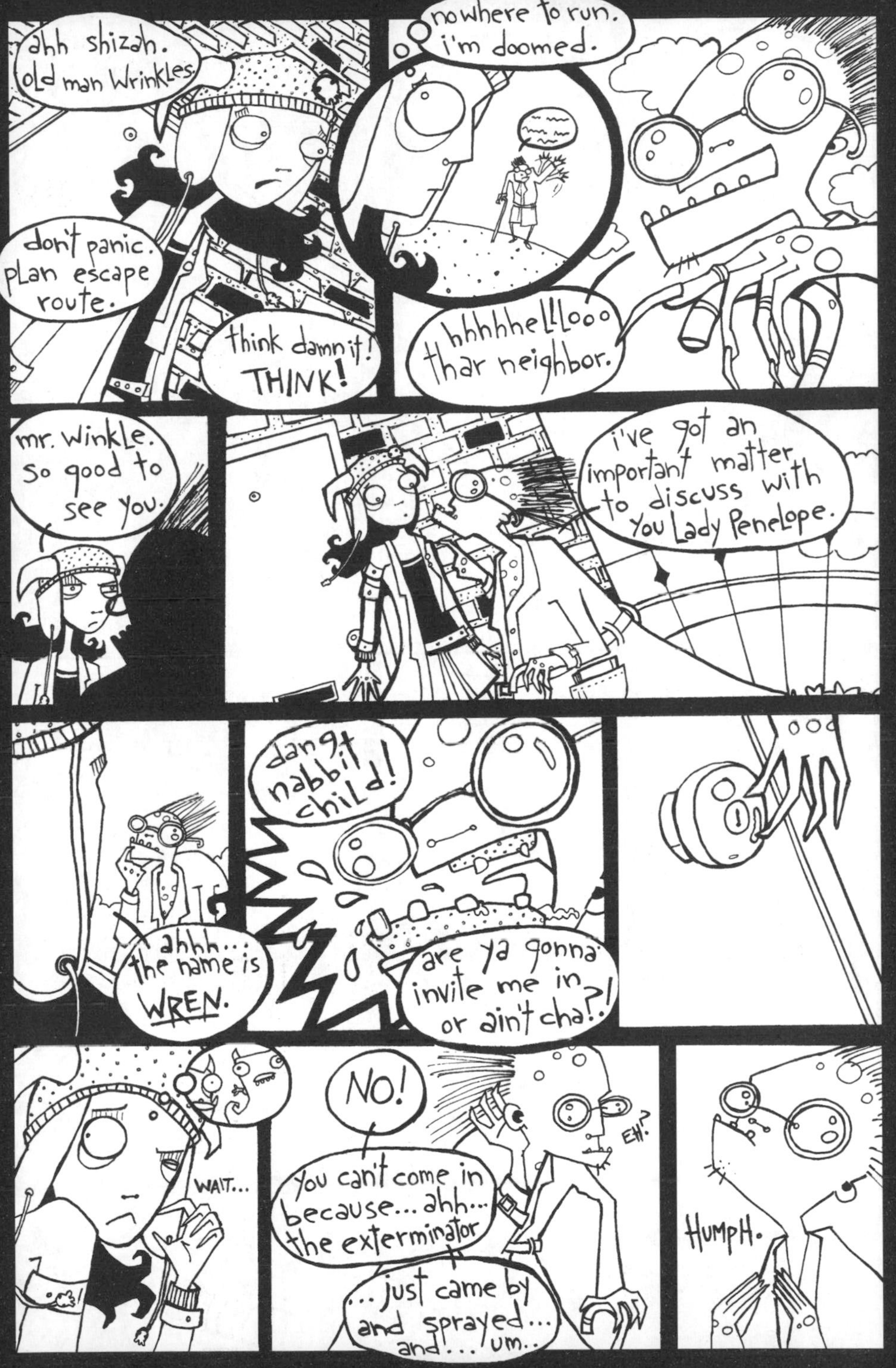
ahh shizah. oLd man Wrinkles.
don't panic. pLan escape route.
think damnit! THINK!
no where to run. i'm doomed.
hhhhheLLLooo thar neighbor.
mr. winkLe. So good to see you.
i've got an important matter to discuss with you Lady PeneLope.
ahhh... the name is WREN.
dangit nabbit chiLd!
are ya gonna invite me in or ain't cha?!
WAIT...
NO!
you can't come in because... ahh... the exterminator
...just came by and sprayed... and... um..
EH?
HUMPH.

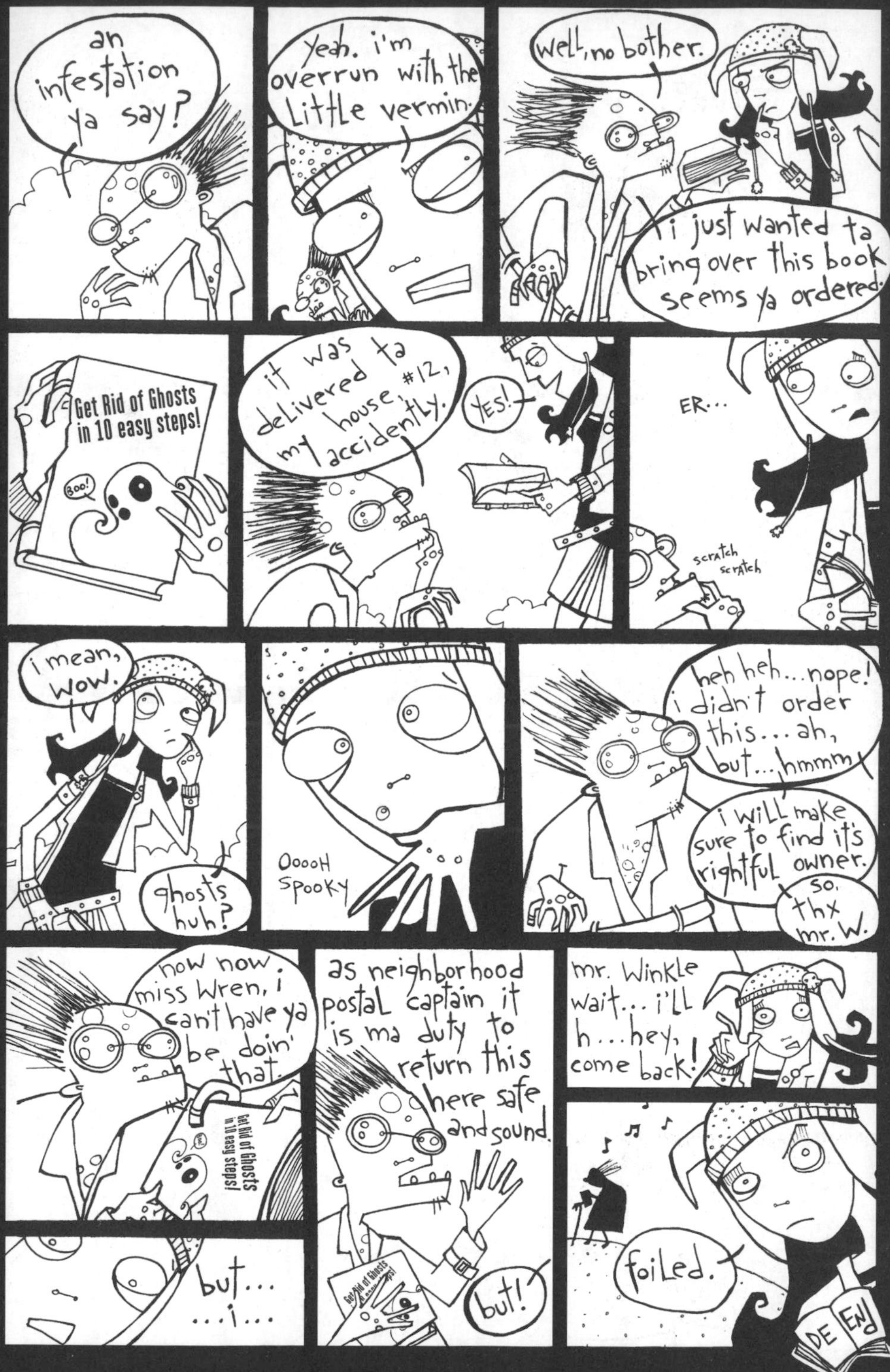
an infestation ya say?
yeah. i'm overrun with the Little vermin.
well, no bother.
i just wanted ta bring over this book seems ya ordered.
Get Rid of Ghosts in 10 easy steps!
BOO!
it was ta delivered my house, #12, accidently.
YES!
ER...
scratch scratch
i mean, wow.
ghosts huh?
OoooH Spooky
heh heh... nope! i didn't order this... ah, but... hmmm
i will make sure to find it's rightful owner.
so. thx mr. W.
now now miss Wren, i can't have ya be doin' that.
Get Rid of Ghosts in 10 easy steps!
as neighborhood postal captain it is ma duty to return this here safe and sound.
mr. Winkle wait... i'll h... hey, come back!
but... ...i...
but!
foiled.
DE END

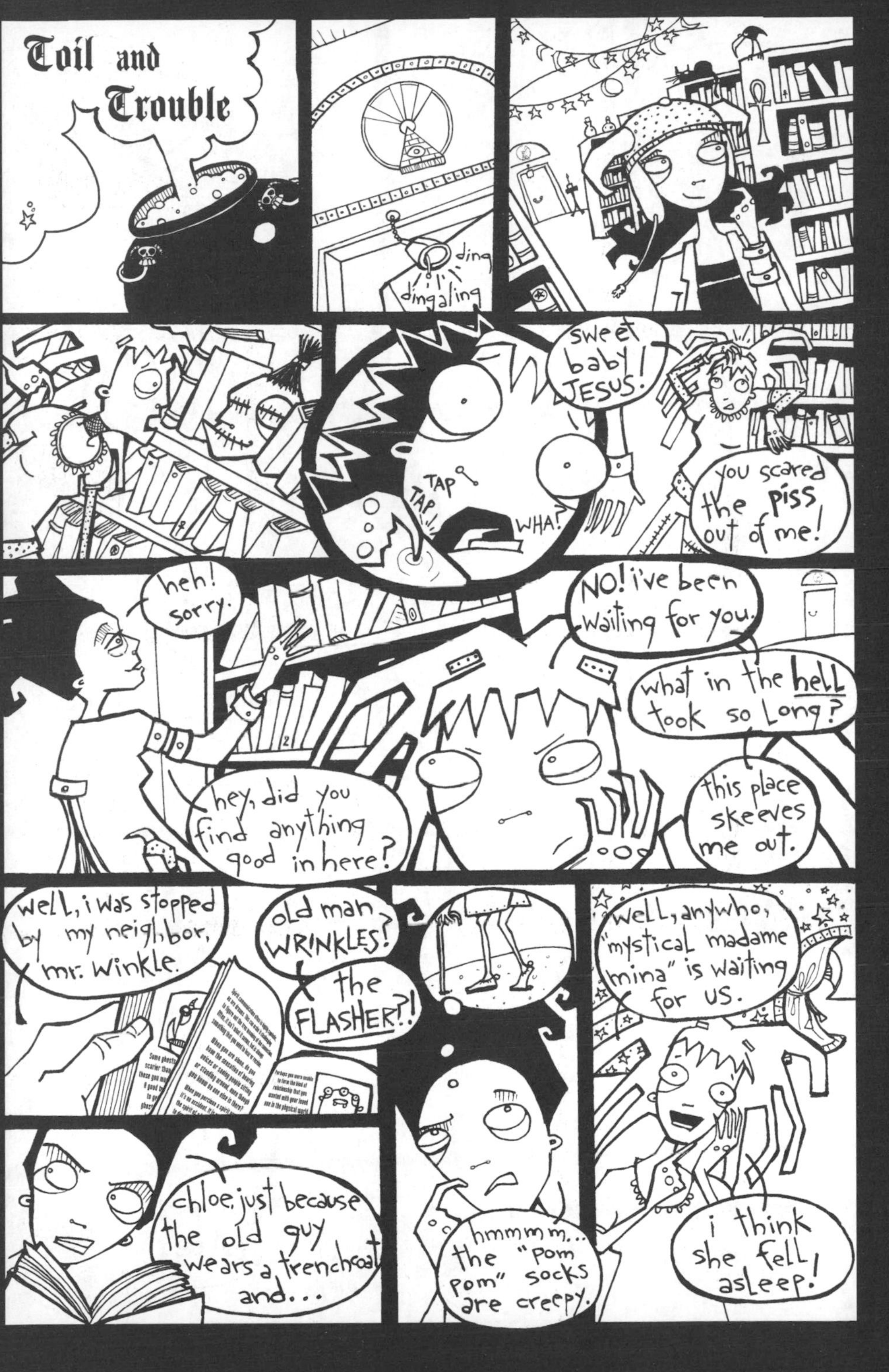
Toil and Trouble
ding
dingaling
sweet baby! JESUS!
TAP TAP
WHA?
you scared the PISS out of me!
heh! sorry.
NO! i've been waiting for you.
what in the hell took so Long?
this place skeeves me out.
hey, did you find anything good in here?
well, i was stopped by my neighbor, mr. winkle.
old man WRINKLES?
the FLASHER?!
well, anywho, "mystical madame mina" is waiting for us.
chloe, just because the old guy wears a trenchcoat and...
hmmmm... the "pom pom" socks are creepy.
i think she fell asleep!

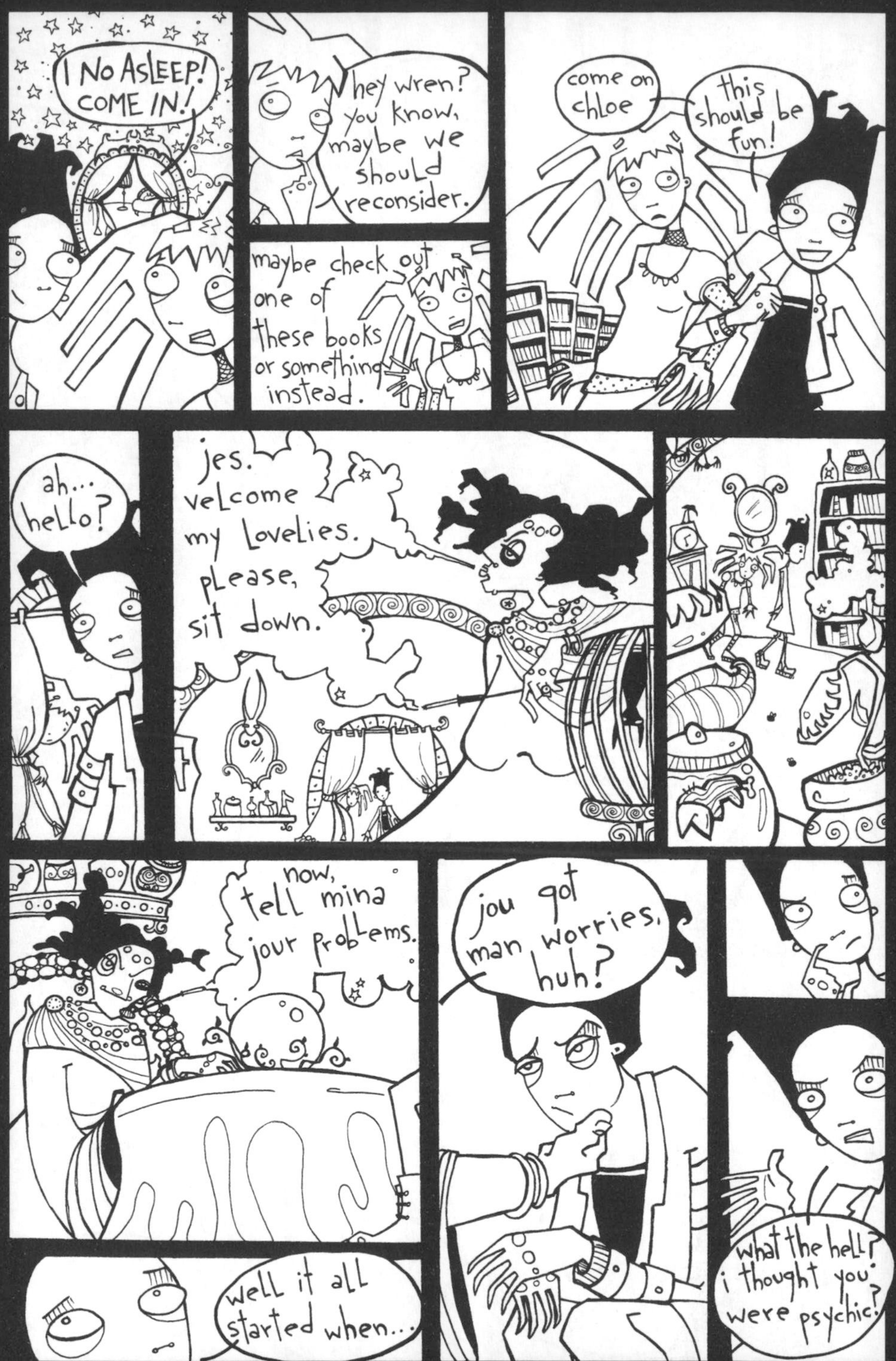
I NO ASLEEP! COME IN!
hey wren? you know, maybe we should reconsider.
maybe check out one of these books or something instead.
come on chloe
this should be fun!
ah... hello?
jes. velcome my lovelies. please, sit down.
now, tell mina jour problems.
well it all started when...
jou got man worries, huh?
what the hell? i thought you were psychic?

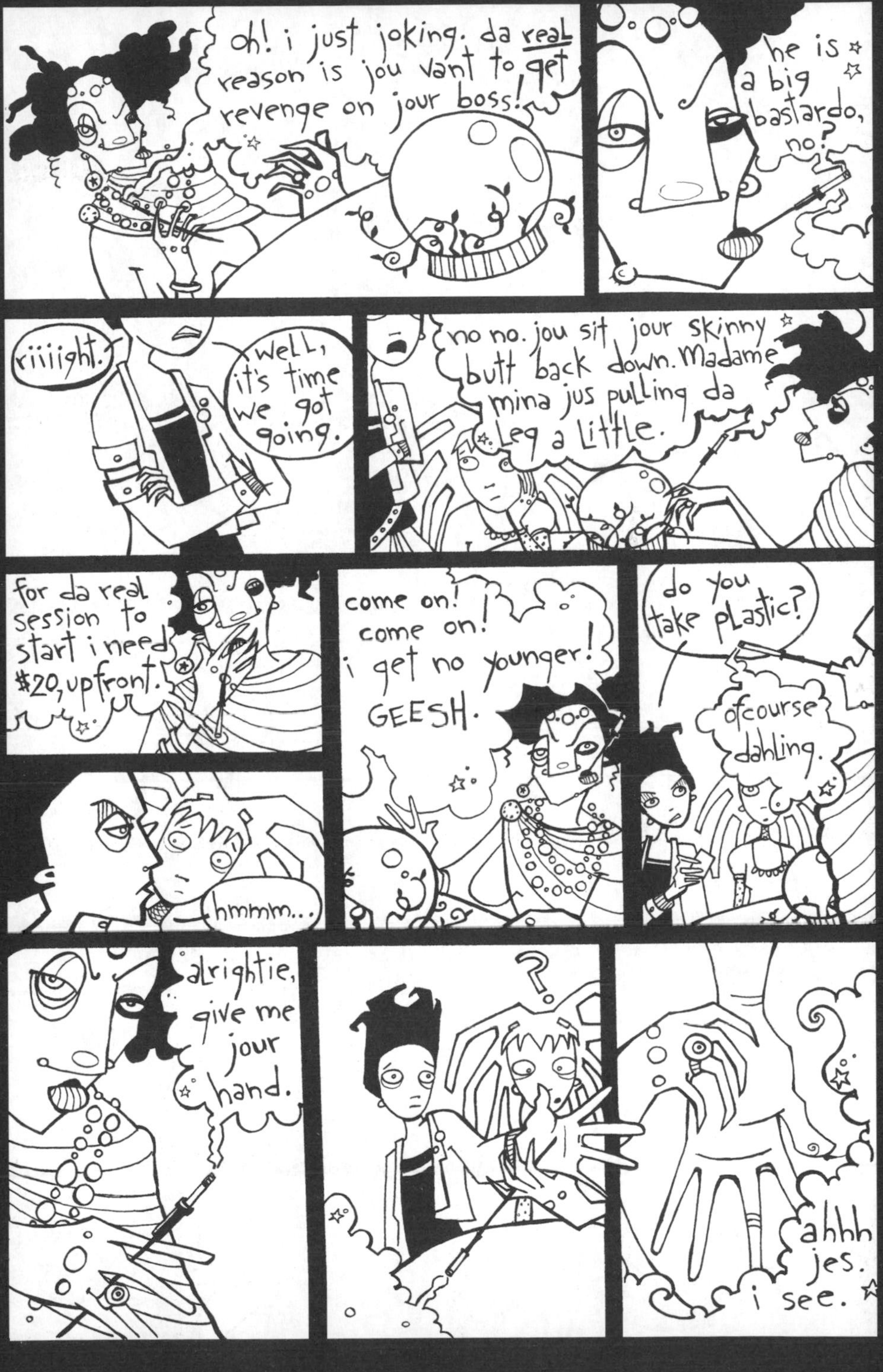
oh! i just joking. da real reason is jou vant to get revenge on jour boss!
he is a big bastardo, no?
riiiight.
well, it's time we got going.
no no. jou sit jour skinny butt back down. Madame mina jus pulling da leg a little.
for da real session to start i need $20, upfront.
hmmm...
come on! come on! i get no younger! GEESH.
do you take plastic?
ofcourse dahling.
alrightie, give me jour hand.
?
ahhh jes. i see.

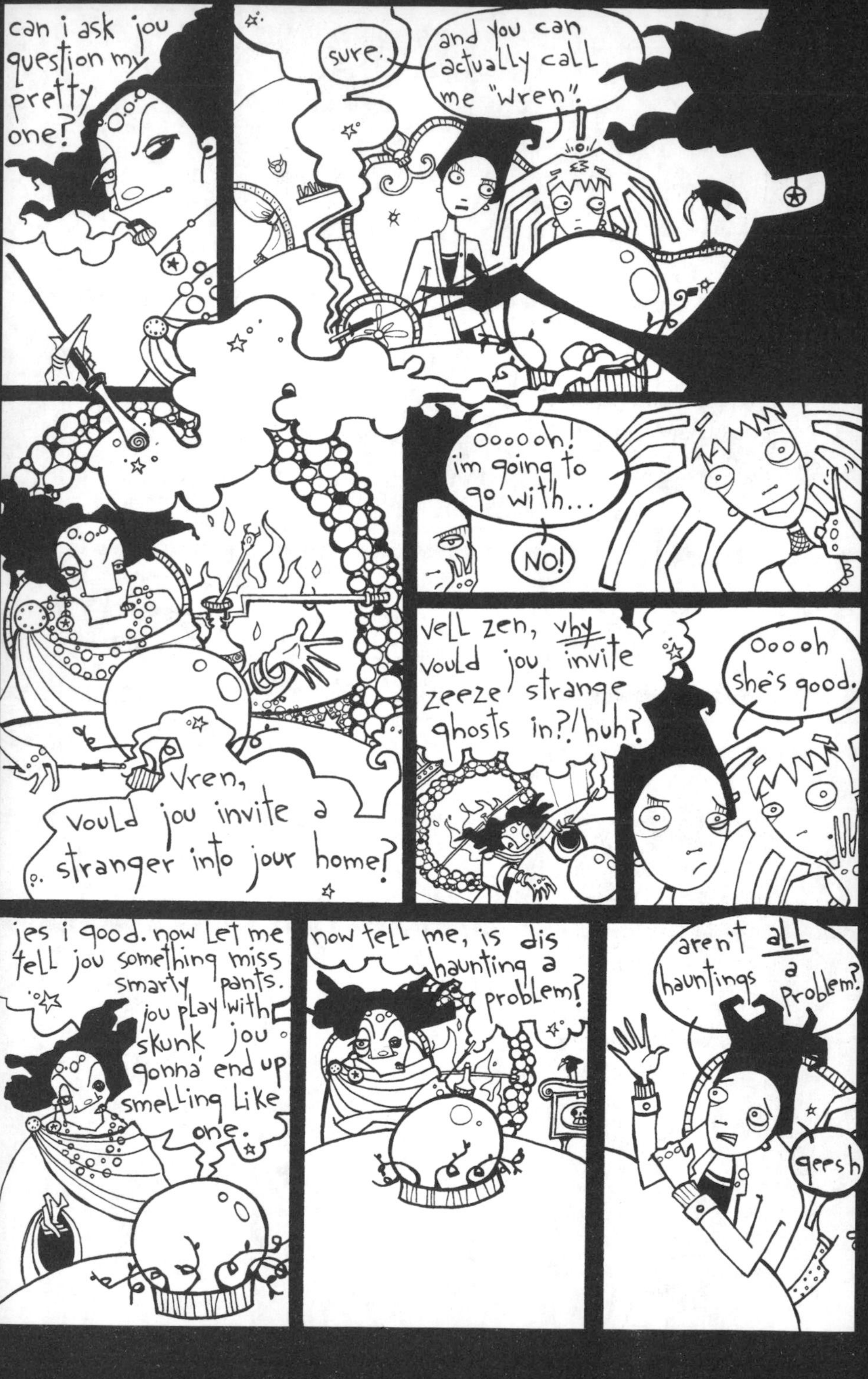
can i ask jou question my pretty one?
sure.
and you can actually call me "wren".
!
Ooooh! i'm going to go with...
NO!
vell zen, vhy vould jou invite zeeze strange ghosts in?/huh?
Ooooh she's good.
Vren, vould jou invite a stranger into jour home?
jes i good. now let me tell jou something miss smarty pants. jou play with skunk jou gonna' end up smelling like one.
now tell me, is dis haunting a problem?
aren't all hauntings a problem?
geesh

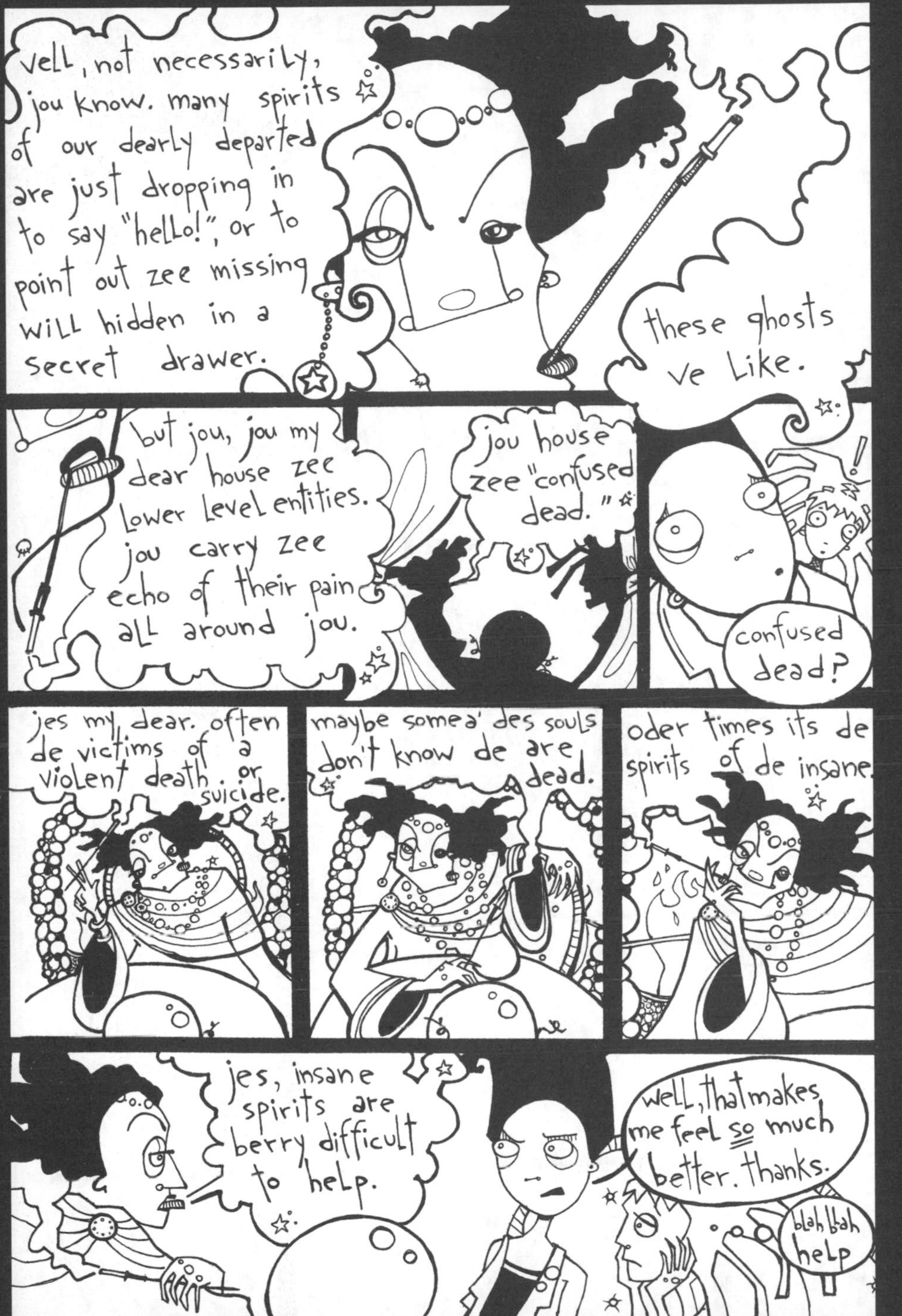
vell, not necessarily, jou know. many spirits of our dearly departed are just dropping in to say "hello!", or to point out zee missing will hidden in a secret drawer.
these ghosts ve like.
but jou, jou my dear house zee lower level entities. jou carry zee echo of their pain all around jou.
jou house zee "confused dead."
confused dead?
jes my dear. often de victims of a violent death or suicide.
maybe somea' des souls don't know de are dead.
oder times its de spirits of de insane.
jes, insane spirits are berry difficult to help.
well, that makes me feel so much better. thanks.
blah blah help

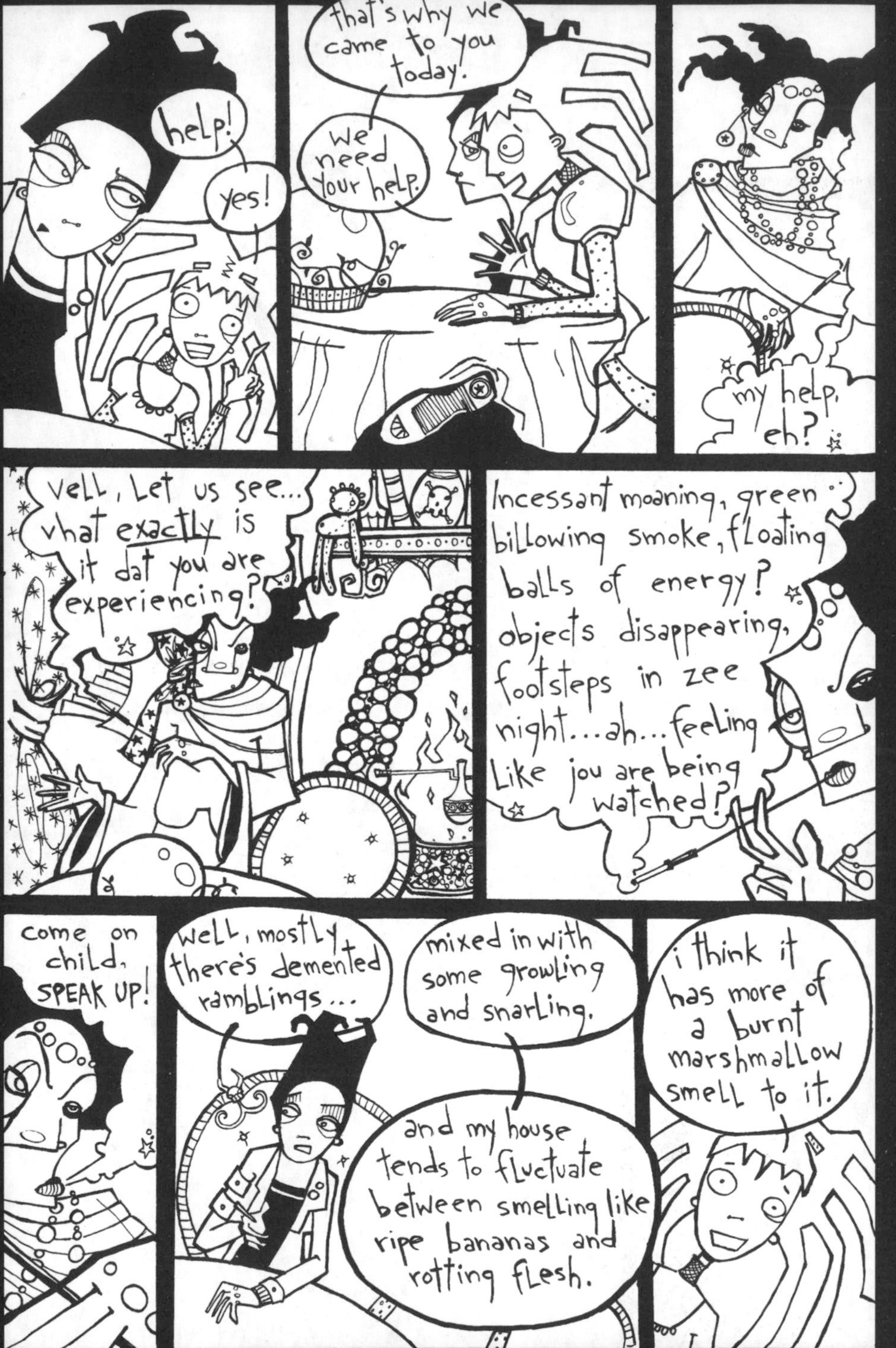
help!
yes!
that's why we came to you today!
we need your help.
my help, eh?
vell, let us see... vhat exactly is it dat you are experiencing?
Incessant moaning, green billowing smoke, floating balls of energy? objects disappearing, footsteps in zee night...ah...feeling like jou are being watched?
come on child, SPEAK UP!
well, mostly there's demented ramblings...
mixed in with some growling and snarling.
and my house tends to fluctuate between smelling like ripe bananas and rotting flesh.
i think it has more of a burnt marshmallow smell to it.

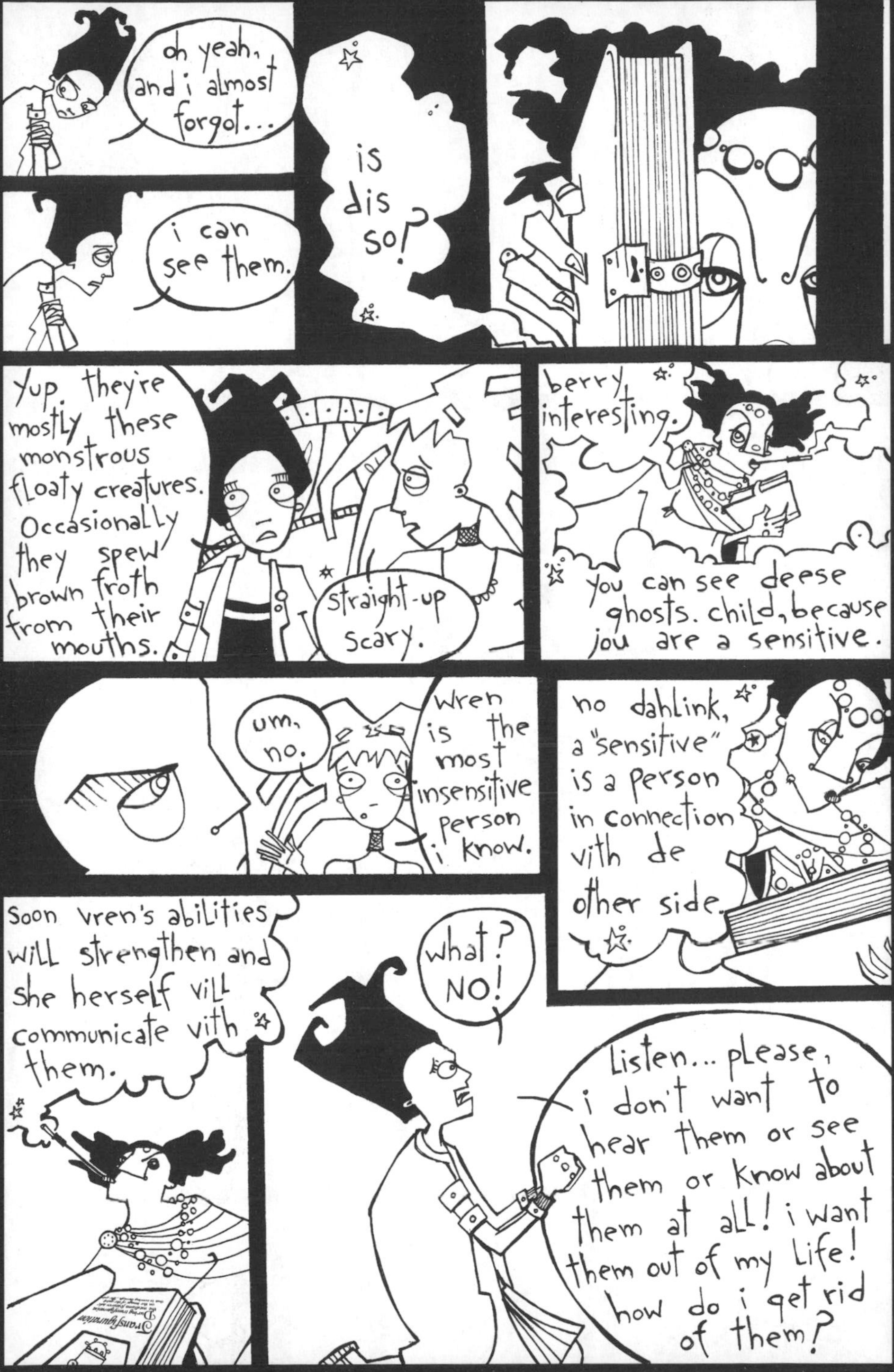
oh yeah, and i almost forgot...
i can see them.
is dis so?
yup, they're mostly these monstrous floaty creatures. Occasionally they spew brown froth from their mouths.
straight-up scary.
berry interesting.
you can see deese ghosts, child, because jou are a sensitive.
um, no.
wren is the most insensitive person i know.
no dahlink, a "sensitive" is a person in connection vith de other side.
Soon vren's abilities will strengthen and she herself vill communicate vith them.
what? NO!
Listen... please, i don't want to hear them or see them or know about them at all! i want them out of my life! how do i get rid of them?

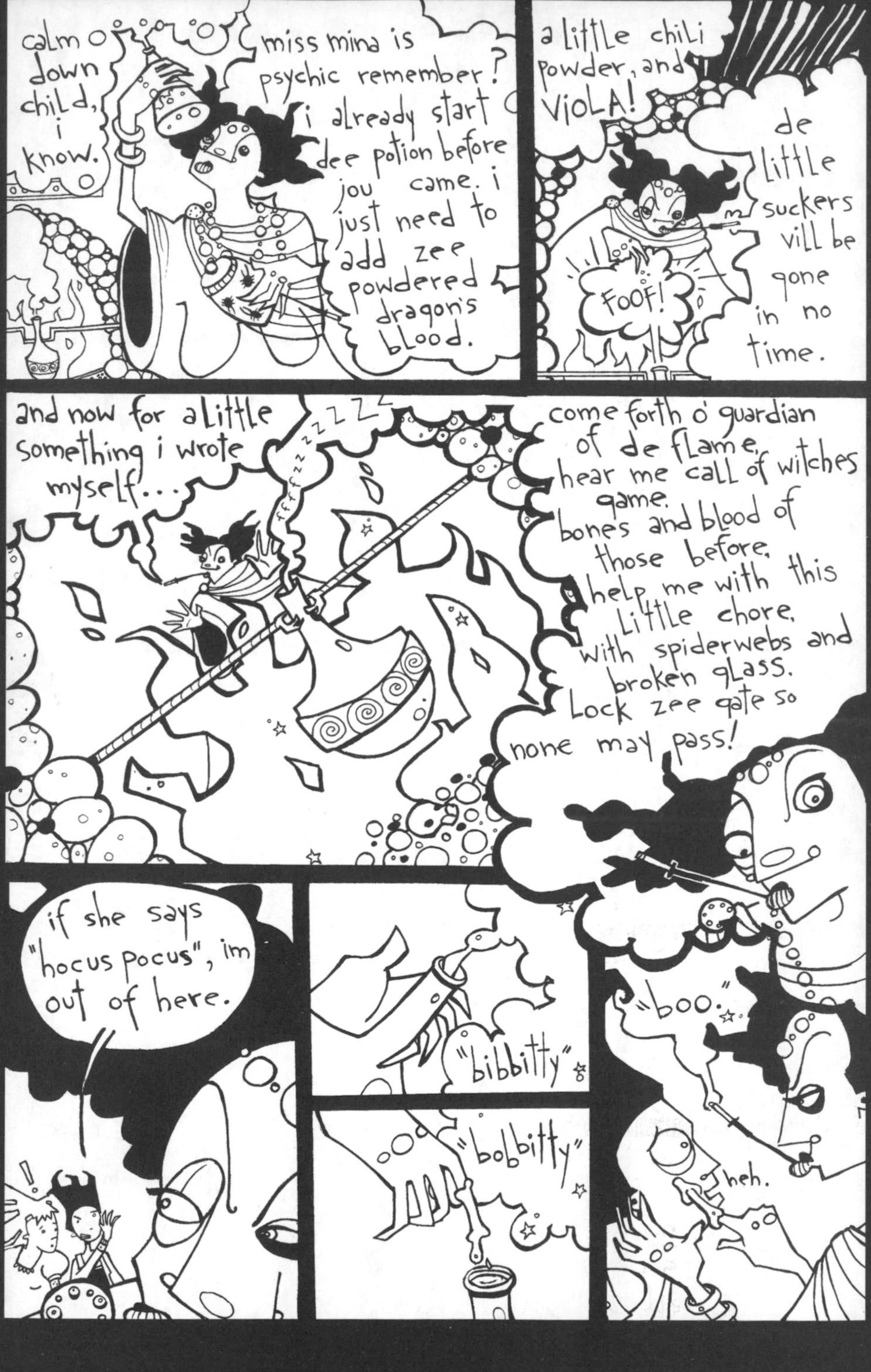

calm down child, i know.
miss mina is psychic remember? i already start dee potion before jou came. i just need to add zee powdered dragon's blood.
a little chili powder, and VIOLA!
FOOF!
de little suckers vill be gone in no time.
and now for a little something i wrote myself...
ffffzzzzzzzZZ
come forth o' guardian of de flame, hear me call of witches game. bones and blood of those before, help me with this little chore. with spiderwebs and broken glass. Lock zee gate so none may pass!
if she says "hocus pocus", im out of here.
!
"bibbitty"
"bobbitty"
"boo."
heh.

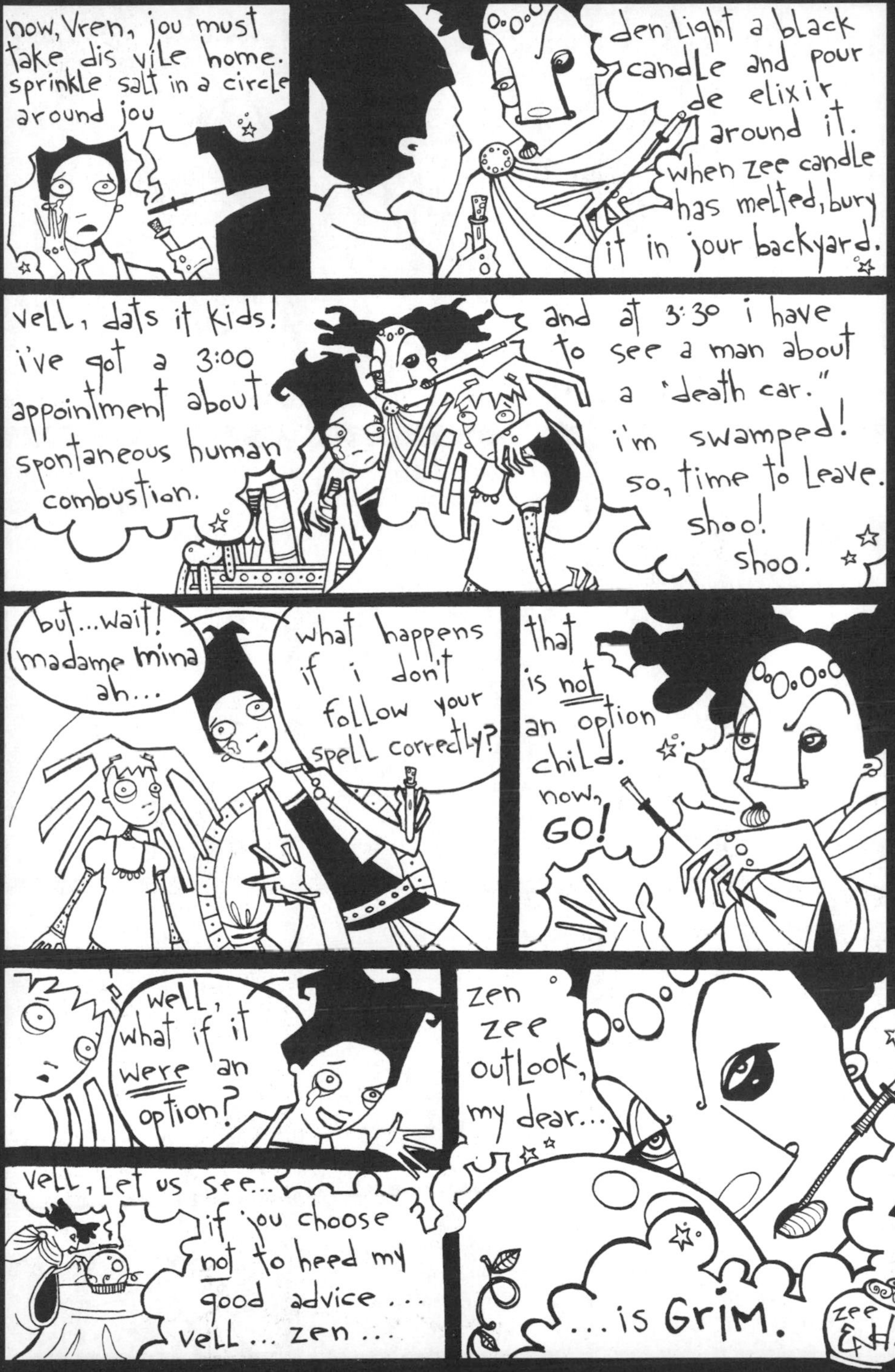
now, Vren, jou must take dis vile home. sprinkle salt in a circle around jou
den light a black candle and pour de elixir around it. when zee candle has melted, bury it in jour backyard.
vell, dats it kids! i've got a 3:00 appointment about spontaneous human combustion.
and at 3:30 i have to see a man about a "death car." i'm swamped! so, time to leave. shoo! shoo!
but...wait! madame mina ah...
what happens if i don't follow your spell correctly?
that is not an option child. now, GO!
well, what if it were an option?
vell, let us see...
if you choose not to heed my good advice... vell... zen...
zen zee outlook, my dear...
...is GRIM.
zee E&H.

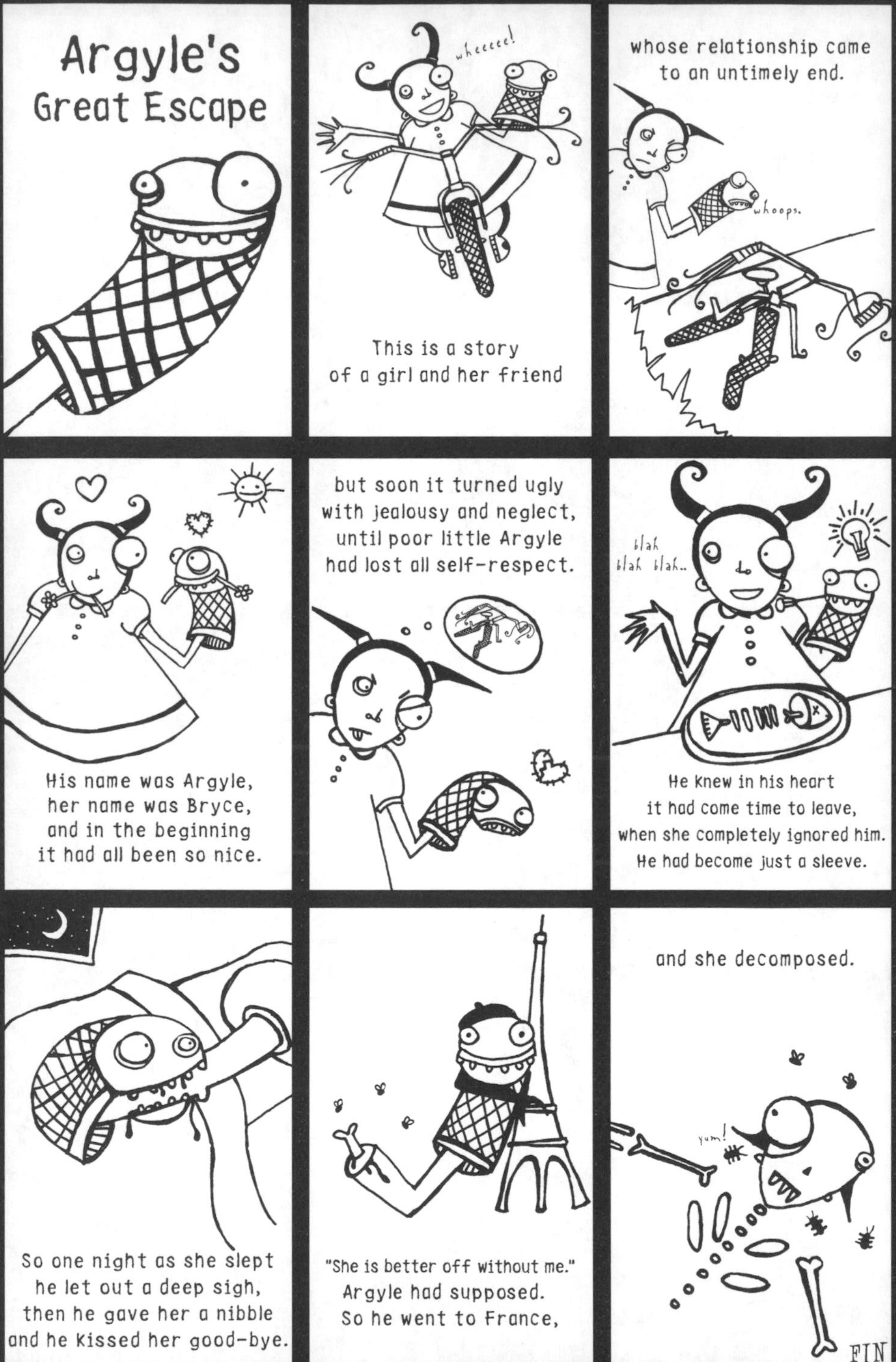

Argyle's
Great Escape
wheeeeee!
This is a story
of a girl and her friend
whose relationship came
to an untimely end.
whoops.
His name was Argyle,
her name was Bryce,
and in the beginning
it had all been so nice.
but soon it turned ugly
with jealousy and neglect,
until poor little Argyle
had lost all self-respect.
blah
blah blah..
He knew in his heart
it had come time to leave,
when she completely ignored him.
He had become just a sleeve.
So one night as she slept
he let out a deep sigh,
then he gave her a nibble
and he kissed her good-bye.
"She is better off without me."
Argyle had supposed.
So he went to France,
and she decomposed.
yum!
FIN

chapter three.

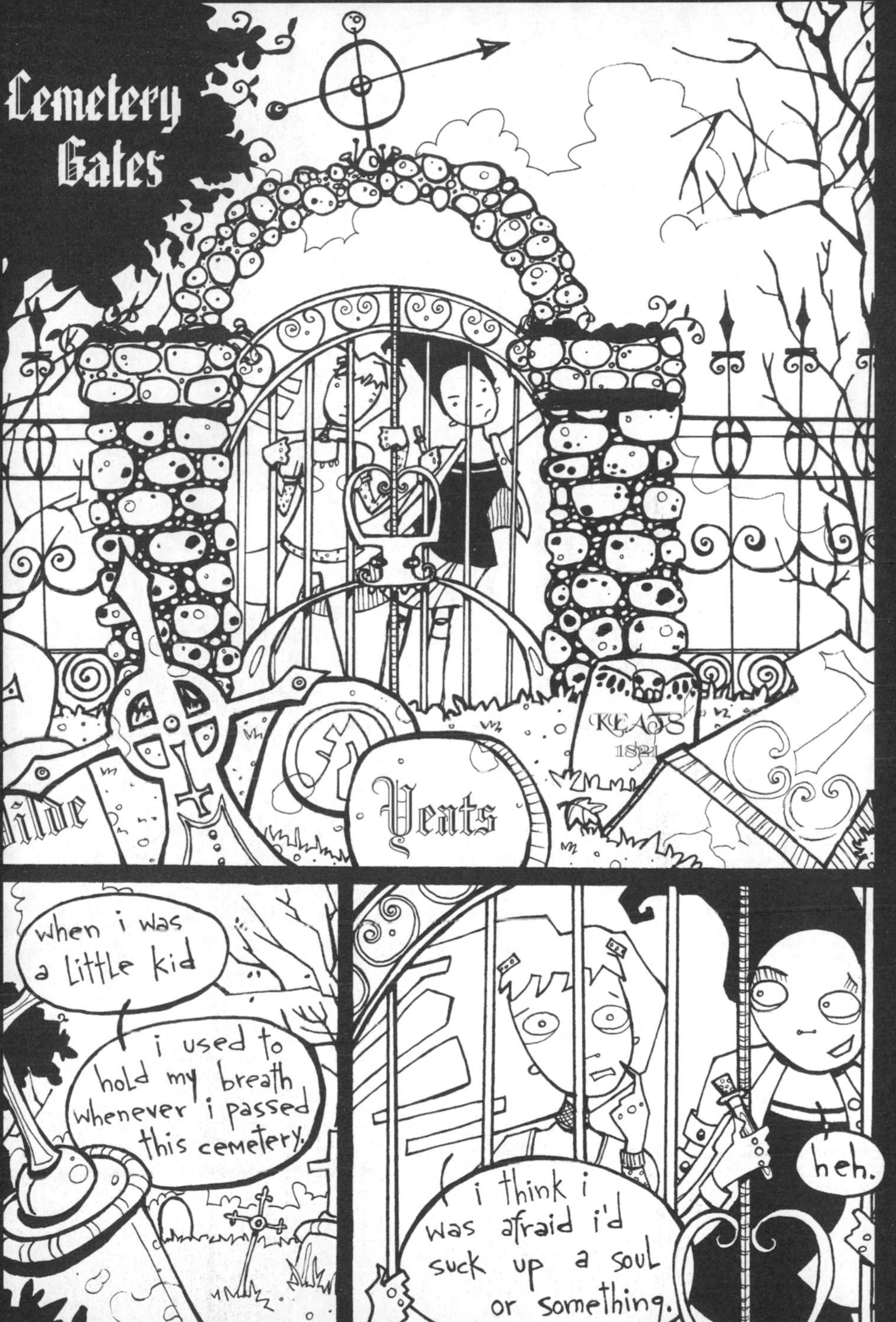
Cemetery Gates
Yeats
KEATS
1821
when i was a little kid
i used to hold my breath whenever i passed this cemetery.
i think i was afraid i'd suck up a soul or something.
heh.

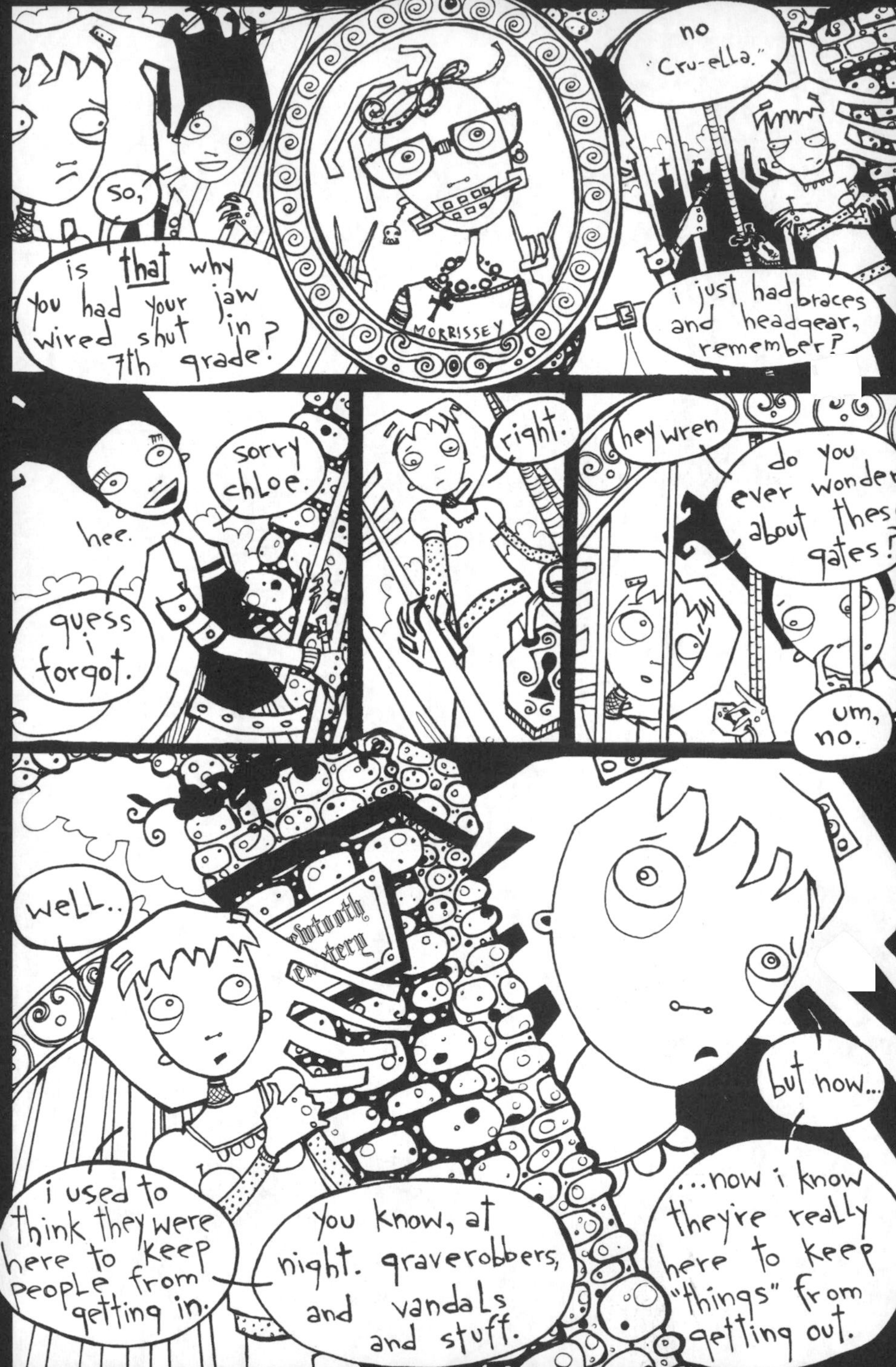
so,
is that why you had your jaw wired shut in 7th grade?
no "Cru-ella."
i just had braces and headgear, remember?
sorry chloe.
hee.
guess i forgot.
right.
hey wren
do you ever wonder about these gates?
um, no.
well..
i used to think they were here to keep people from getting in.
you know, at night. graverobbers, and vandals and stuff.
but now...
...now i know they're really here to keep "things" from getting out.

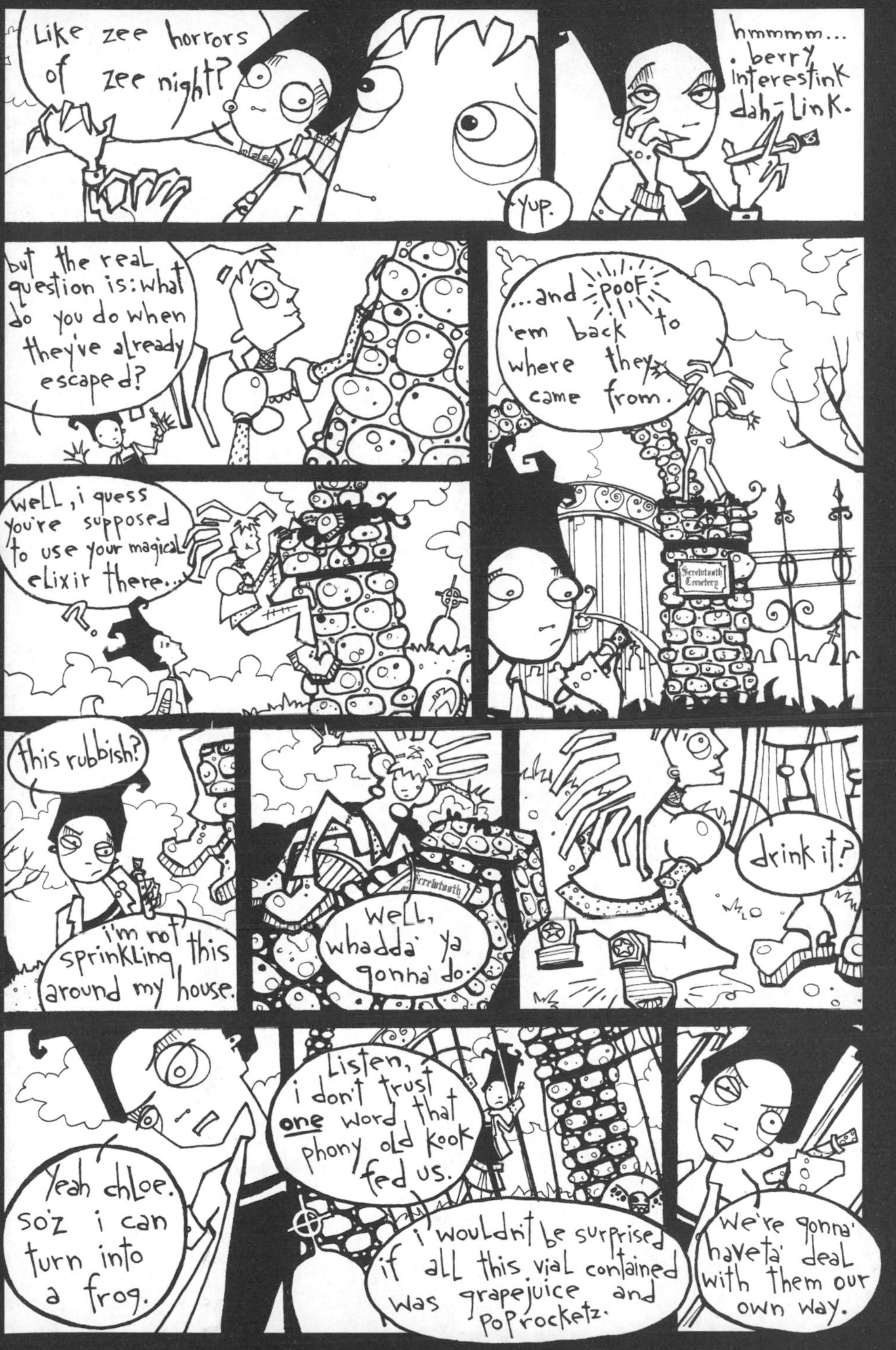
Like zee horrors of zee night?
yup.
hmmmm... berry interestink dah-Link.
but the real question is: what do you do when they've already escaped?
...and poof 'em back to where they came from.
well, i guess you're supposed to use your magical elixir there...
?
this rubbish?
i'm not sprinkling this around my house.
well, whadda' ya gonna' do..
drink it?
Yeah chloe. so'z i can turn into a frog.
Listen, i don't trust one word that phony old kook fed us.
i wouldn't be surprised if all this vial contained was grapejuice and poprocketz.
we're gonna' haveta' deal with them our own way.

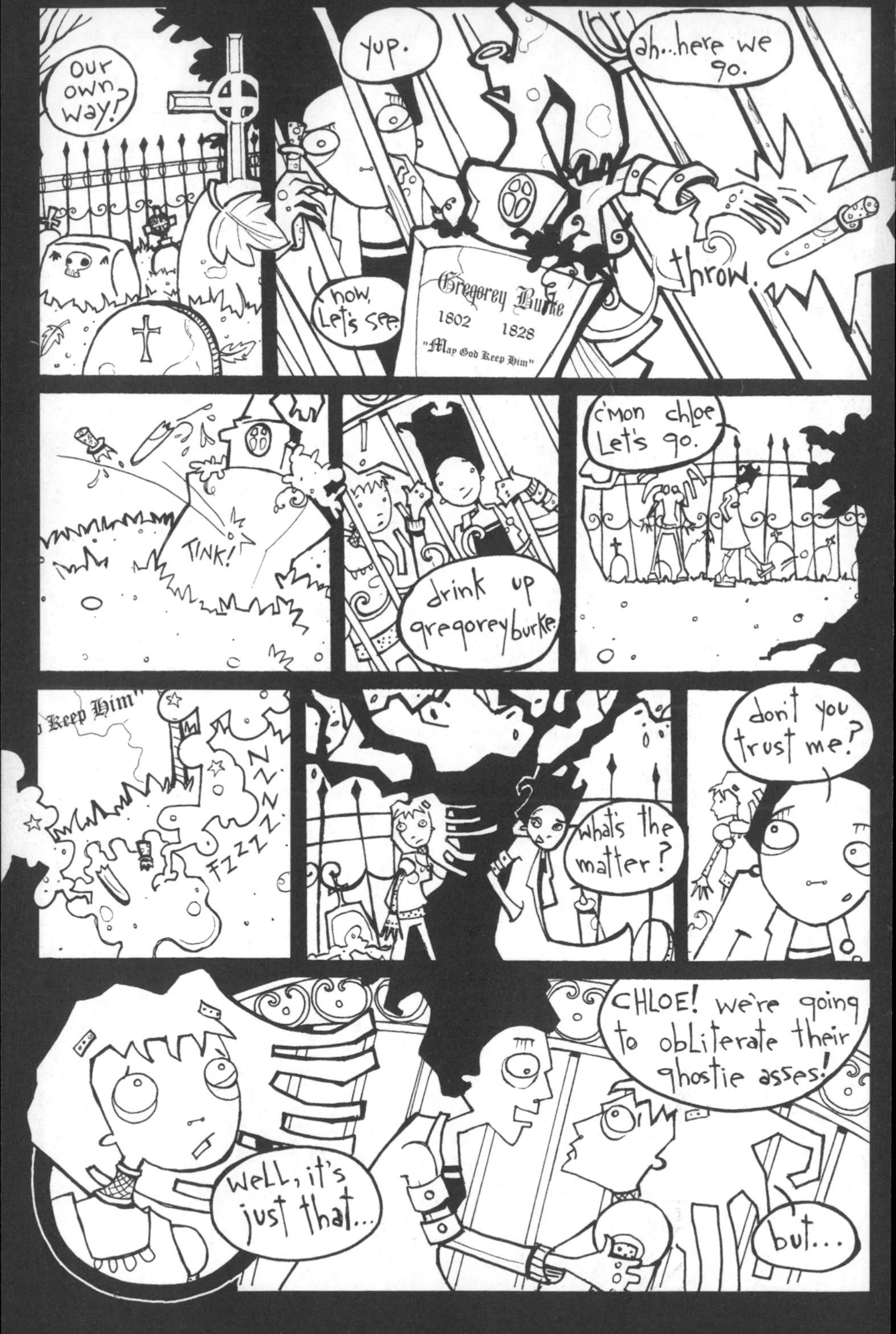

our own way?
yup.
ah...here we go.
now, Let's see.
Gregorey Burke
1802 1828
"May God Keep Him"
throw.
TINK!
drink up gregoreyburke.
c'mon chloe Let's go.
Keep Him
NZZZ
FZZZ
what's the matter?
don't you trust me?
CHLOE! we're going to obLiterate their ghostie asses!
weLL, it's just that...
but...

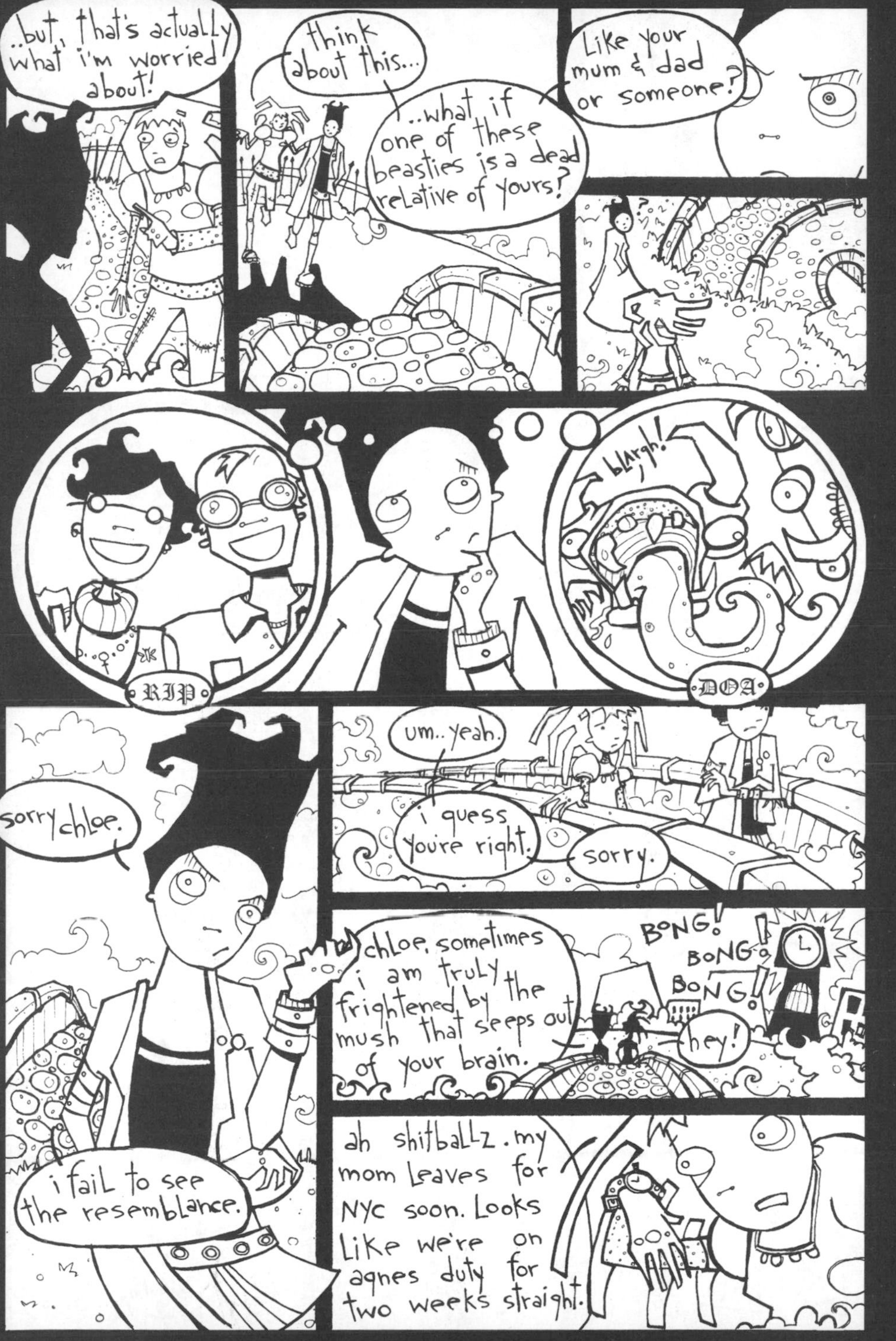
..but, that's actually what i'm worried about!
think about this...
..what if one of these beasties is a dead relative of yours?
Like your mum & dad or someone?
blargh!
RIP
DOA
sorry chloe.
i fail to see the resemblance.
um.. yeah.
i guess you're right.
sorry.
chloe, sometimes i am truly frightened by the mush that seeps out of your brain.
BONG! BONG! BONG!
hey!
ah shitballz. my mom leaves for NYC soon. Looks like we're on agnes duty for two weeks straight.

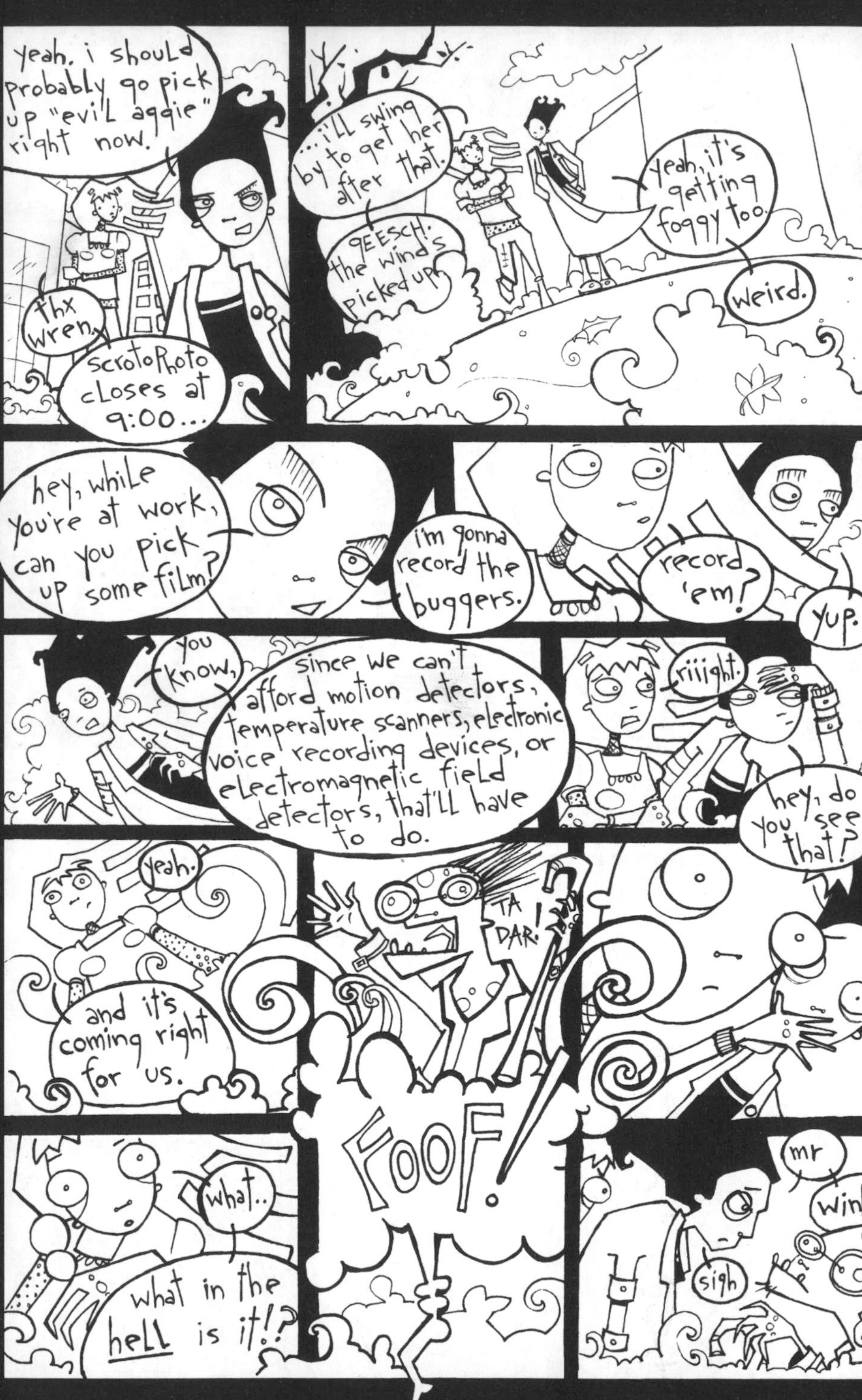
yeah, i should probably go pick up "evil aggie" right now.
thx wren.
scrotoPhoto closes at 9:00...
...i'll swing by to get her after that.
GEESCH! the wind's picked up.
yeah, it's getting foggy too.
weird.
hey, while you're at work, can you pick up some film?
i'm gonna record the buggers.
record 'em?
yup.
you know,
since we can't afford motion detectors, temperature scanners, electronic voice recording devices, or electromagnetic field detectors, that'll have to do.
riiight.
hey, do you see that?
yeah.
and it's coming right for us.
TA DAR!
FOOF!
what..
what in the hell is it!?
mr
winkle.
sigh

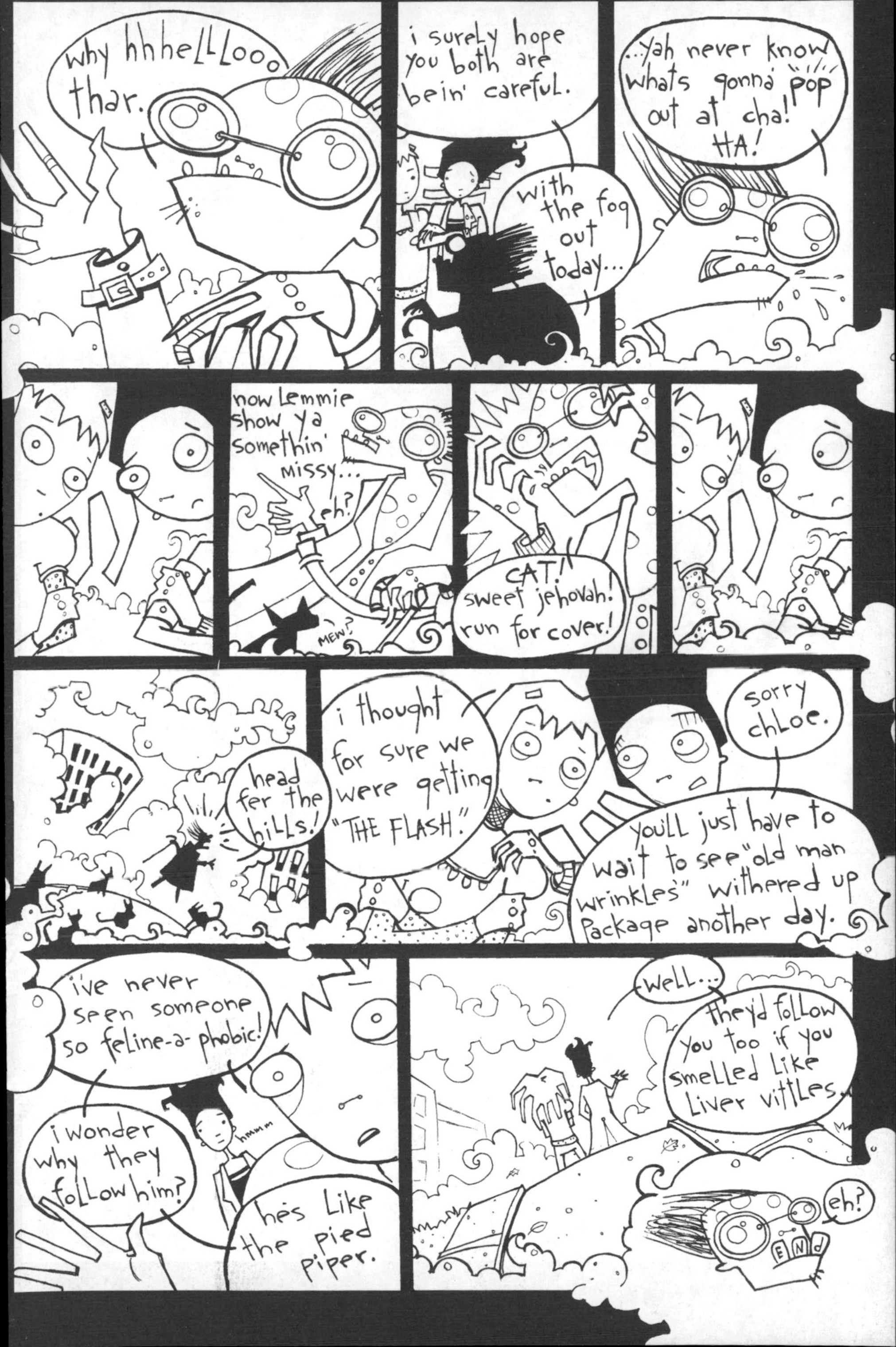
why hhhellLooo thar.
i sureLy hope you both are bein' carefuL.
with the fog out today...
...yah never know whats gonna "pop" out at cha! HA!
now Lemmie show ya somethin' missy...
eh?
MEW?
CAT!! sweet jehovah! run for cover!
head fer the hiLLs!
i thought for sure we were getting "THE FLASH."
sorry chLoe.
you'LL just have to wait to see "oLd man wrinkLes" withered up package another day.
i've never seen someone so feline-a-phobic!
i wonder why they foLLow him?
hmmm
he's Like the pied piper.
WeLL...
they'd foLLow you too if you smeLLed Like Liver vittLes.
eh?
END

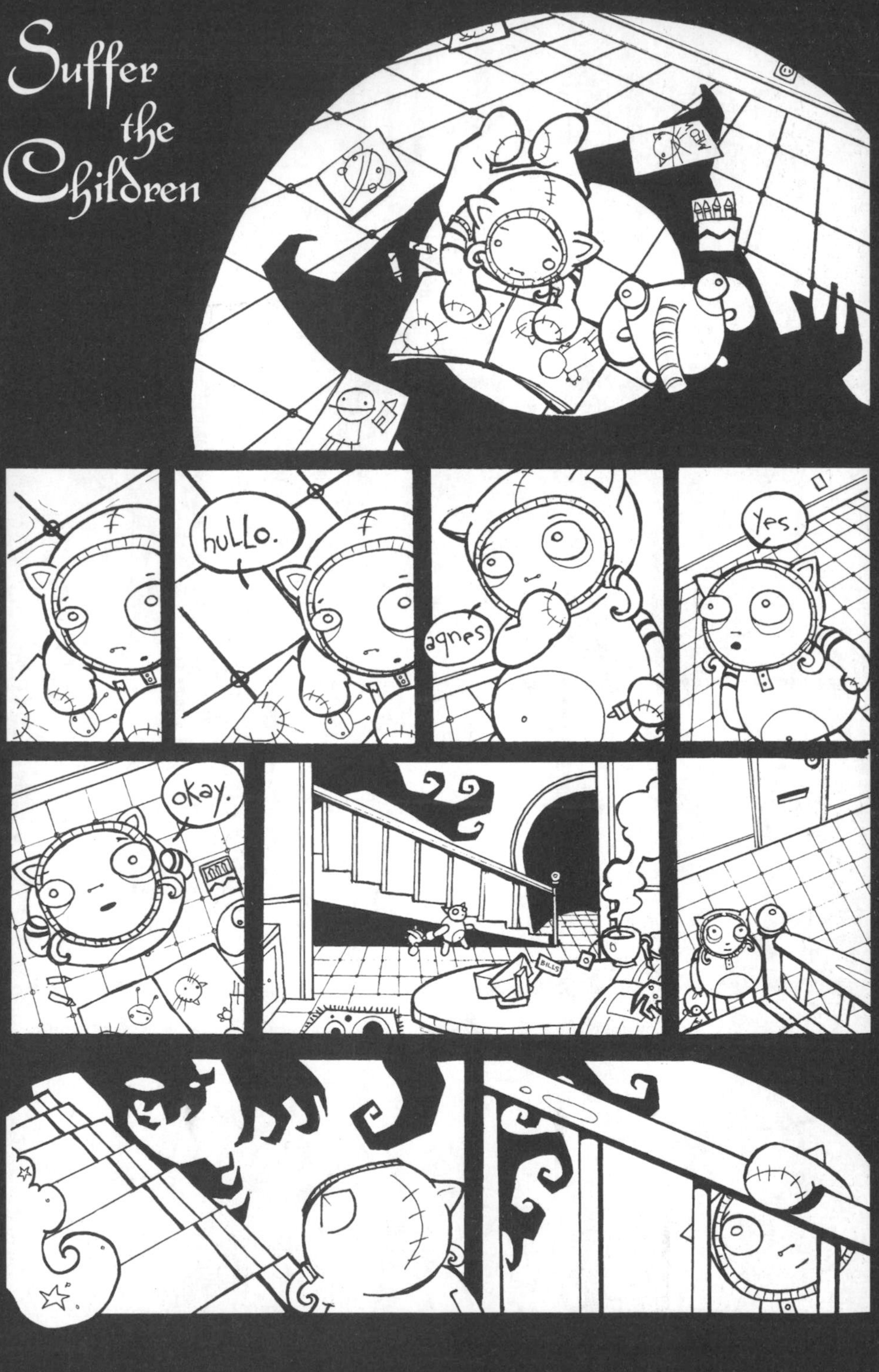
Suffer the Children
hullo.
agnes
yes.
okay.
BILLS

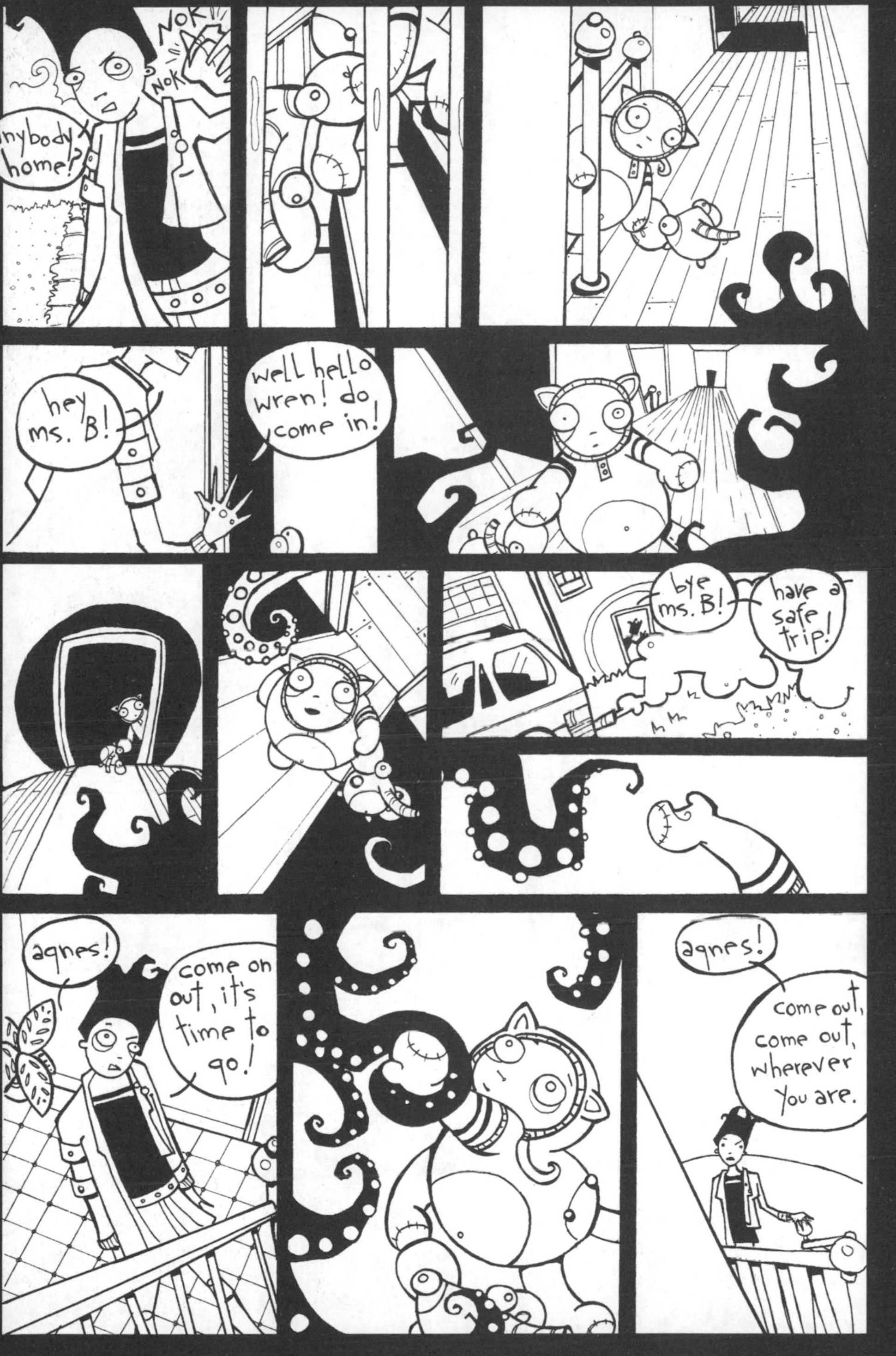
NOK
NOK
anybody home?
hey ms. B!
well hello wren! do come in!
bye ms. B!
have a safe trip!
agnes!
come on out, it's time to go!
agnes!
come out, come out, wherever you are.

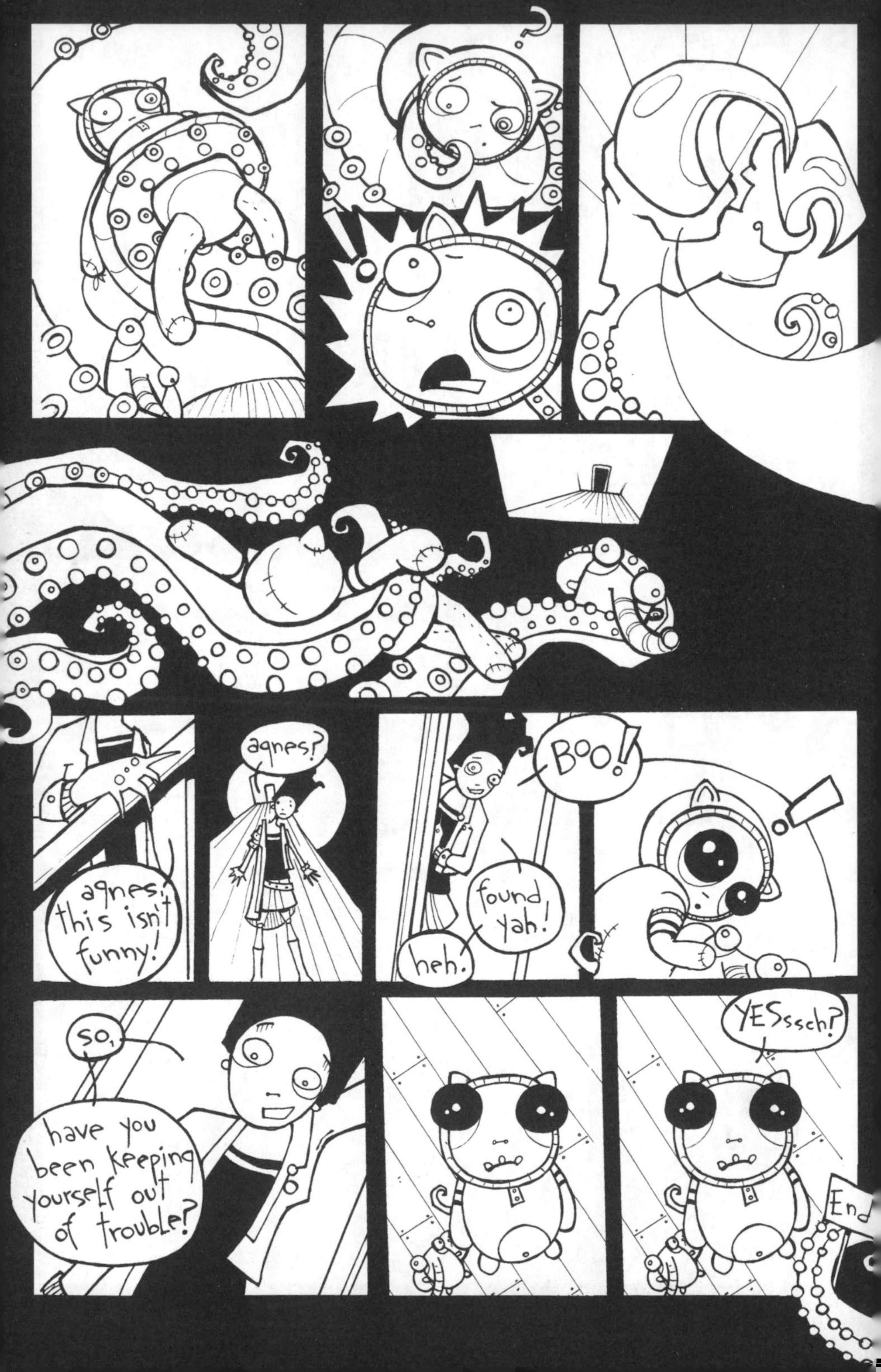
?
!
aqnes, this isn't funny!
aqnes?
BOO!
found yah!
heh.
!
so,
have you been keeping yourself out of trouble?
YESssch?
End

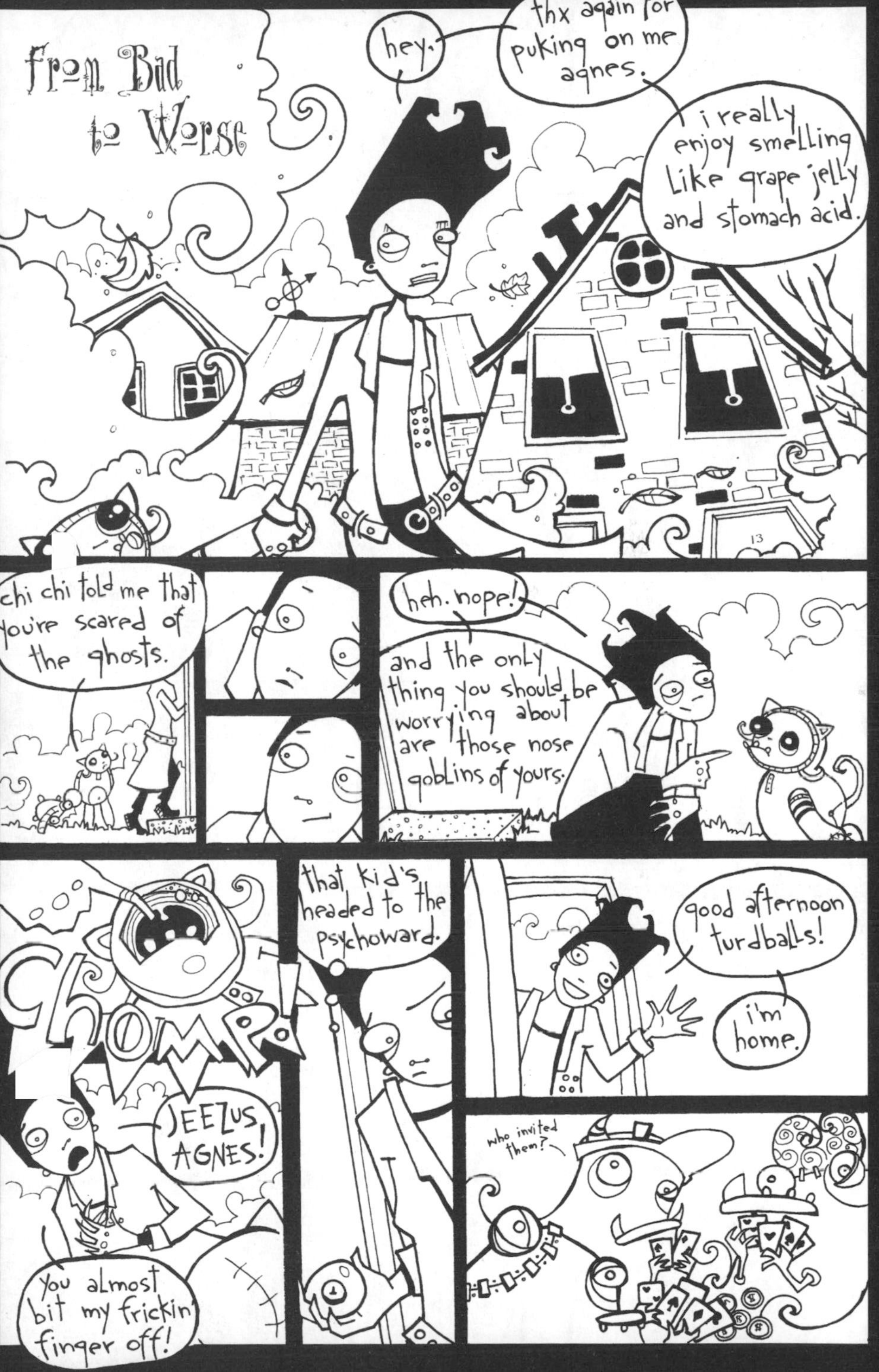
From Bad to Worse
hey.
thx again for puking on me agnes.
i really enjoy smelling like grape jelly and stomach acid.
chi chi told me that you're scared of the ghosts.
heh. nope!
and the only thing you should be worrying about are those nose goblins of yours.
CHOMP!
JEEZUS AGNES!
you almost bit my frickin' finger off!
that kid's headed to the psychoward.
good afternoon turdballs!
i'm home.
who invited them?

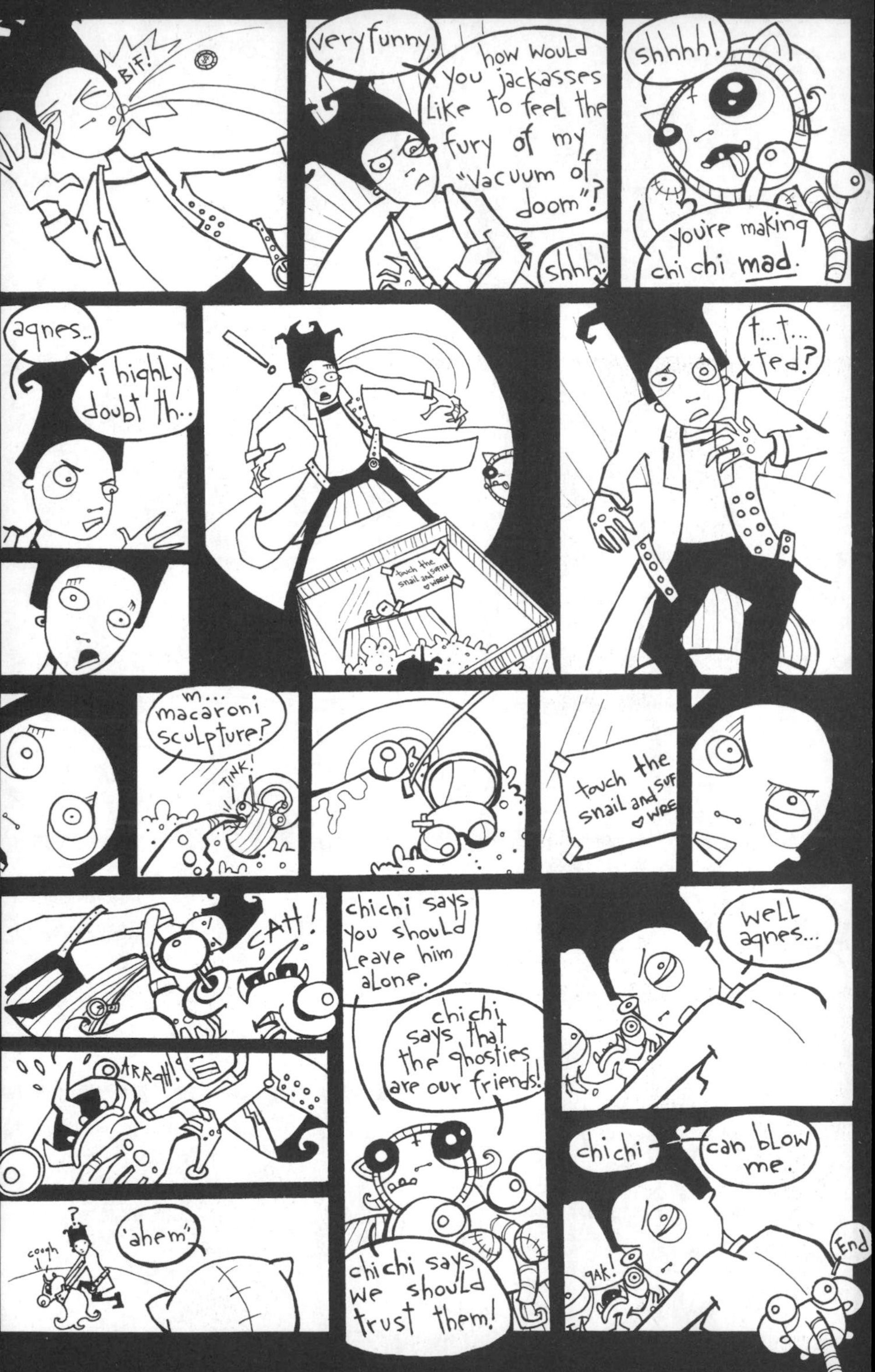
BIF!
very funny.
how would you jackasses like to feel the fury of my "vacuum of doom"?
shhh!
shhhh!
you're making chi chi mad.
agnes..
i highly doubt th..
!
touch the snail and SUFFER ♡ WREN
t... t... ted?
m... macaroni sculpture?
TINK!
touch the snail and SUF ♡ WRE
GAH!
ARRGH!
chichi says you should leave him alone.
chichi says that the ghosties are our friends!
chichi says we should trust them!
well agnes...
chichi
can blow me.
'ahem'
cough
GAK!
End

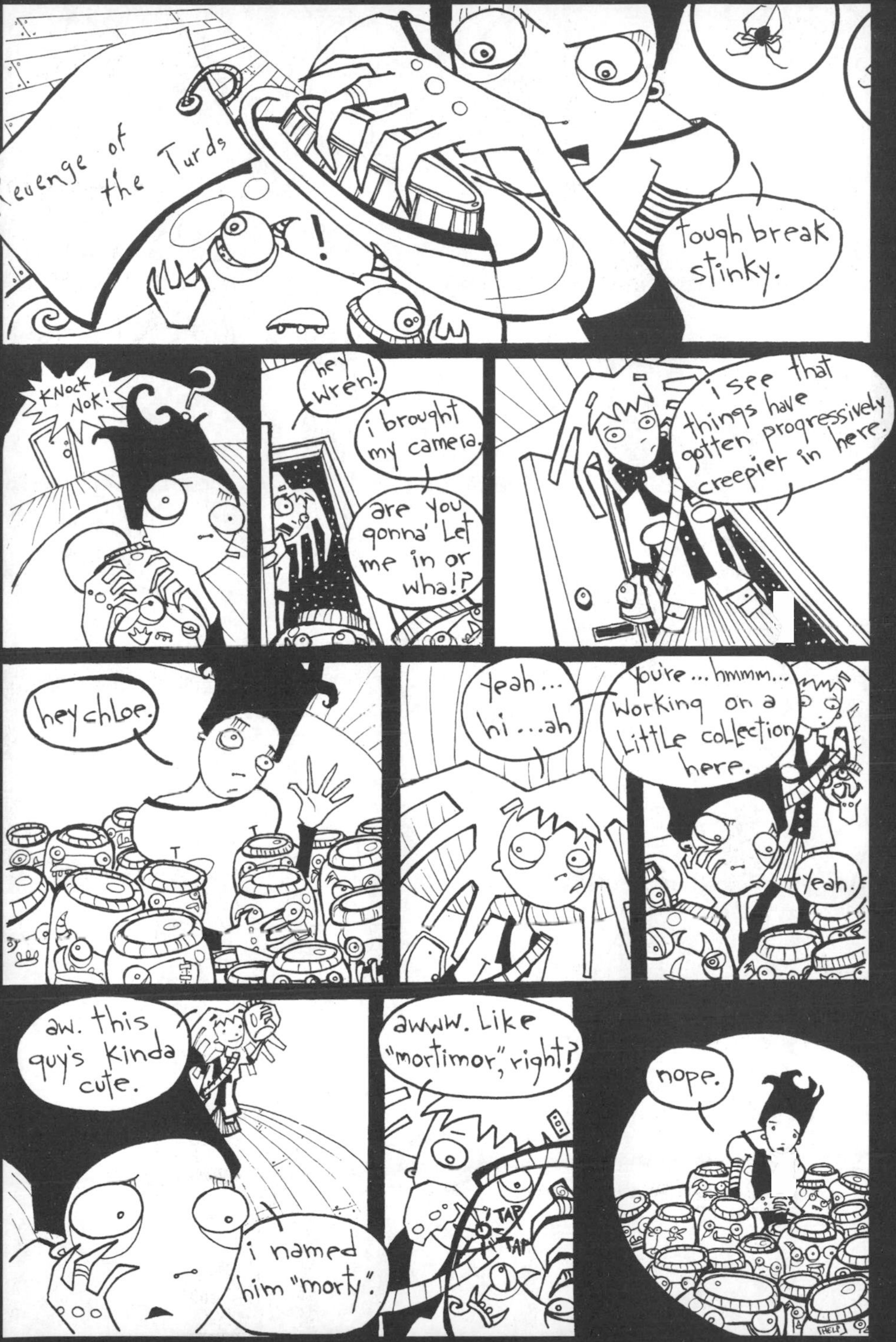
Revenge of the Turds
!
tough break stinky.
KNOCK NOK!
hey wren!
i brought my camera.
are you gonna' let me in or wha!?
i see that things have gotten progressively creepier in here.
hey chloe.
yeah... hi ...ah
you're ... hmmm... working on a little collection here.
yeah.
aw. this guy's kinda cute.
i named him "morty".
awww. like "mortimor," right?
TAP TAP
nope.
HELP

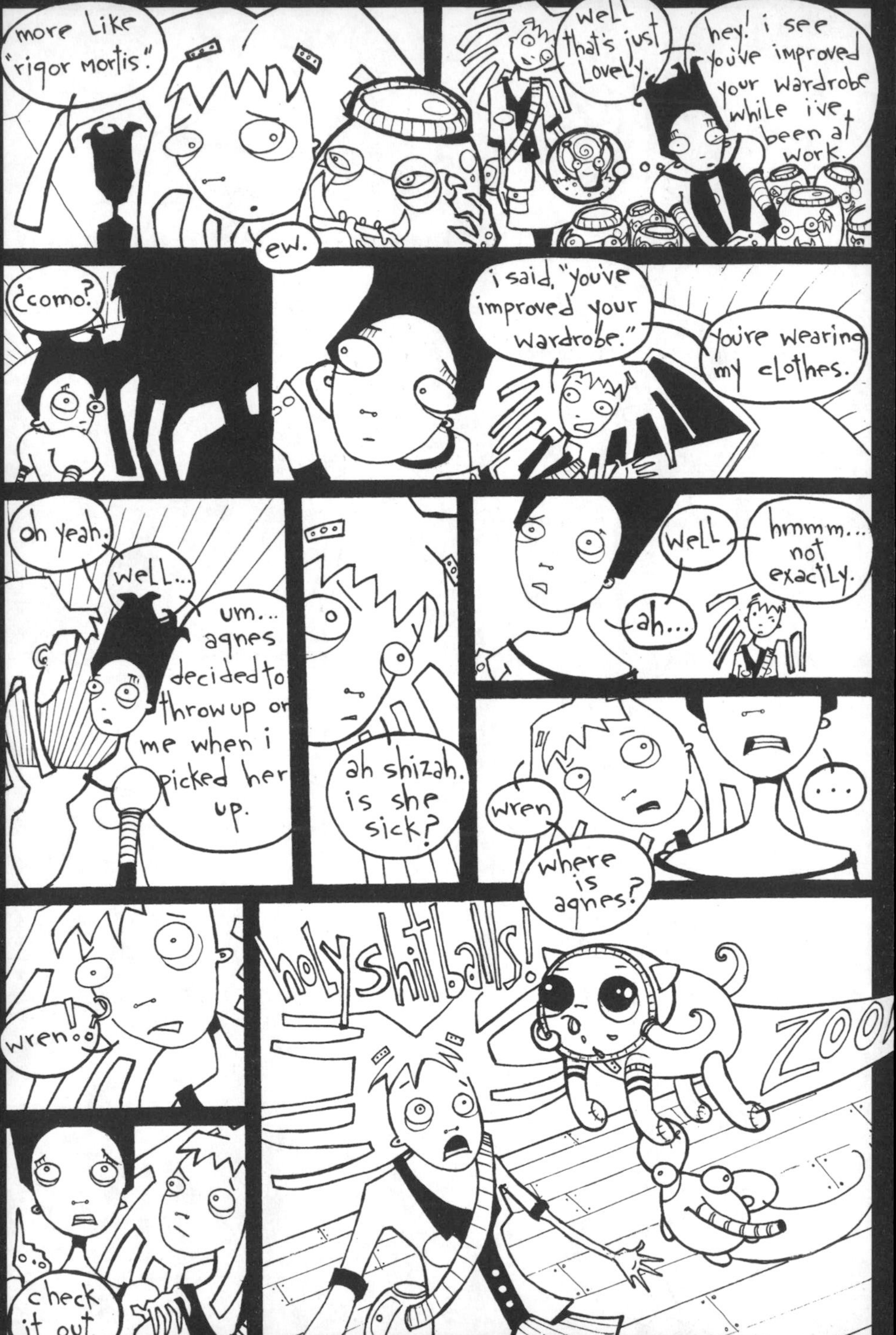
more like "rigor mortis."
ew.
well that's just lovely.
hey! i see you've improved your wardrobe while i've been at work.
¿como?
i said, "you've improved your wardrobe."
you're wearing my clothes.
oh yeah.
well...
um... agnes decided to throw up on me when i picked her up.
ah shizah. is she sick?
well
hmmm... not exactly.
ah...
wren
...
where is agnes?
wren
check it out.
holy shit balls!
ZOO

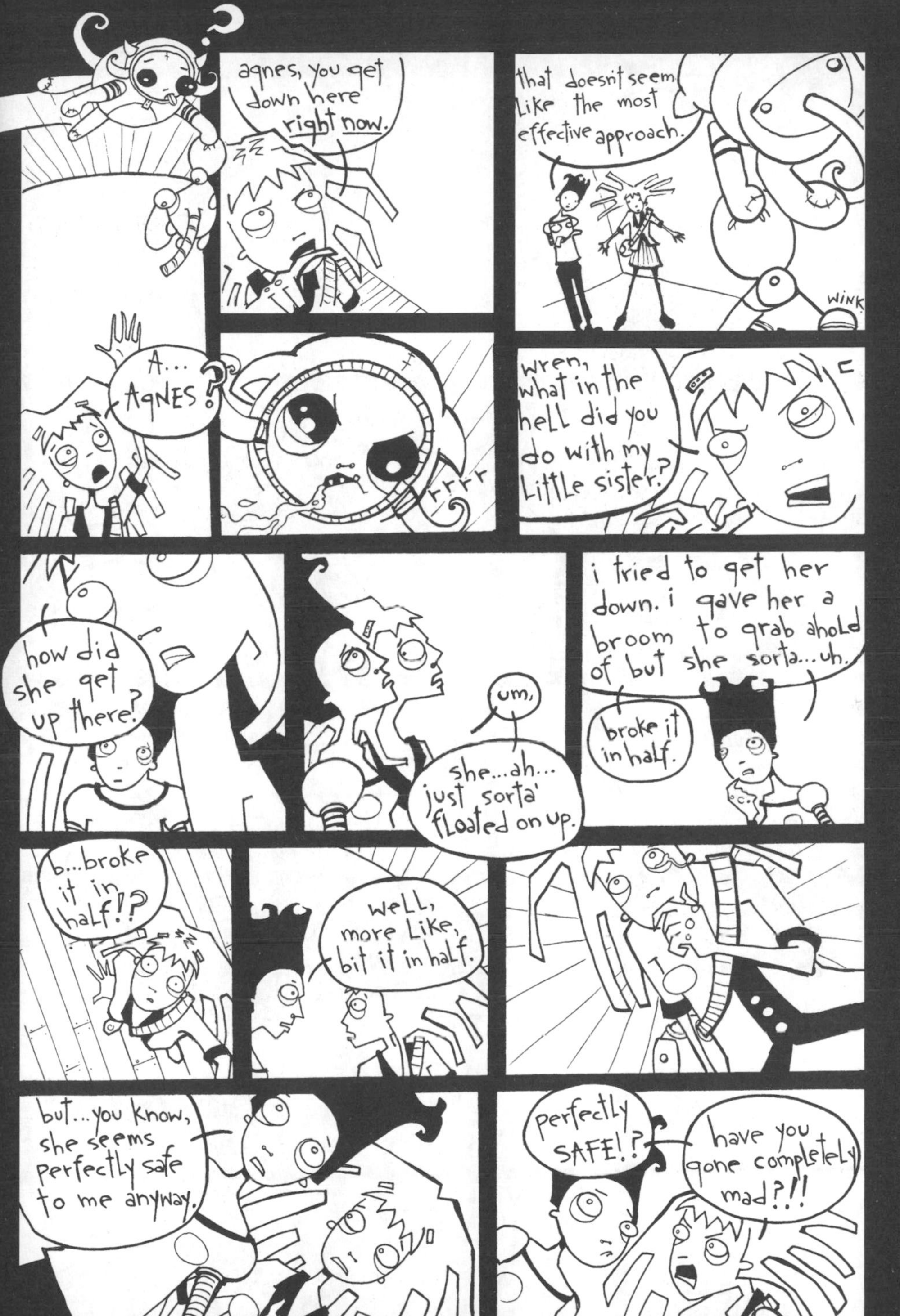

agnes, you get down here right now.
that doesn't seem like the most effective approach.
WINK
A... AGNES?
rrrr
wren, what in the hell did you do with my little sister?
how did she get up there?
um,
she...ah... just sorta' floated on up.
i tried to get her down. i gave her a broom to grab ahold of but she sorta...uh.
broke it in half.
b...broke it in half!?
well, more like, bit it in half.
but...you know, she seems perfectly safe to me anyway.
perfectly SAFE!?
have you gone completely mad?!!

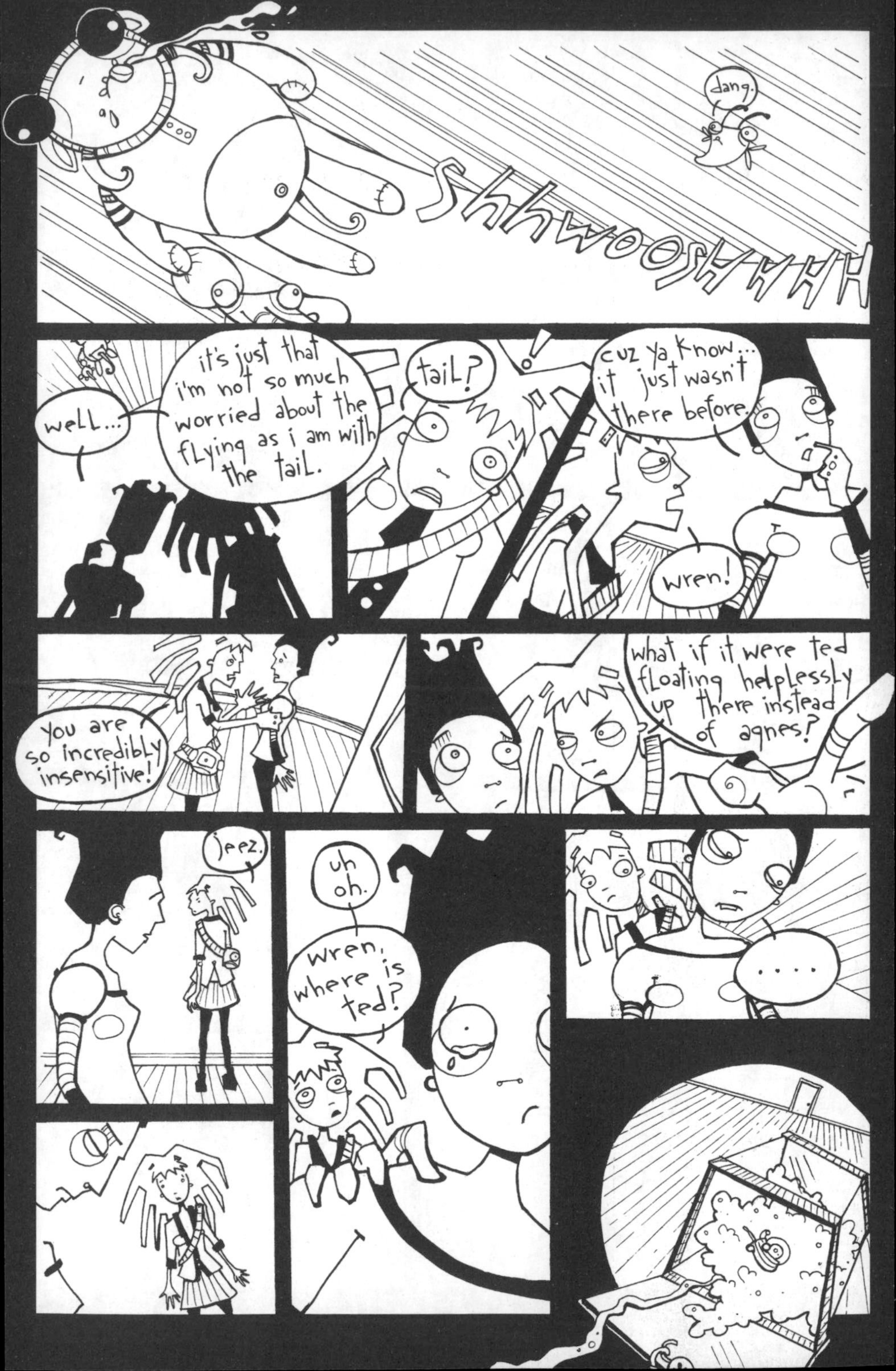

dang.
SHHWOOSHHHHH
well...
it's just that i'm not so much worried about the flying as i am with the tail.
tail?
!
cuz ya know... it just wasn't there before.
wren!
you are so incredibly insensitive!
what if it were ted floating helplessly up there instead of agnes?
jeez.
uh oh.
wren, where is ted?
....

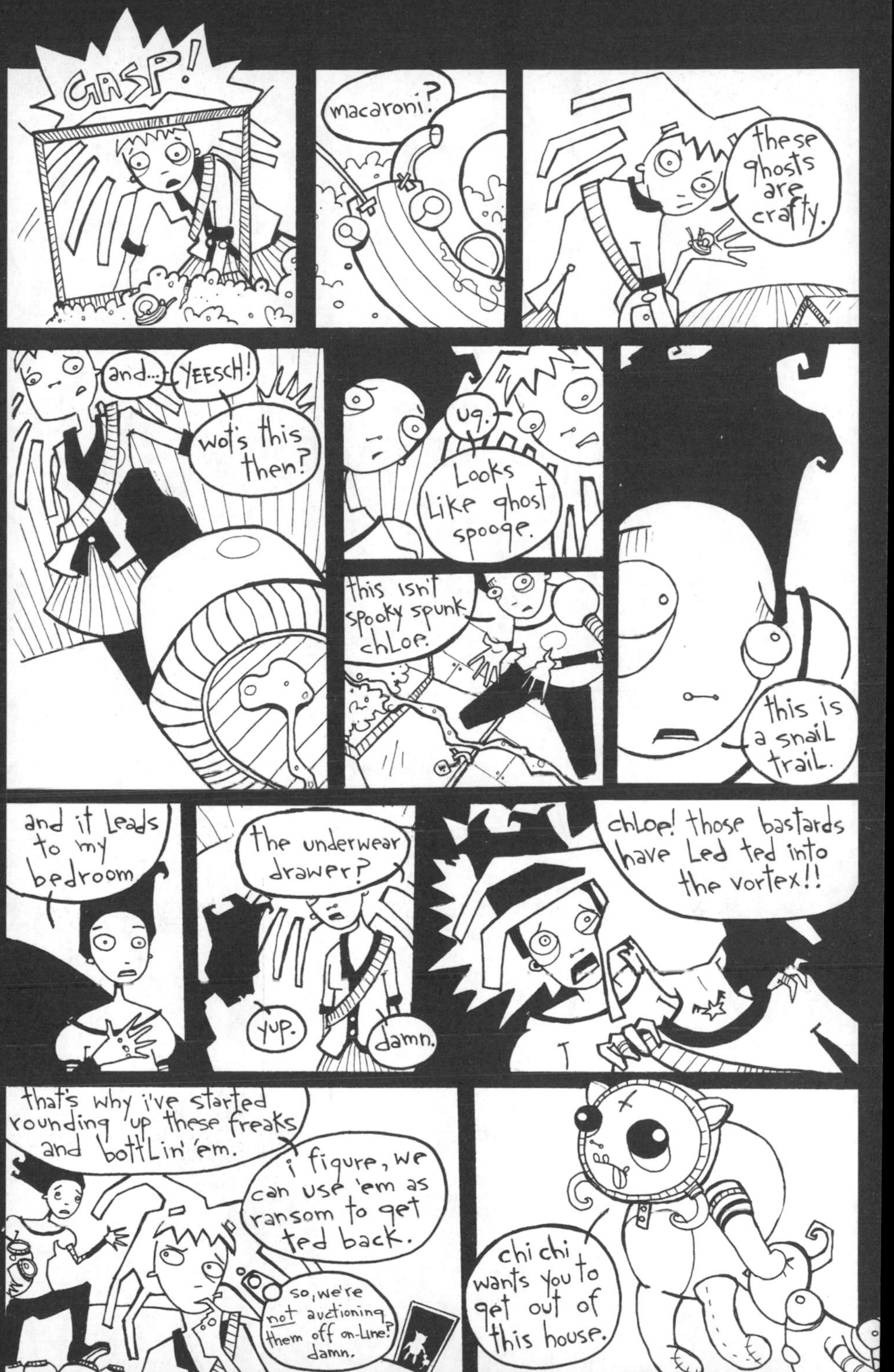
GASP!
macaroni?
these ghosts are crafty.
and...
YEESCH!
wot's this then?
ug.
Looks Like ghost spooge.
this isn't spooky spunk chLoe.
this is a snaiL traiL.
and it Leads to my bedroom
the underwear drawer?
yup.
damn.
chLoe! those bastards have Led ted into the vortex!!
that's why i've started rounding up these freaks and bottLin' 'em.
i figure, we can use 'em as ransom to get ted back.
so, we're not auctioning them off on-Line? damn.
chi chi wants you to get out of this house.

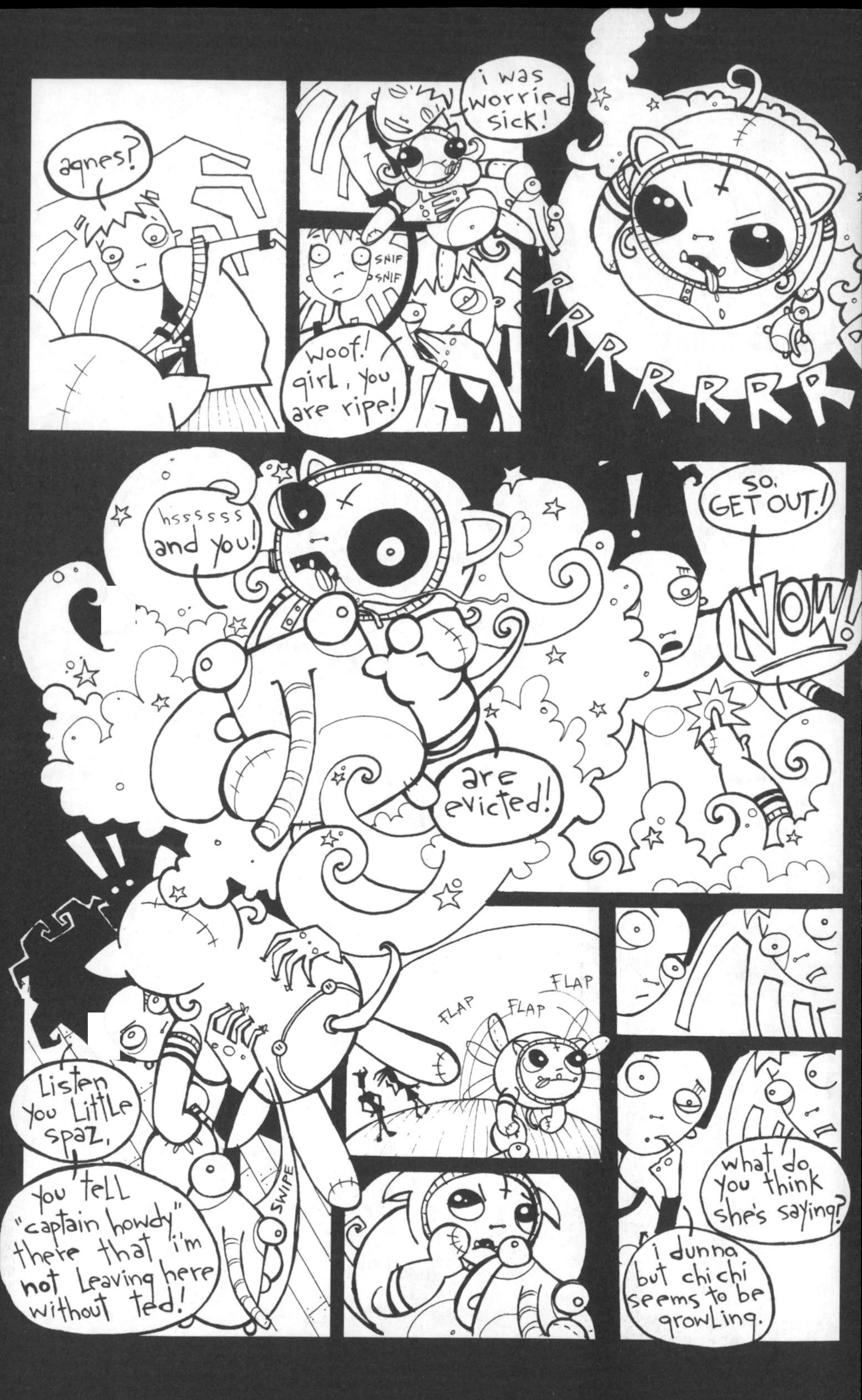

agnes?
i was worried sick!
SNIF SNIF
woof! girl, you are ripe!
RRRRRRRR
hssssss and you!
are evicted!
so, GET OUT!
NOW!
Listen you Little spaz,
you tell "captain howdy" there that i'm not leaving here without ted!
SWIPE
FLAP FLAP FLAP
what do you think she's saying?
i dunno but chi chi seems to be growling.

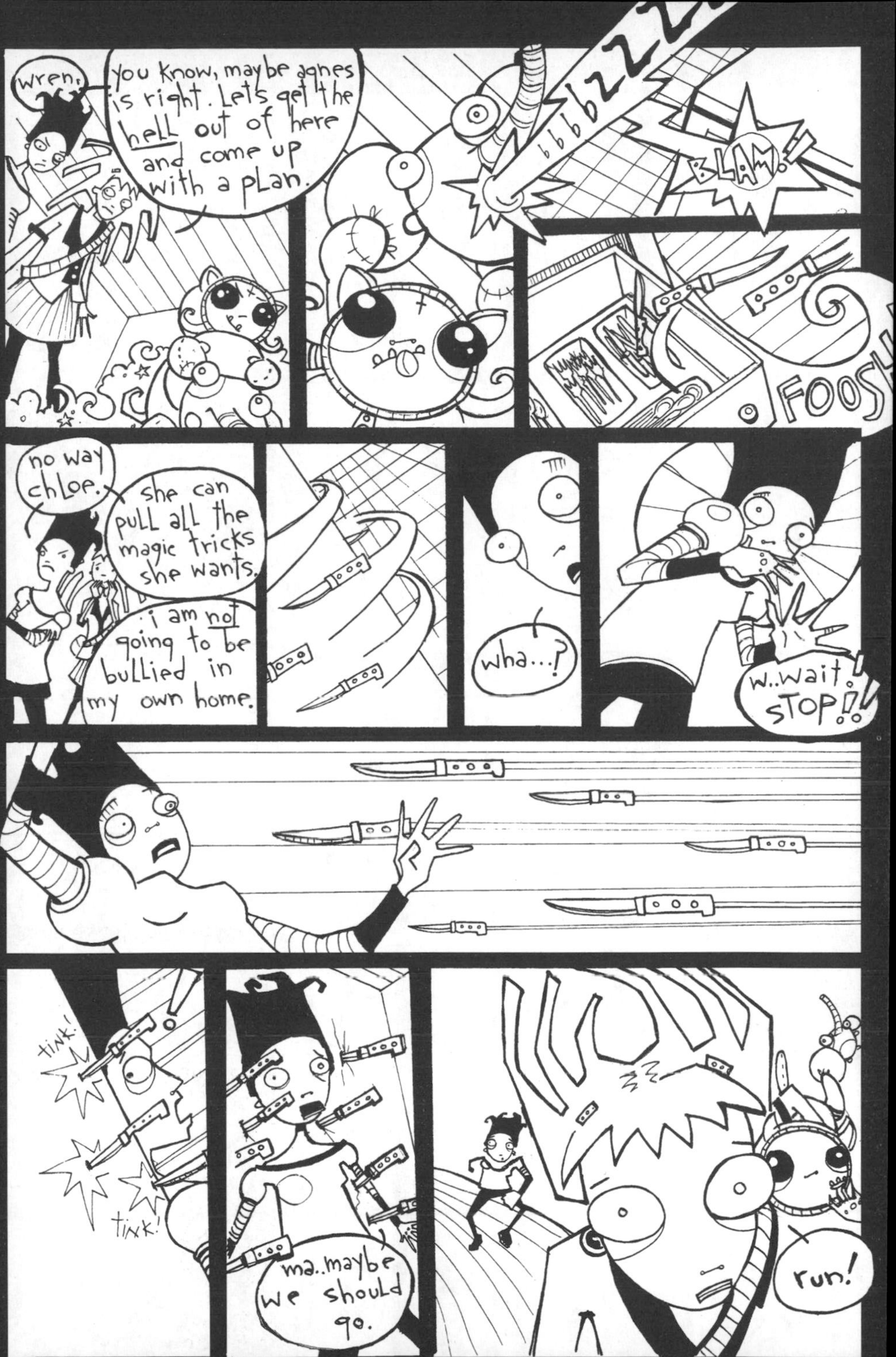
wren,
you know, maybe agnes is right. Let's get the hell out of here and come up with a plan.
bbbbzzzz
BLAM!
FOOSH
no way chloe.
she can pull all the magic tricks she wants.
i am not going to be bullied in my own home.
wha...?
w..wait! STOP!!
tink!
tink!
ma..maybe we should go.
run!

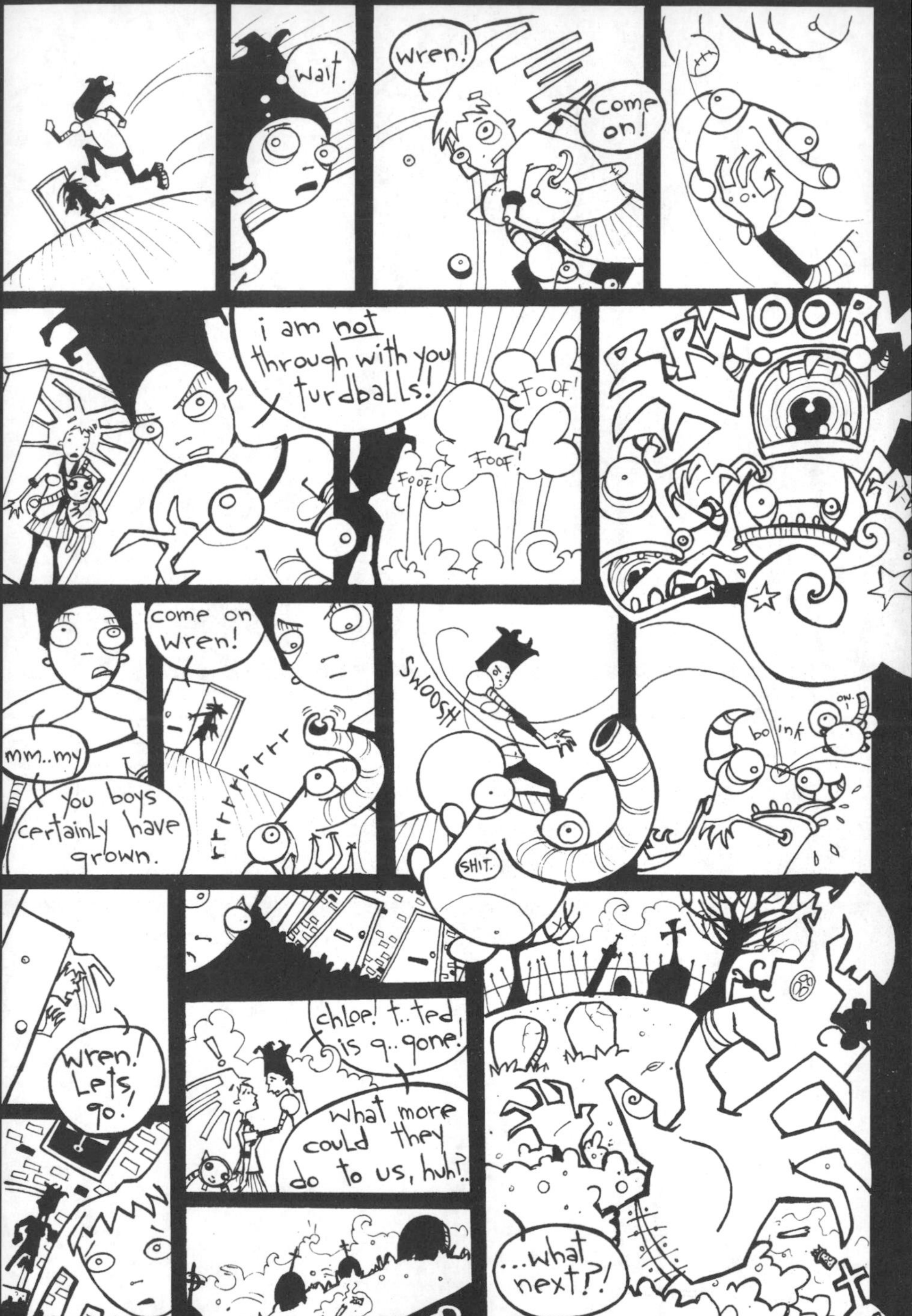
wait.
wren!
come on!
i am not through with you turdballs!
FOOF!
FOOF!
FOOF!
BRWOOR
mm..my
you boys certainly have grown.
come on wren!
rrrrrrrrrrr
SWOOSH
SHIT.
boink
ow.
wren! Lets, go.
chloe! t.. ted is g.. gone!
what more could they do to us, huh?..
...what next?!
END

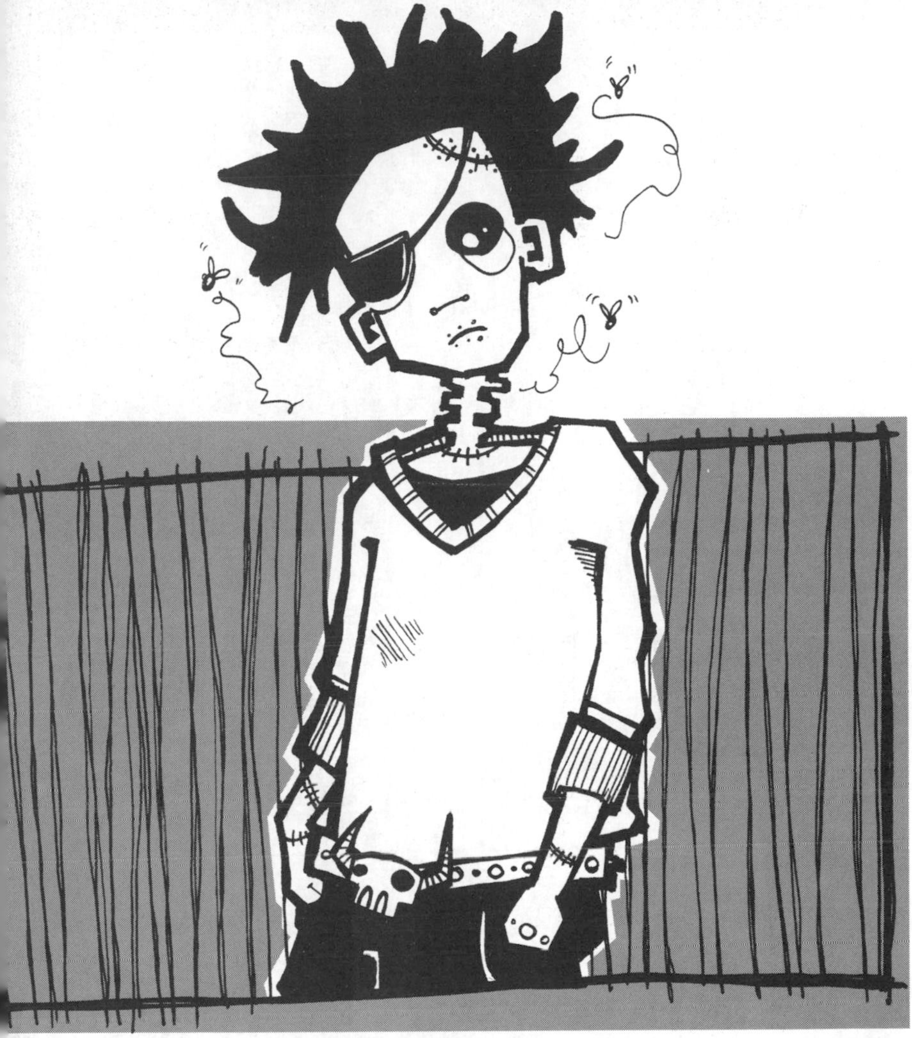

chapter four.

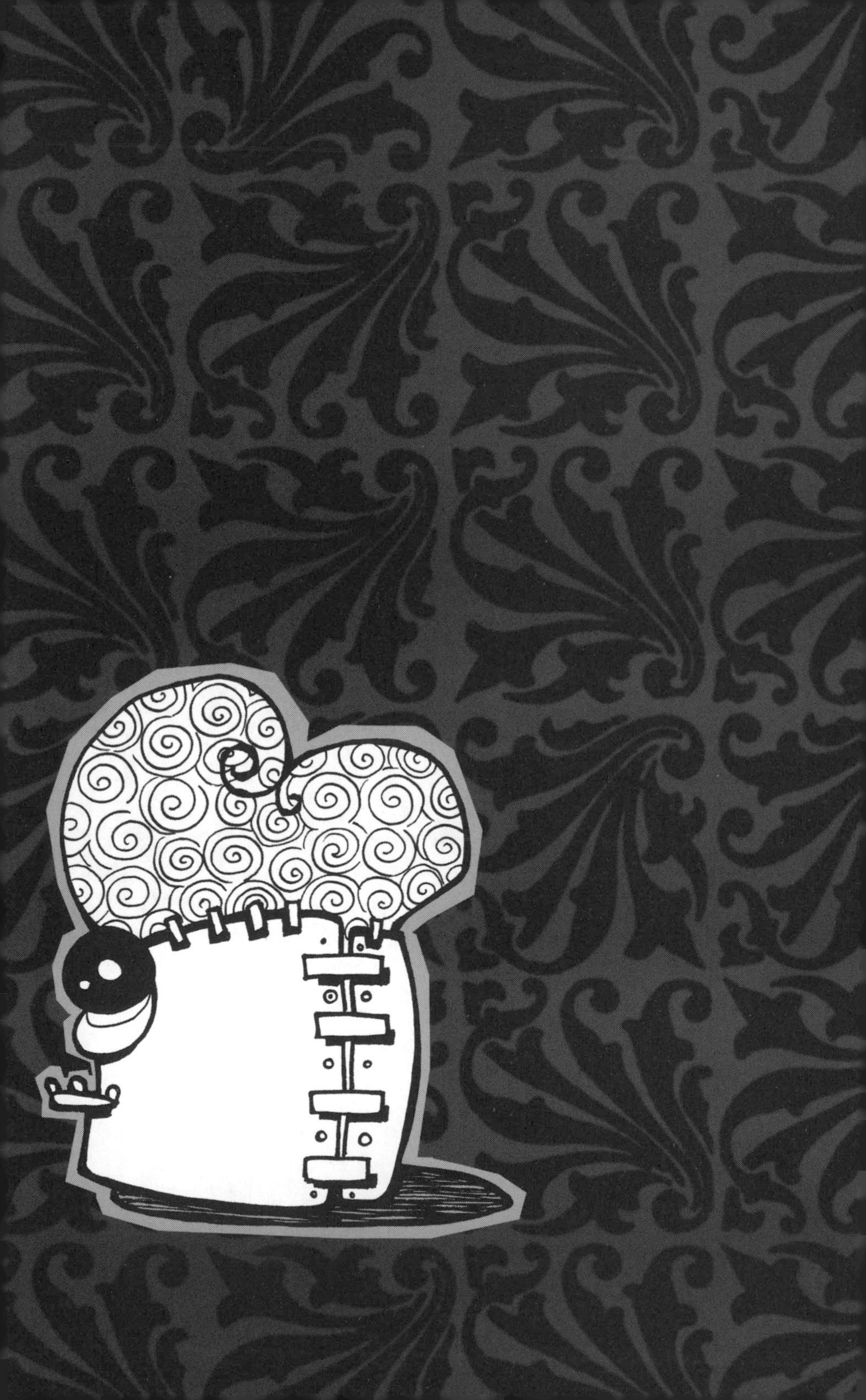

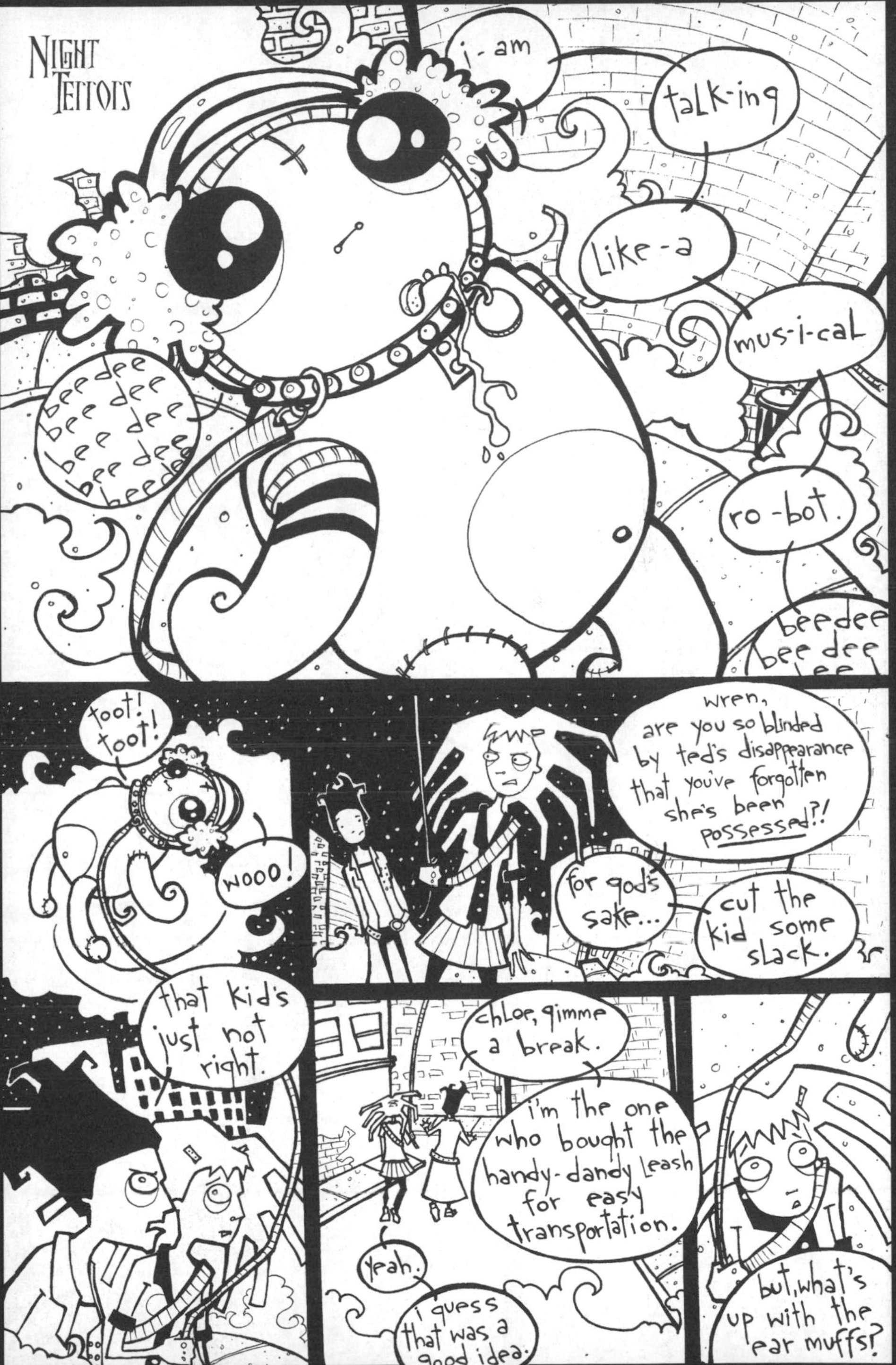
Night Terrors
i-am
talk-ing
like-a
mus-i-cal
ro-bot.
beedee bee dee bee dee bee dee bee dee beedee
beedee bee dee
toot! toot!
wooo!
wren, are you so blinded by ted's disappearance that you've forgotten she's been possessed?!
for god's sake...
cut the kid some slack.
that kid's just not right.
chloe, gimme a break.
i'm the one who bought the handy-dandy leash for easy transportation.
yeah.
i guess that was a good idea.
but, what's up with the ear muffs?

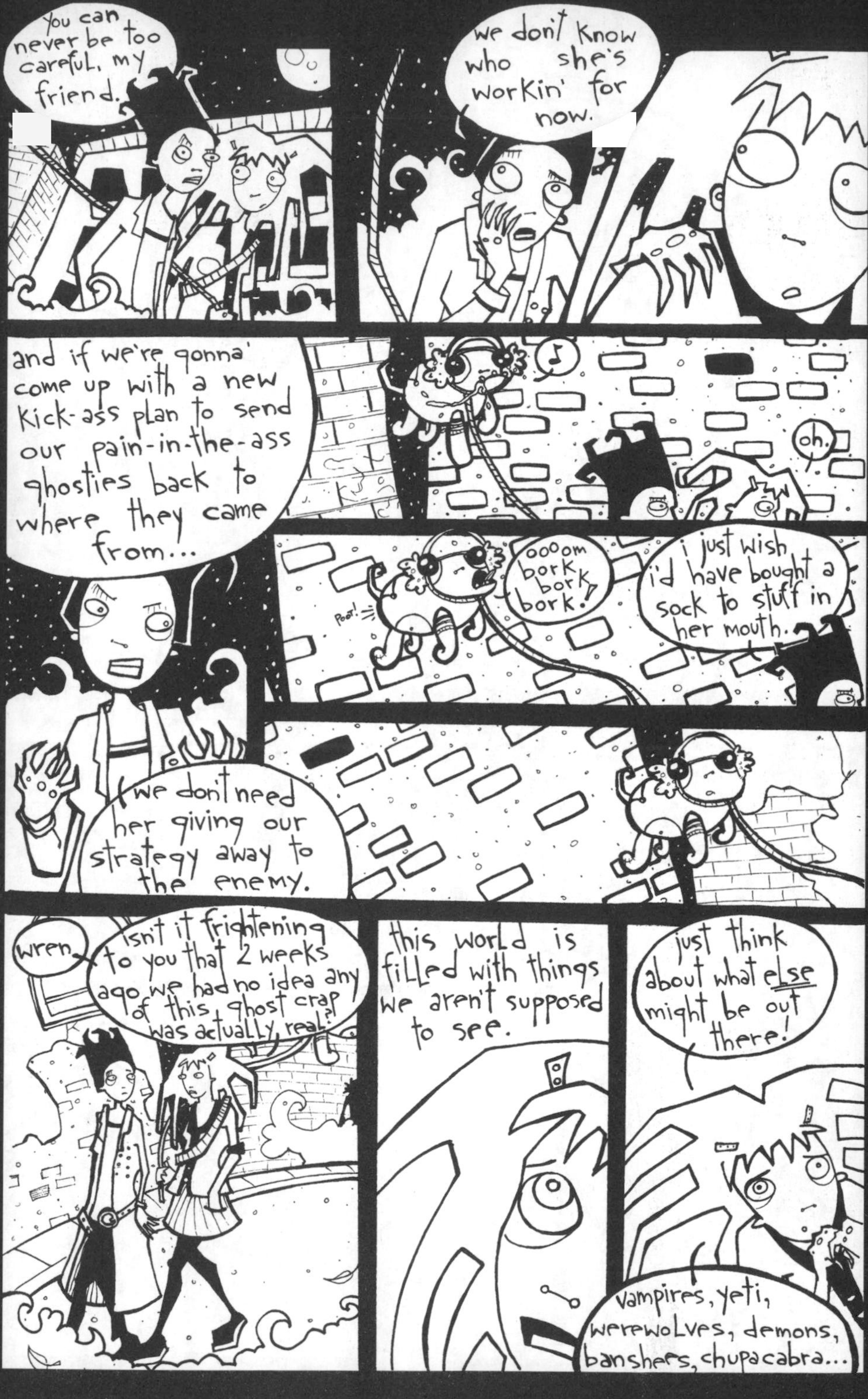
you can never be too careful, my friend.
we don't know who she's workin' for now.
and if we're gonna' come up with a new kick-ass plan to send our pain-in-the-ass ghosties back to where they came from...
oh.
oooom bork bork bork!
i just wish i'd have bought a sock to stuff in her mouth.
we don't need her giving our strategy away to the enemy.
wren,
isn't it frightening to you that 2 weeks ago we had no idea any of this ghost crap was actually real?
this world is filled with things we aren't supposed to see.
just think about what else might be out there!
vampires, yeti, werewolves, demons, banshees, chupacabra...

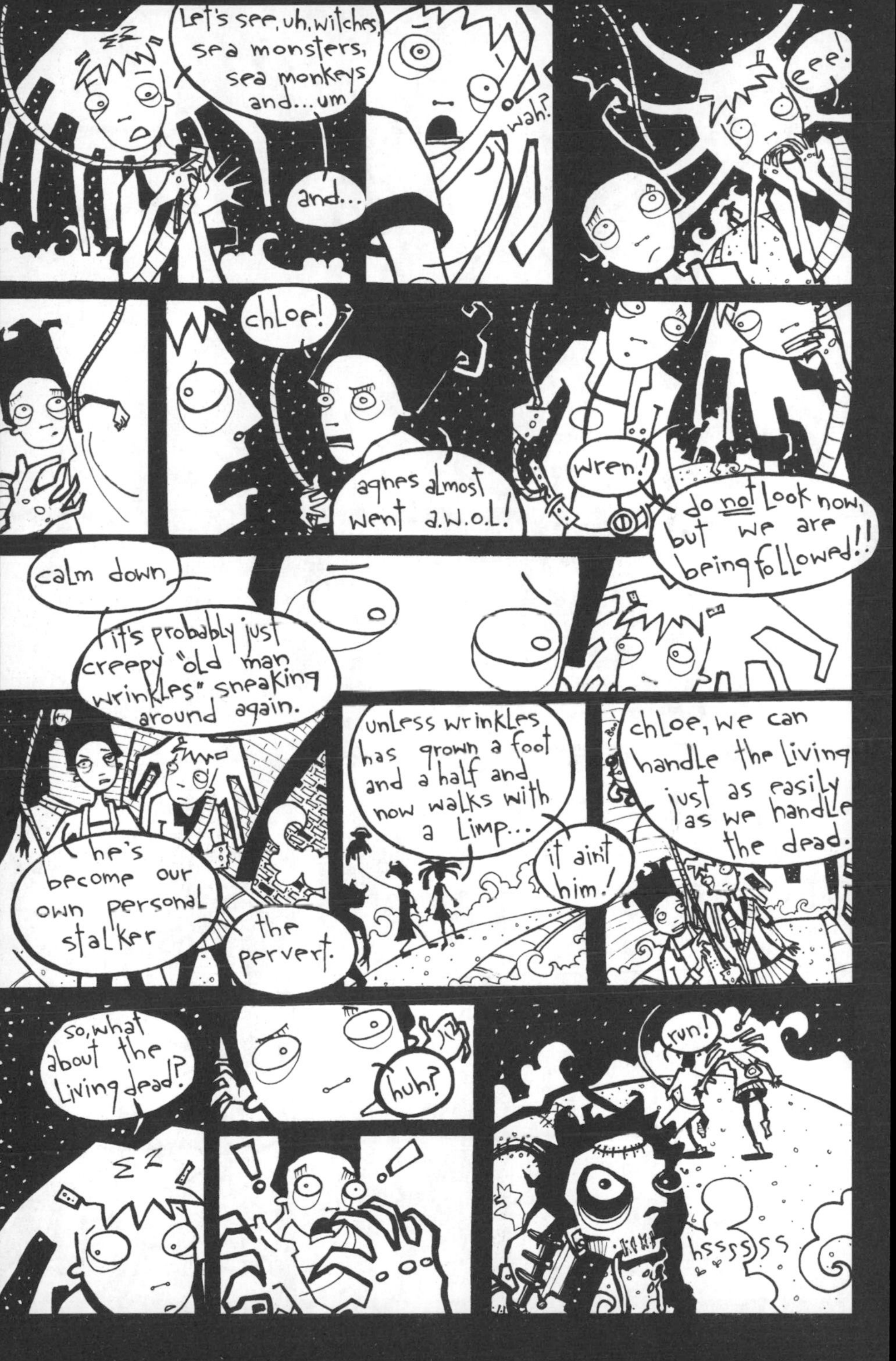

Let's see, uh, witches, sea monsters, sea monkeys and...um
and...
wah?
eee!
chloe!
agnes almost went a.w.o.l.!
wren!
do not look now, but we are being followed!!
calm down
it's probably just creepy "old man wrinkles" sneaking around again.
he's become our own personal stalker
the pervert.
unless wrinkles has grown a foot and a half and now walks with a limp...
it ain't him!
chloe, we can handle the living just as easily as we handle the dead.
so, what about the living dead?
huh?
run!
hssssss

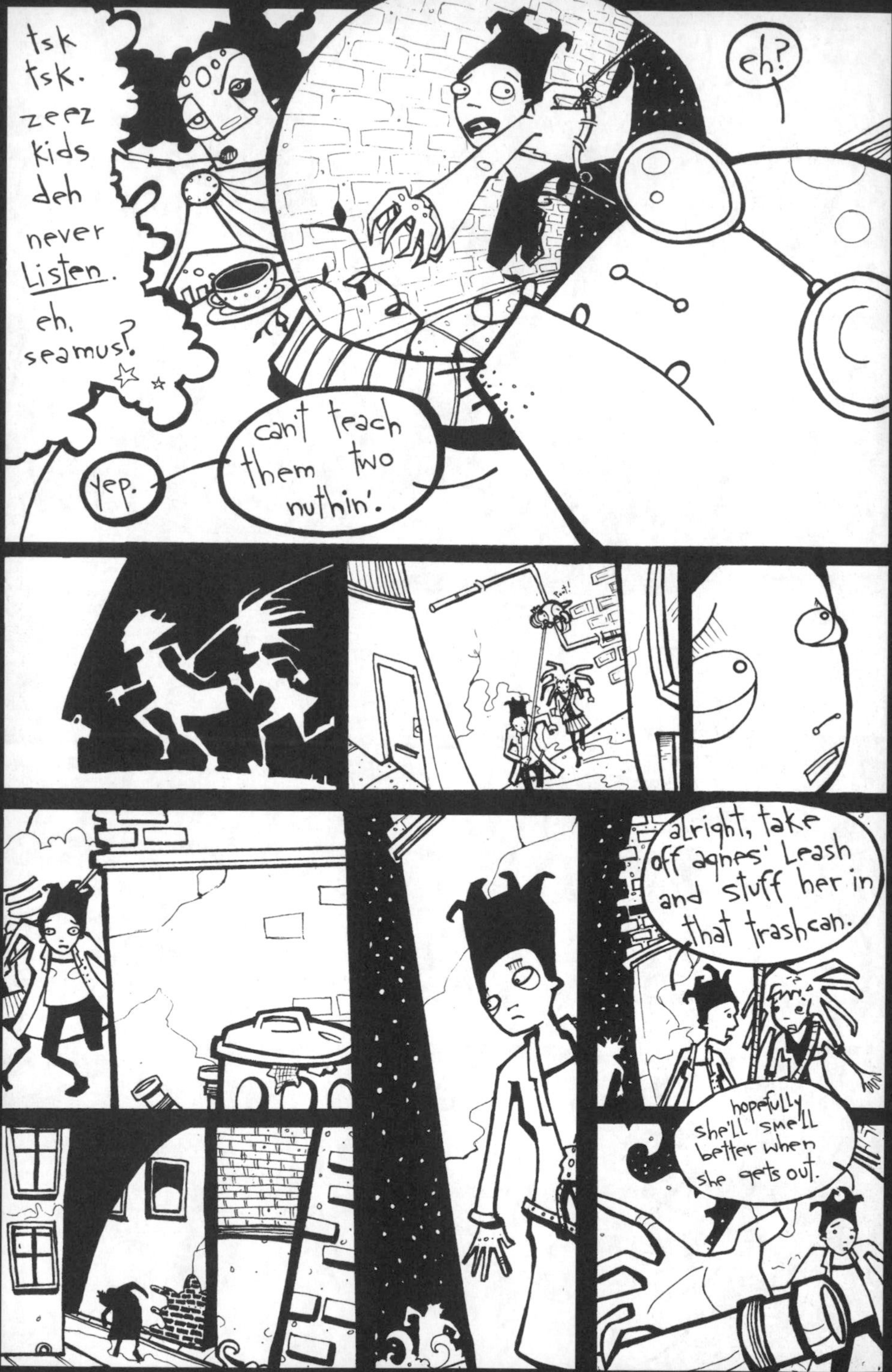
tsk tsk. zeez kids deh never Listen. eh, seamus?
eh?
yep.
can't teach them two nuthin'.
Poot!
alright, take off agnes' Leash and stuff her in that trashcan.
hopefully she'll smell better when she gets out.

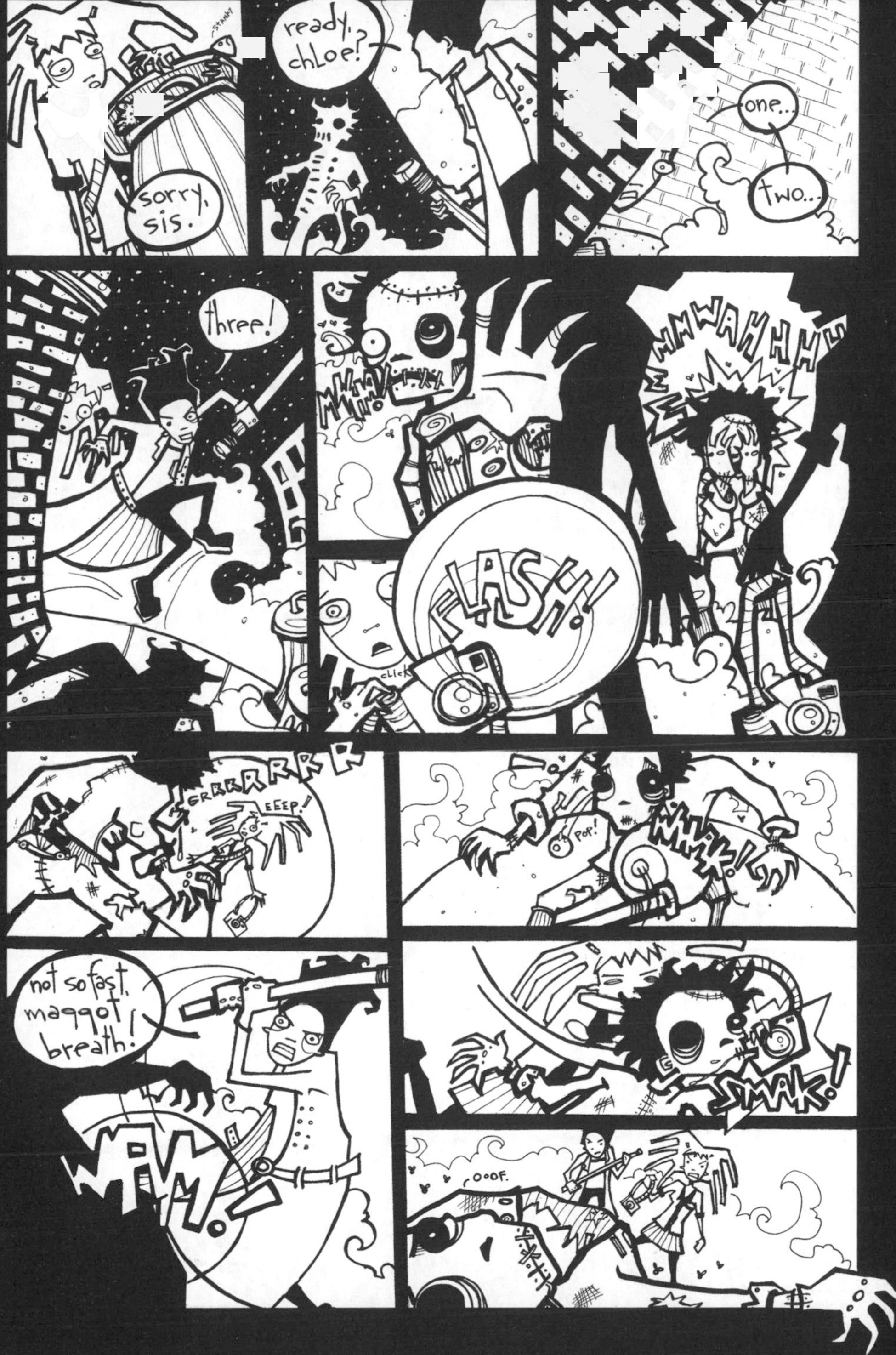
sorry, sis.
ready, chloe?
one...
two...
three!
FLASH!
click
GRRRRRRRR
EEEP!
POP!
not so fast, maggot breath!
SMAK!
OOOF.

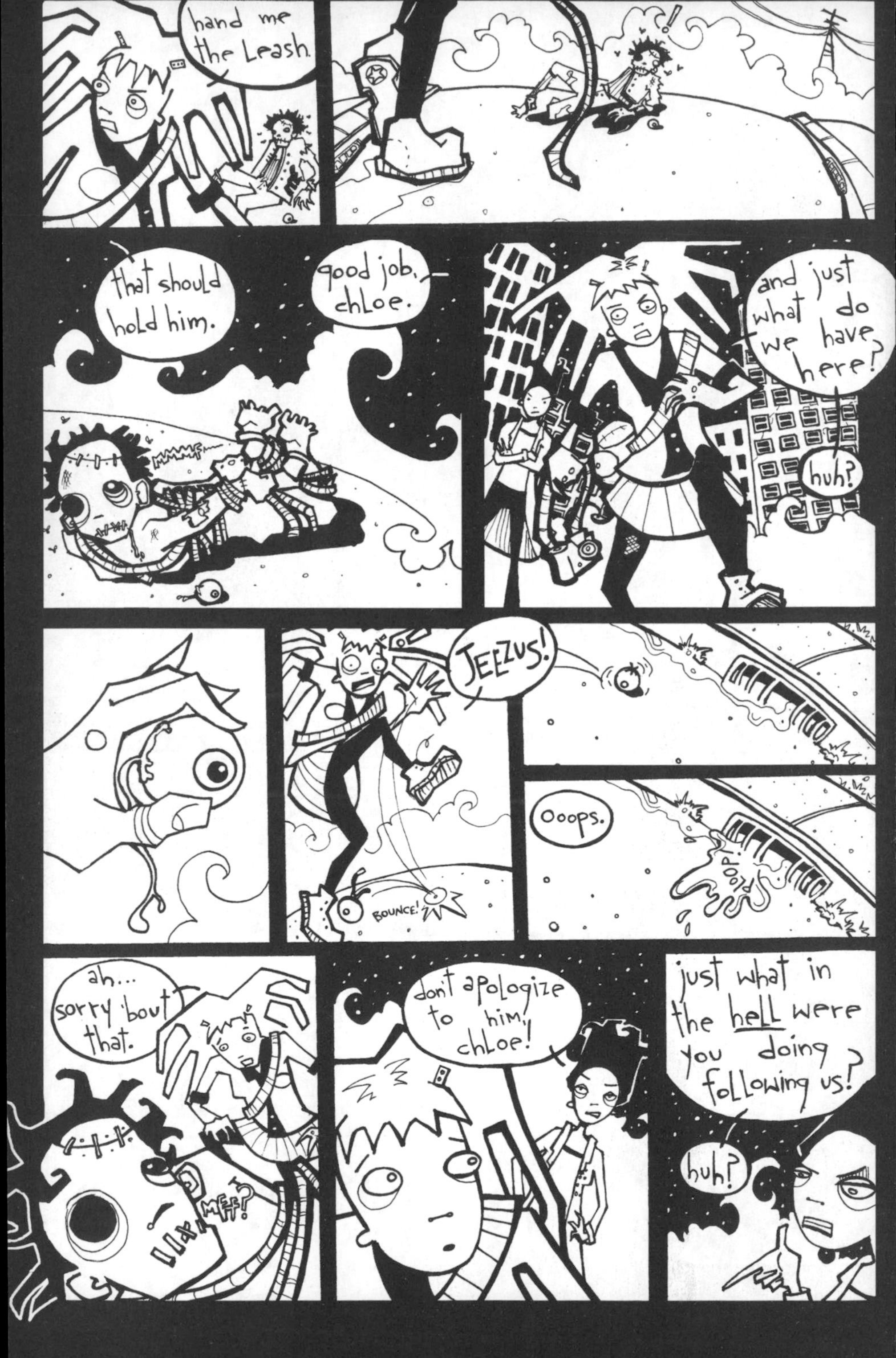
hand me the Leash.
!
that should hold him.
good job, chloe.
MMMF
and just what do we have here?
huh?
JEEZUS!
BOUNCE!
Ooops.
PLOOP!
ah... sorry 'bout that.
MFF?
don't apologize to him, chloe!
just what in the hell were you doing following us?
huh?

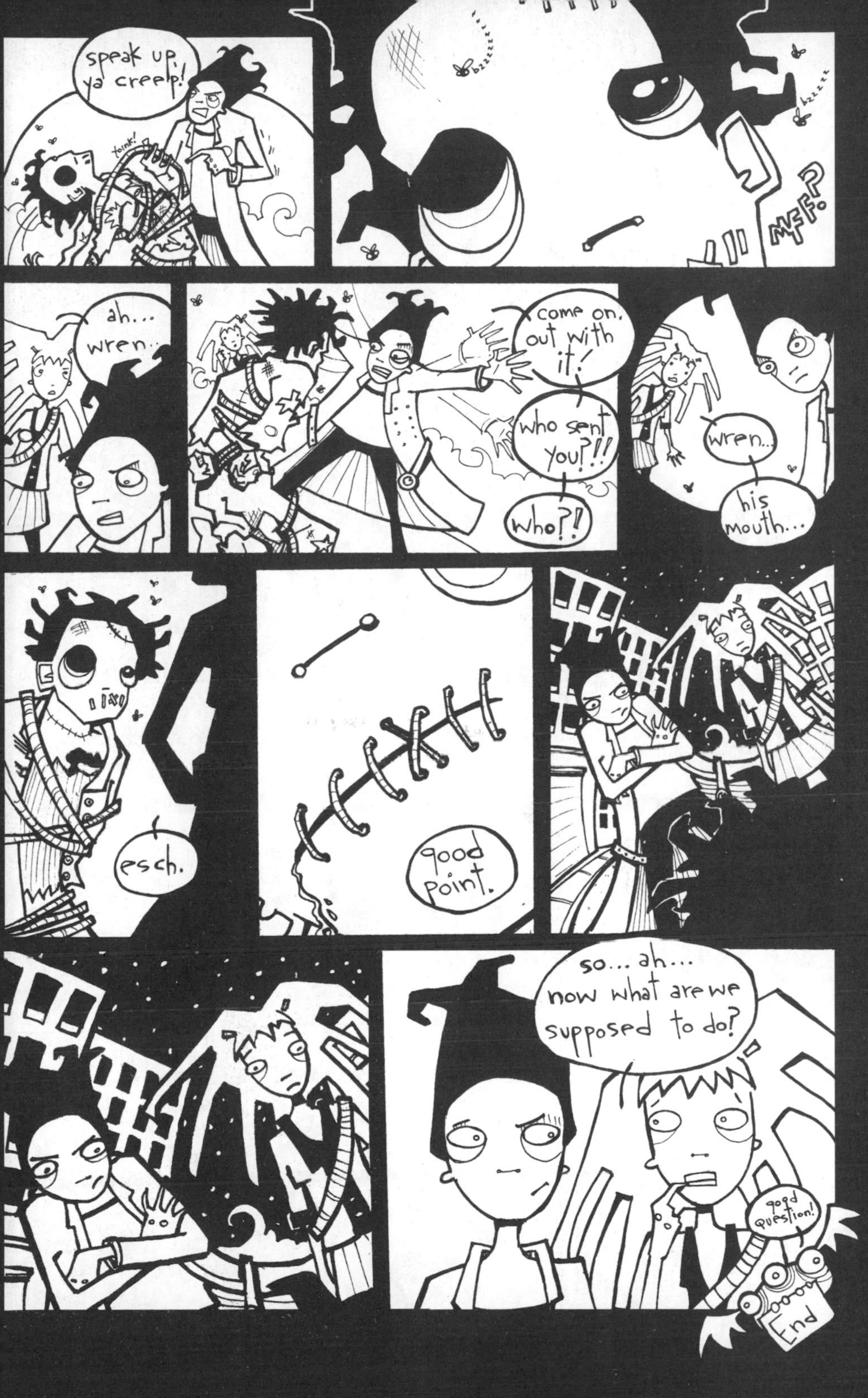
speak up, ya creep!
toink!
bzzzzz
bzzzzz
MFF?
ah... wren...
come on, out with it!
who sent you?!!
who?!
wren...
his mouth...
esch.
good point.
so... ah... now what are we supposed to do?
good question!
End

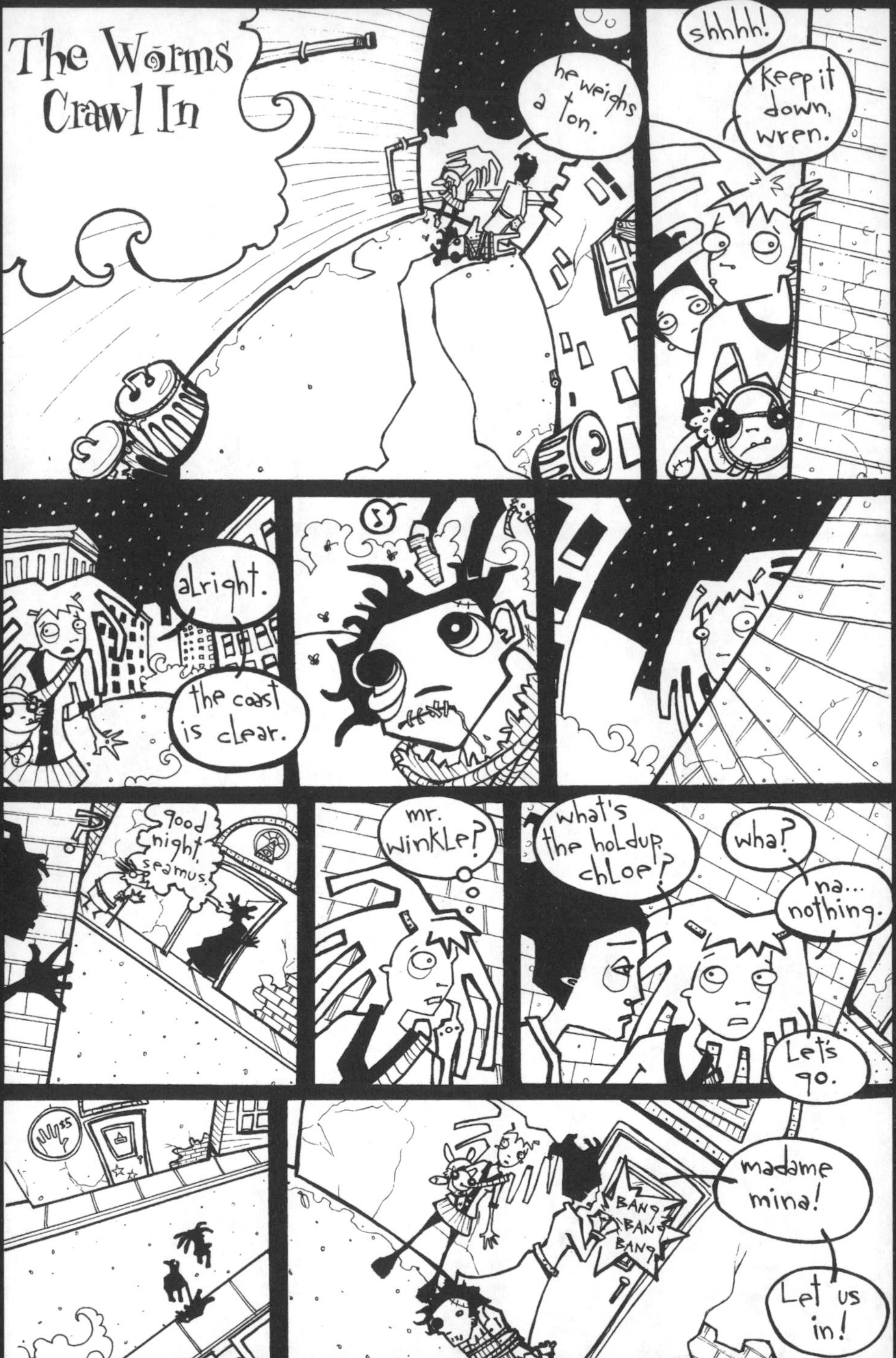
The Worms Crawl In
he weighs a ton.
shhhh!
Keep it down, wren.
alright.
the coast is clear.
good night, seamus.
mr. winkle?
what's the holdup, chloe?
wha?
na... nothing.
Let's go.
madame mina!
BANG BANG BANG
Let us in!

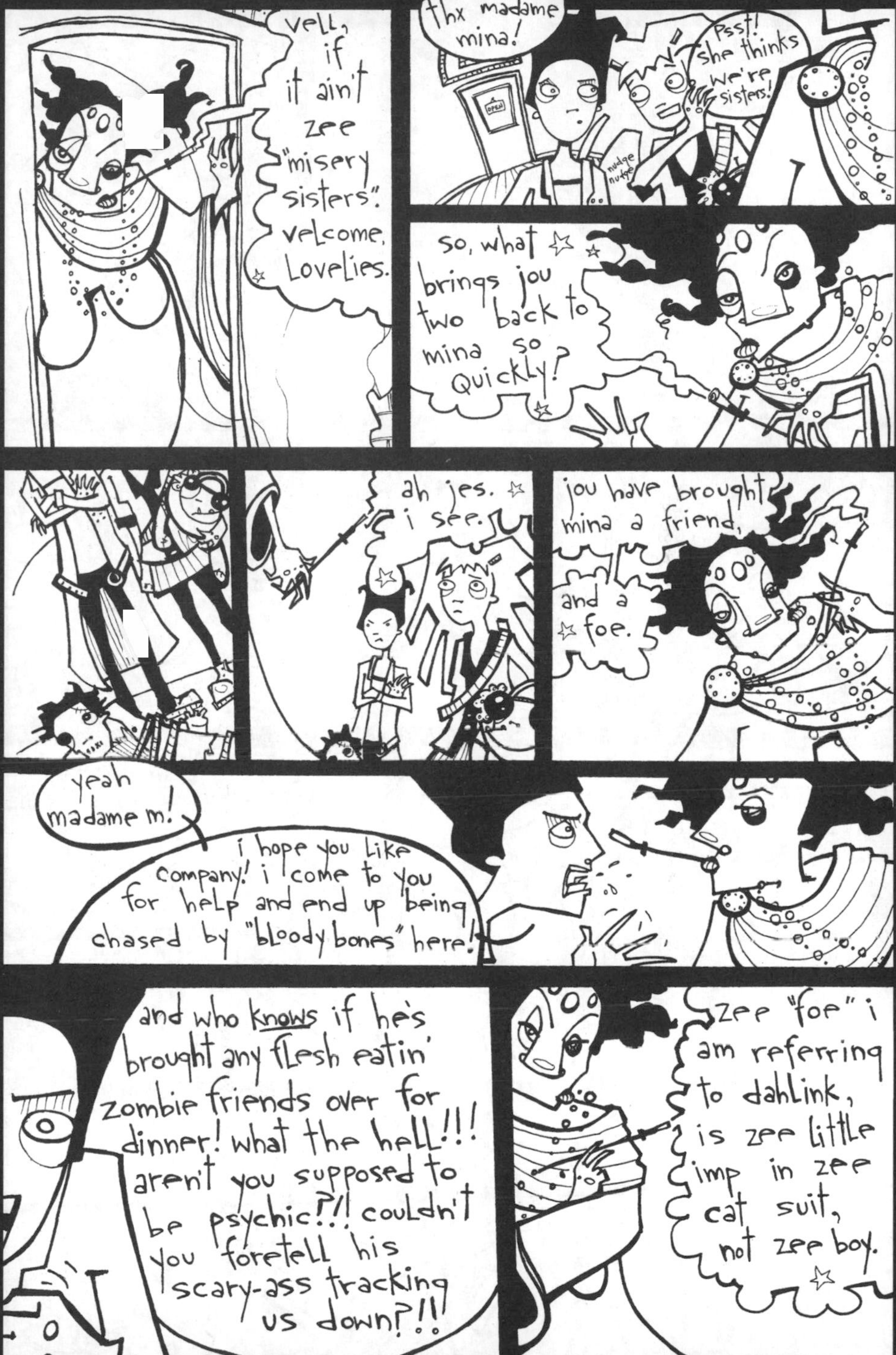
vell, if it ain't zee "misery sisters". velcome, Lovelies.
thx madame mina!
Psst! she thinks we're sisters!
nudge nudge
so, what brings jou two back to mina so Quickly?
ah jes. i see.
jou have brought mina a friend,
and a foe.
yeah madame m!
i hope you Like company! i come to you for help and end up being chased by "bloody bones" here!
and who knows if he's brought any flesh eatin' zombie friends over for dinner! what the hell!!! aren't you supposed to be psychic?!! couldn't you foretell his scary-ass tracking us down?!!
zee "foe" i am referring to dahLink, is zee Little imp in zee cat suit, not zee boy.

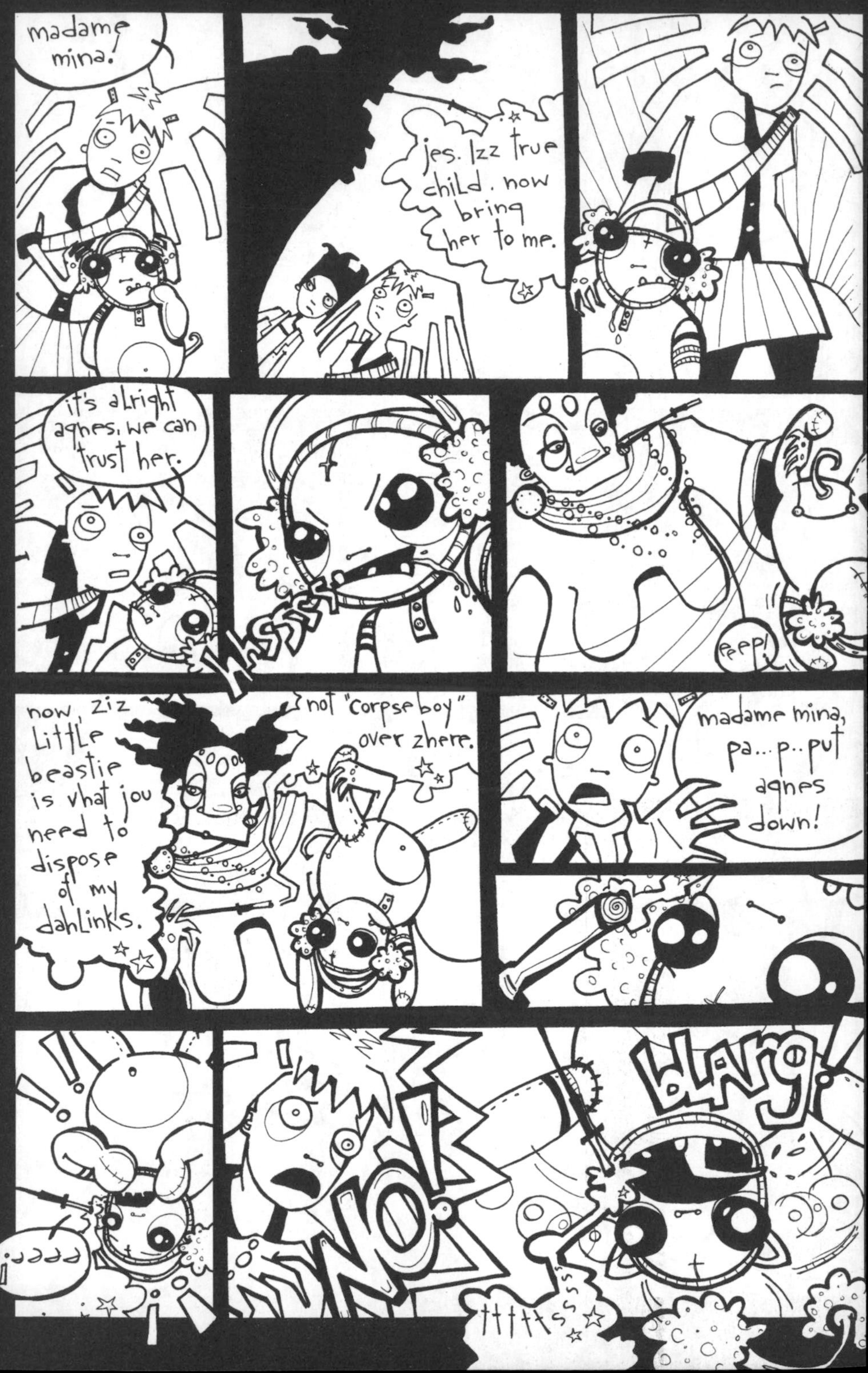

madame mina!
jes. Izz true child. now bring her to me.
it's alright agnes. we can trust her.
whsss
peep!
now, ziz little beastie is vhat jou need to dispose of my dahlinks.
not "corpse boy" over zhere.
madame mina, pa... p.. put agnes down!
!
peep!
NO!
blarg!
tttttsss

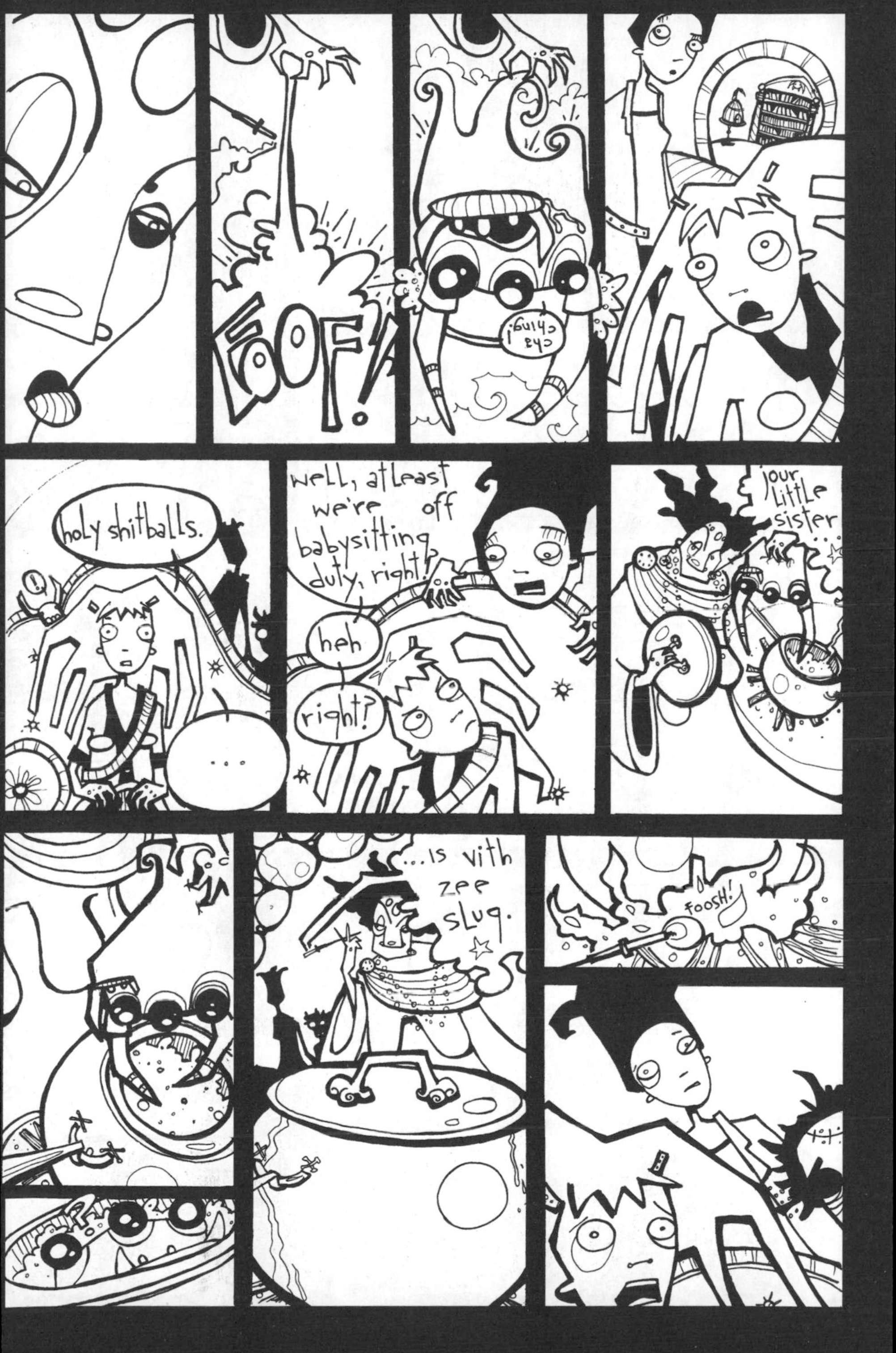
cha ching!
holy shitballs.
well, atleast we're off babysitting duty, right?
heh
right?
jour little sister
...is vith zee slug.
FOOSH!

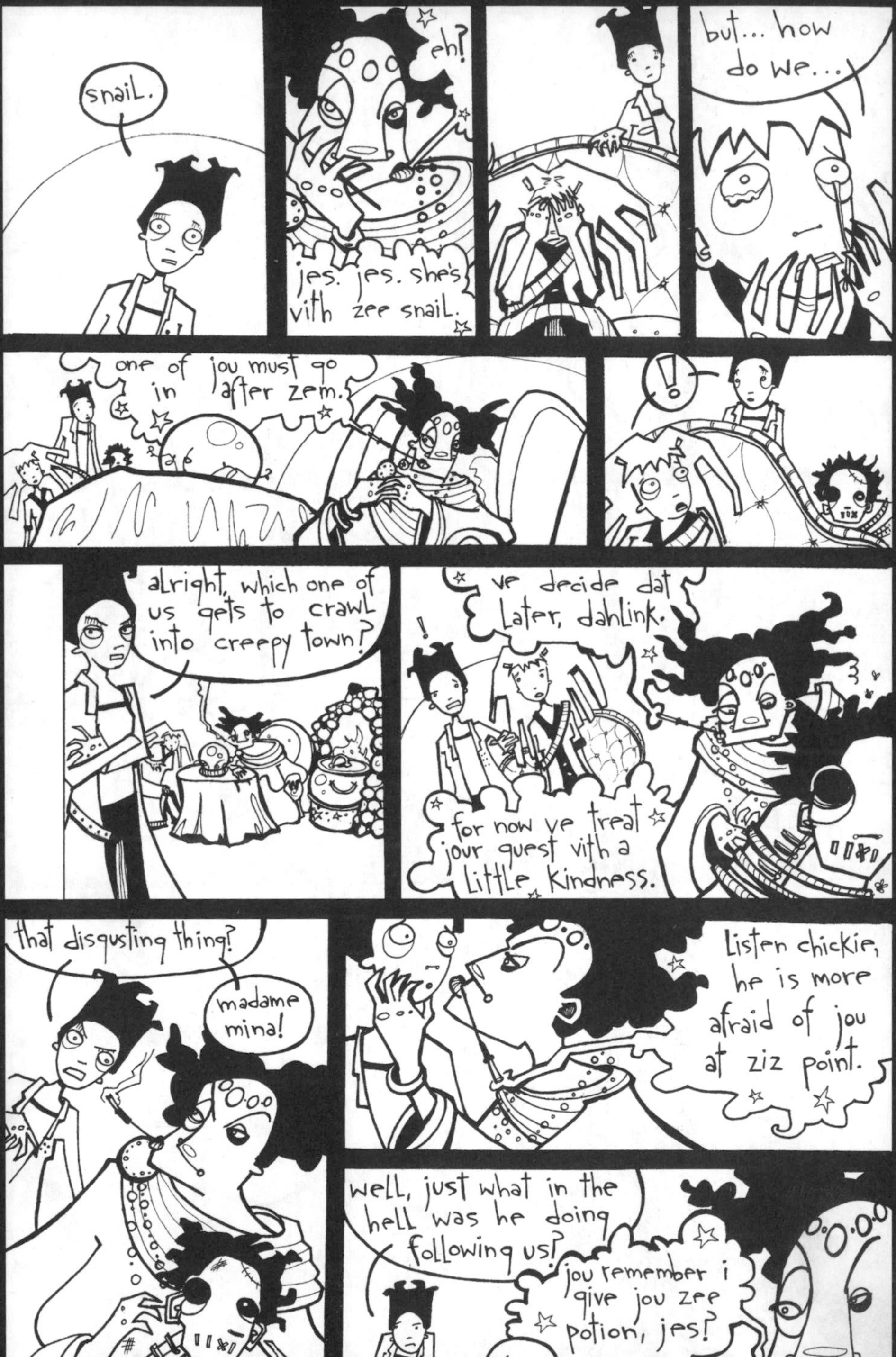
snaiL.
eh?
jes. jes. she's vith zee snaiL.
but... how do we...
one of jou must go in after zem.
!
aLright, which one of us gets to crawL into creepy town?
ve decide dat Later, dahLink.
!
for now ve treat jour guest vith a LittLe Kindness.
that disgusting thing?
madame mina!
Listen chickie, he is more afraid of jou at ziz point.
weLL, just what in the heLL was he doing foLLowing us?
jou remember i give jou zee potion, jes?
yes.

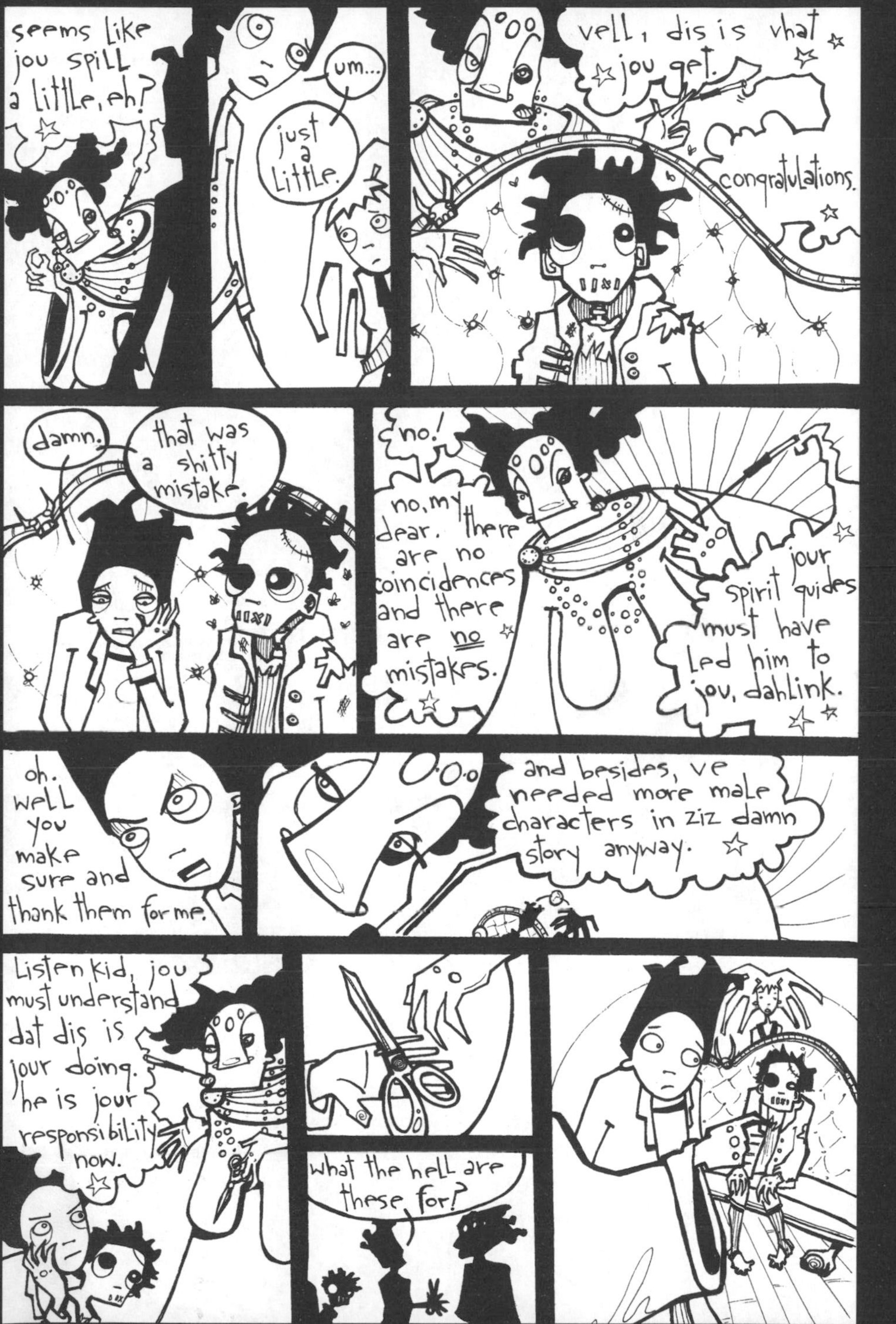
seems like jou spill a little, eh?
um...
just a little.
vell, dis is vhat jou get.
congratulations.
damn.
that was a shitty mistake.
no!
no, my dear. there are no coincidences and there are no mistakes.
jour spirit guides must have led him to jou, dahlink.
oh. well you make sure and thank them for me.
and besides, ve needed more male characters in ziz damn story anyway.
Listen kid, jou must understand dat dis is jour doing. he is jour responsibility now.
what the hell are these for?

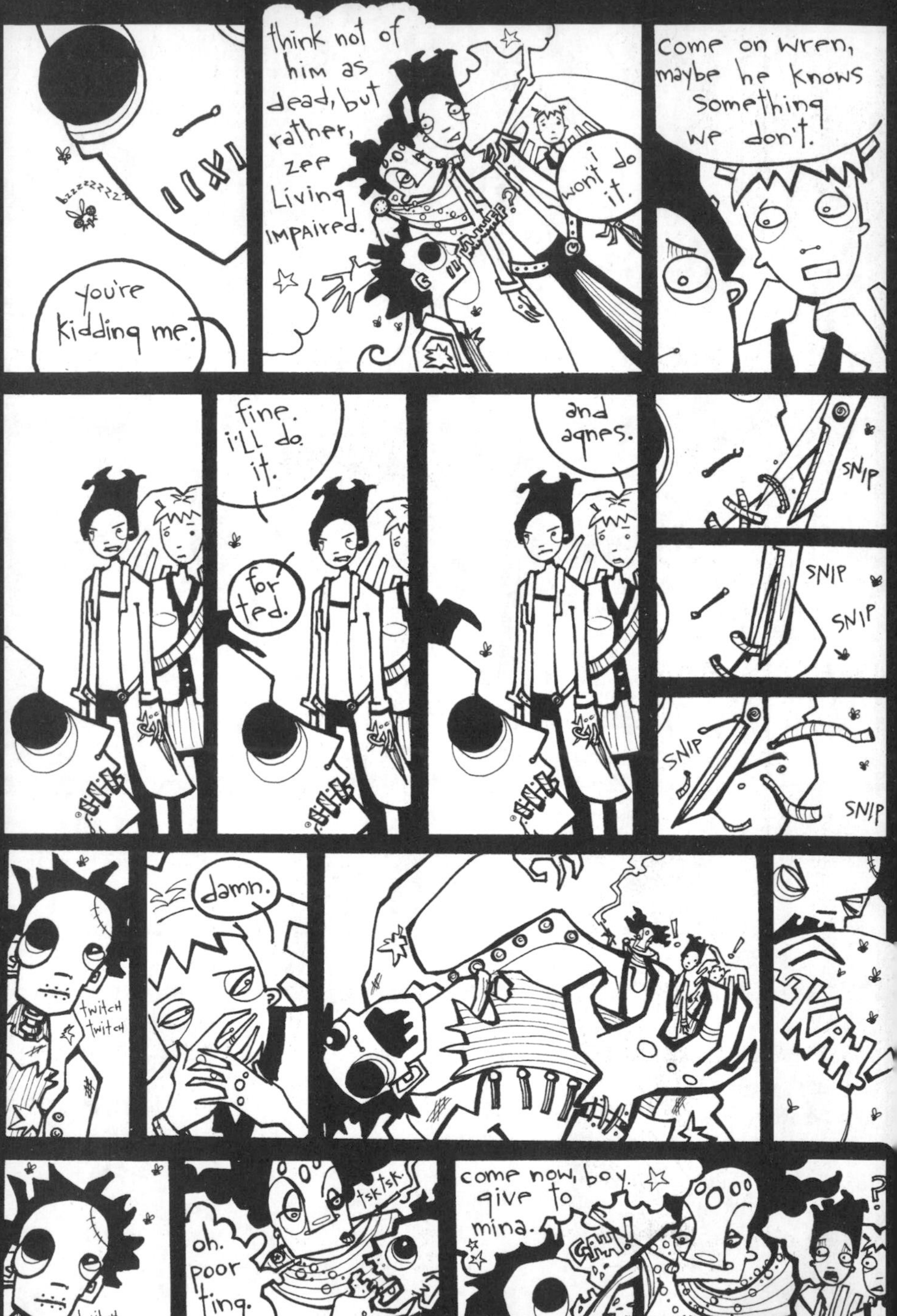
bzzzzzzzz
you're kidding me.
think not of him as dead, but rather, zee Living impaired.
i won't do it.
come on wren, maybe he knows something we don't.
fine. i'll do it.
for ted.
and agnes.
SNIP
SNIP
SNIP
SNIP
SNIP
twitch
twitch
damn.
twitch
oh. poor ting.
tsk tsk.
come now, boy. give to mina.

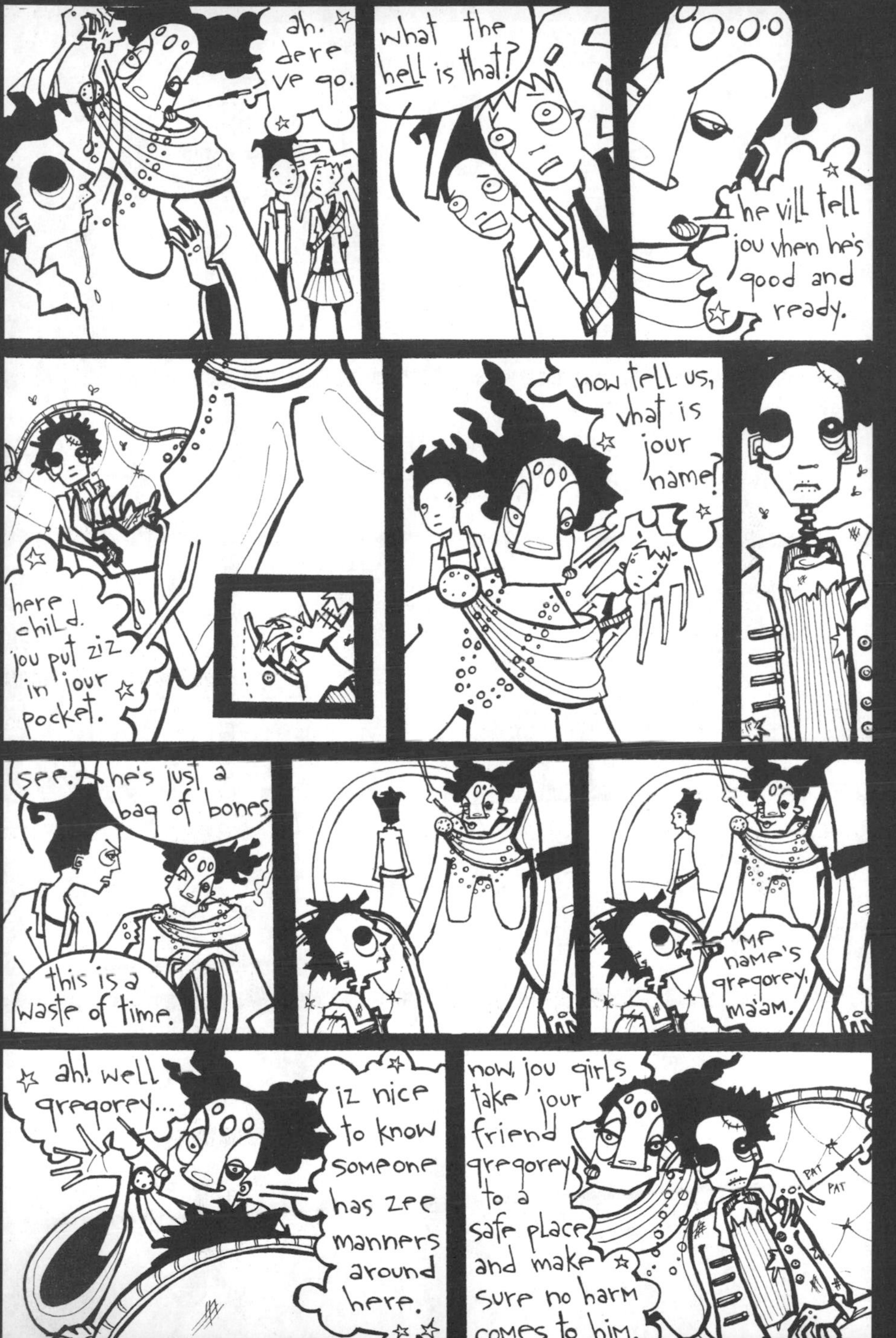
ah. dere ve go.
what the hell is that?
he vill tell jou vhen he's good and ready.
here child. jou put ziz in jour pocket.
now tell us, vhat is jour name?
see.
he's just a bag of bones.
this is a waste of time.
my name's gregorey, ma'am.
ah! well gregorey...
iz nice to know someone has zee manners around here.
now, jou girls take jour friend gregorey to a safe place and make sure no harm comes to him.
PAT PAT

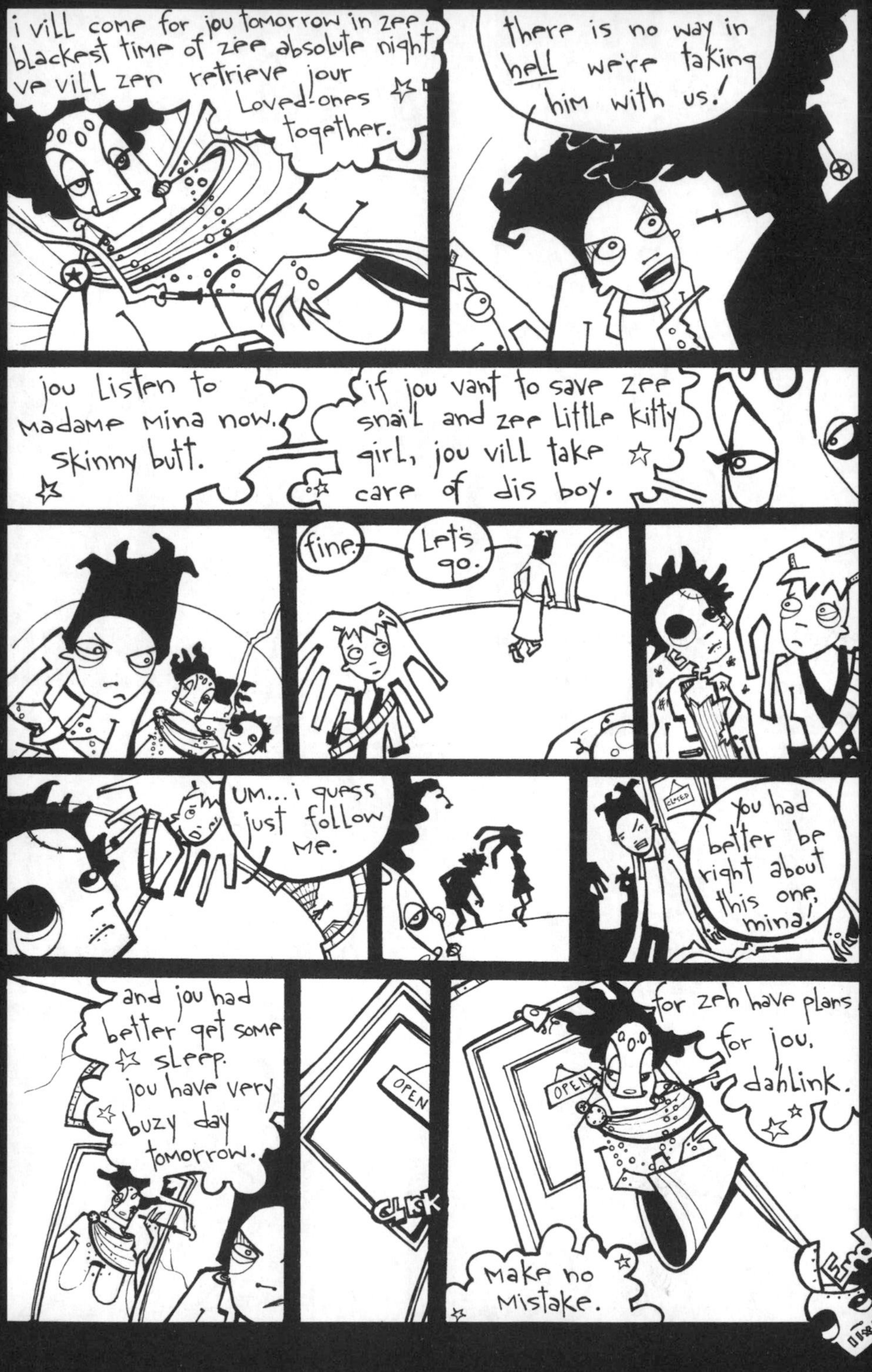
i viLL come for jou tomorrow in zee blackest time of zee absolute night. ve viLL zen retrieve jour Loved-ones together.
there is no way in hell we're taking him with us!
jou Listen to Madame Mina now, skinny butt.
if jou vant to save zee snaiL and zee Little kitty girL, jou viLL take care of dis boy.
fine.
Let's go.
UM... i guess just follow me.
CLOSED
you had better be right about this one, mina!
and jou had better get some sLeep. jou have very buzy day tomorrow.
OPEN
CLIK
OPEN
for zeh have plans for jou, dahLink.
Make no Mistake.

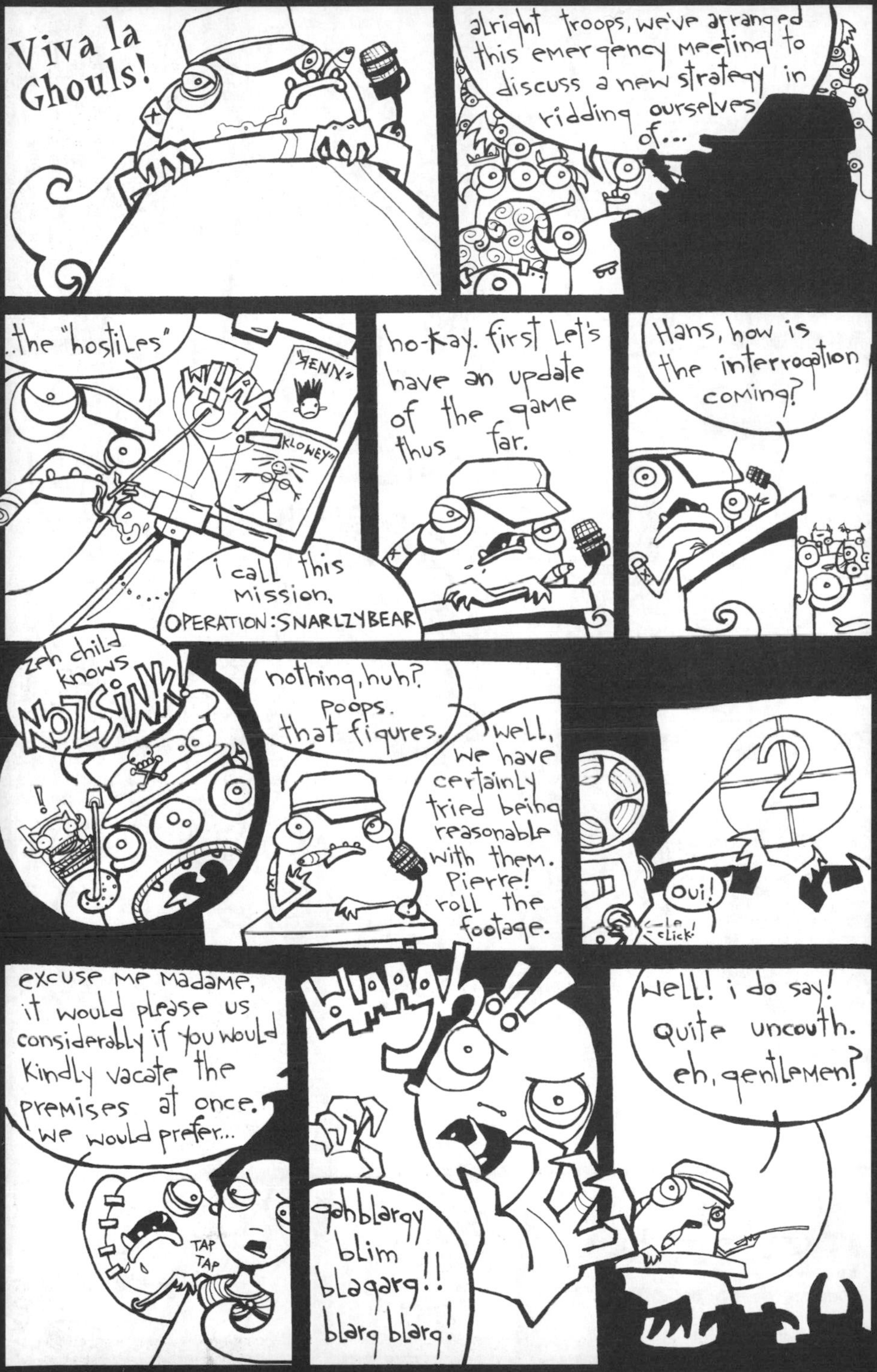
Viva la Ghouls!
alright troops, we've arranged this emergency meeting to discuss a new strategy in ridding ourselves of...
..the "hostiles"
WHAK
"JENNY"
"KLOWEY"
i call this mission, OPERATION:SNARLZYBEAR
ho-kay. first let's have an update of the game thus far.
Hans, how is the interrogation coming?
zeh child knows NOZSINK!
nothing, huh? poops. that figures.
well, we have certainly tried being reasonable with them. Pierre! roll the footage.
2
Oui!
click!
excuse me madame, it would please us considerably if you would kindly vacate the premises at once. we would prefer...
TAP TAP
gahblargy blim blagarg!! blarg blarg!
well! i do say! quite uncouth. eh, gentlemen?

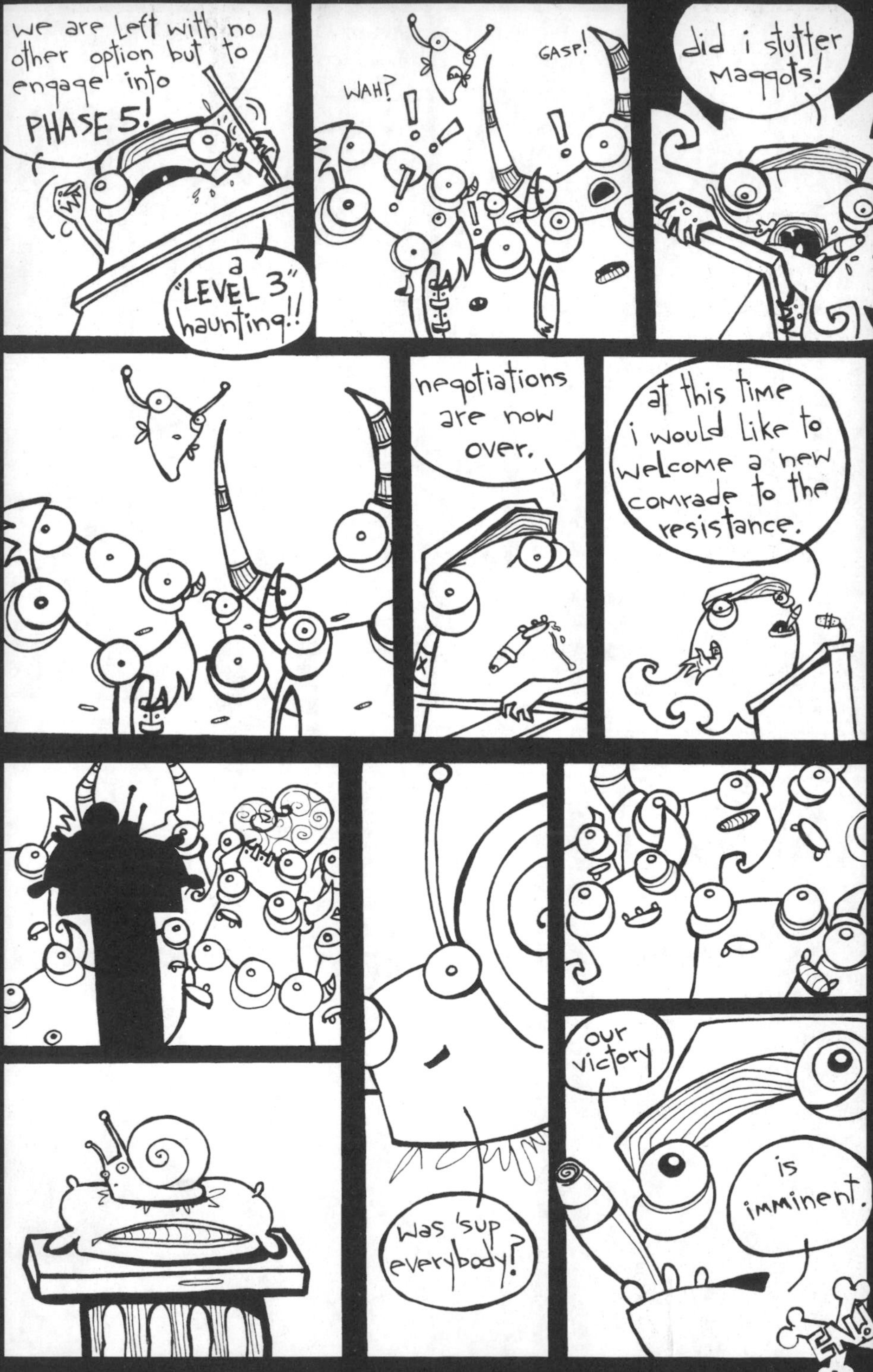
we are left with no other option but to engage into PHASE 5!
a "LEVEL 3" haunting!!
WAH?
GASP!
did i stutter Maggots!
negotiations are now over.
at this time i would like to welcome a new comrade to the resistance.
was 'sup everybody?
our victory
is imminent.
END

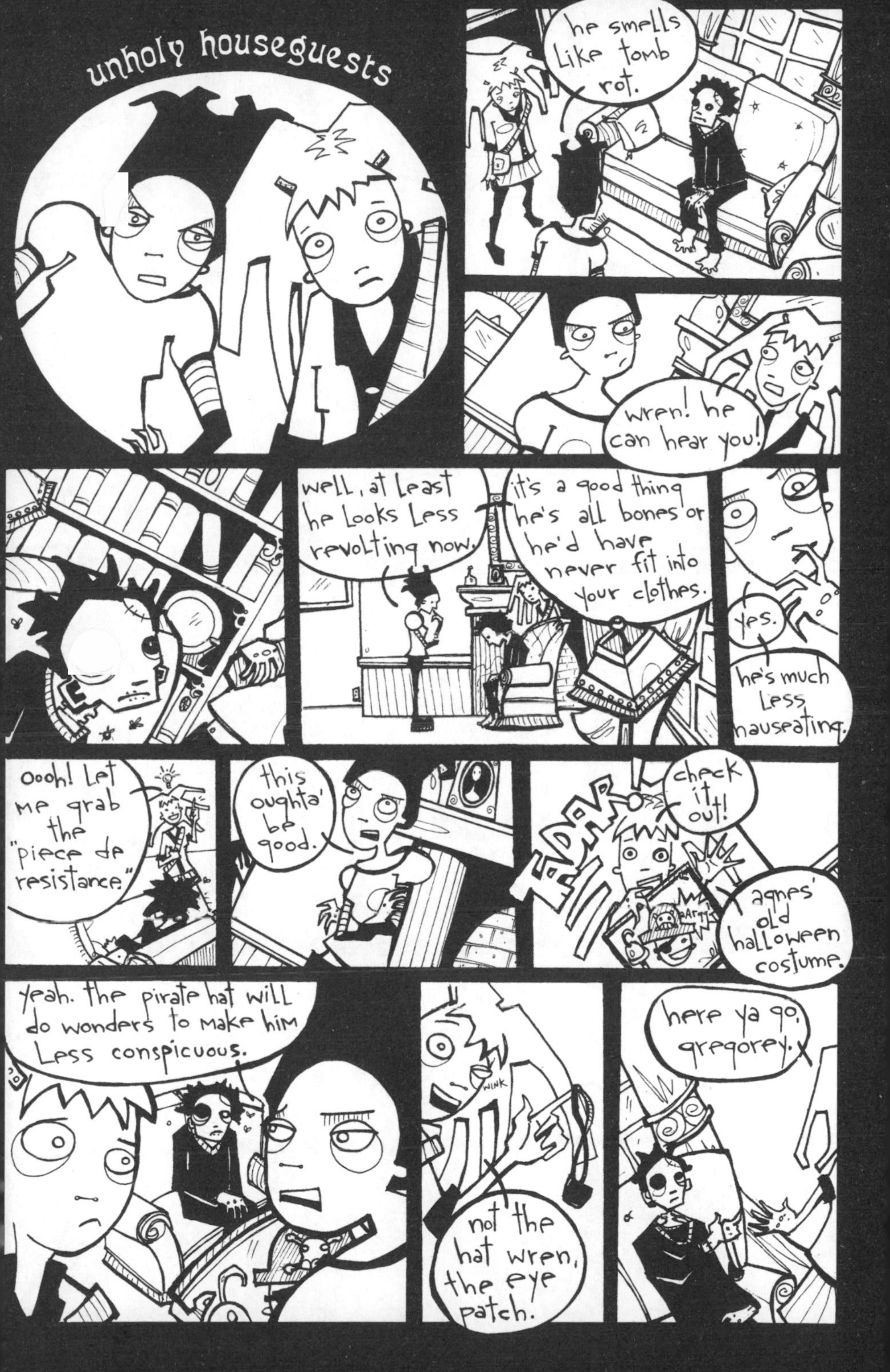
unholy houseguests
he smells like tomb rot.
wren! he can hear you!
well, at least he looks less revolting now.
it's a good thing he's all bones or he'd have never fit into your clothes.
yes.
he's much less nauseating.
oooh! let me grab the "piece de resistance."
this oughta' be good.
TA DAA!
check it out!
agnes' old halloween costume.
yeah. the pirate hat will do wonders to make him less conspicuous.
WINK
not the hat wren, the eye patch.
here ya go, gregorey.

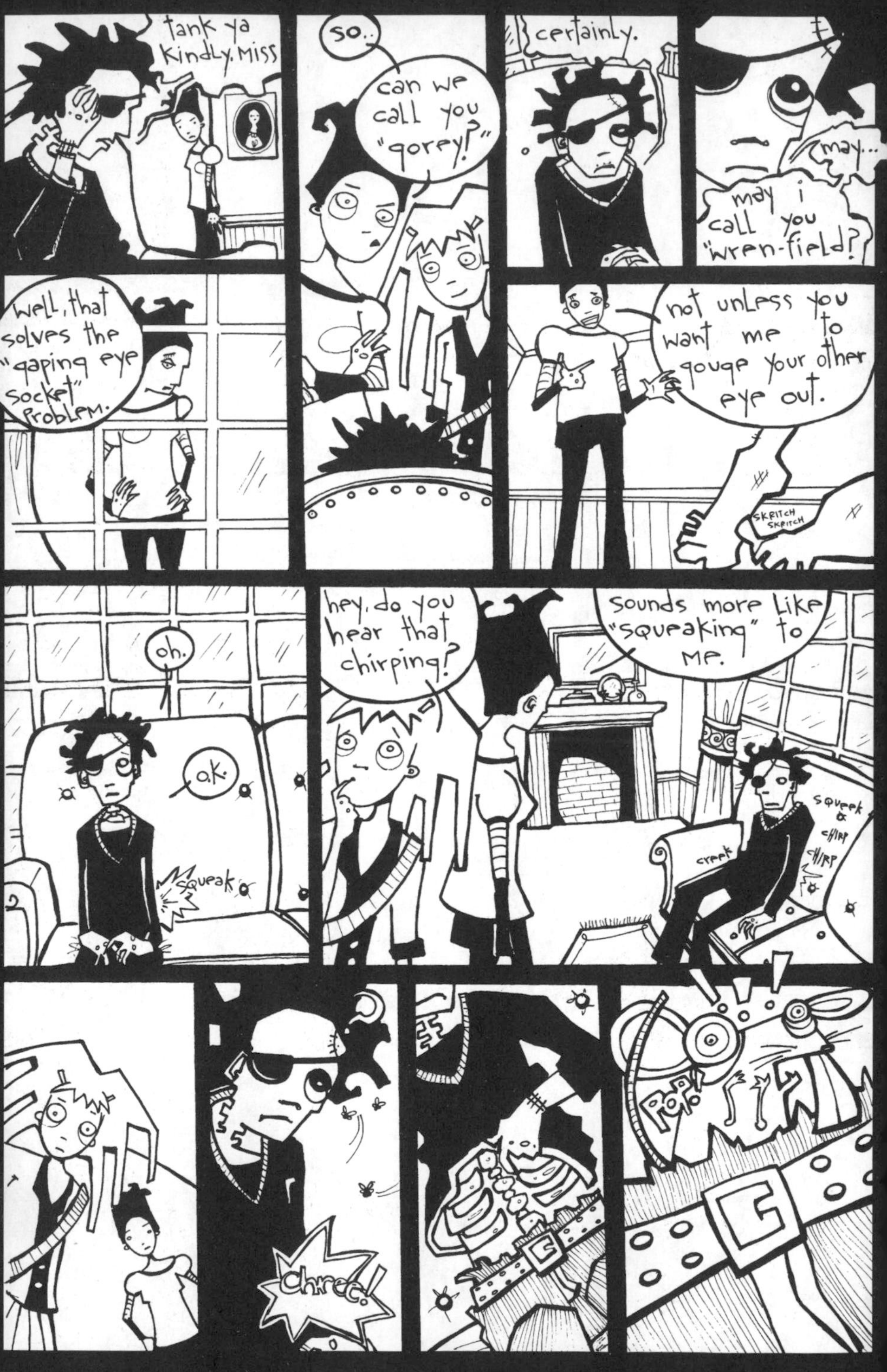
tank ya kindly, miss
so..
can we call you "gorey?"
certainly.
may...
may i call you "wren-field?
well, that solves the "gaping eye socket" problem.
not unless you want me to gouge your other eye out.
SKRITCH SKRITCH
oh.
o.k.
squeak
hey, do you hear that chirping?
sounds more like "squeaking" to me.
creek
squeek
chirp
chirp
chreee!
POP!

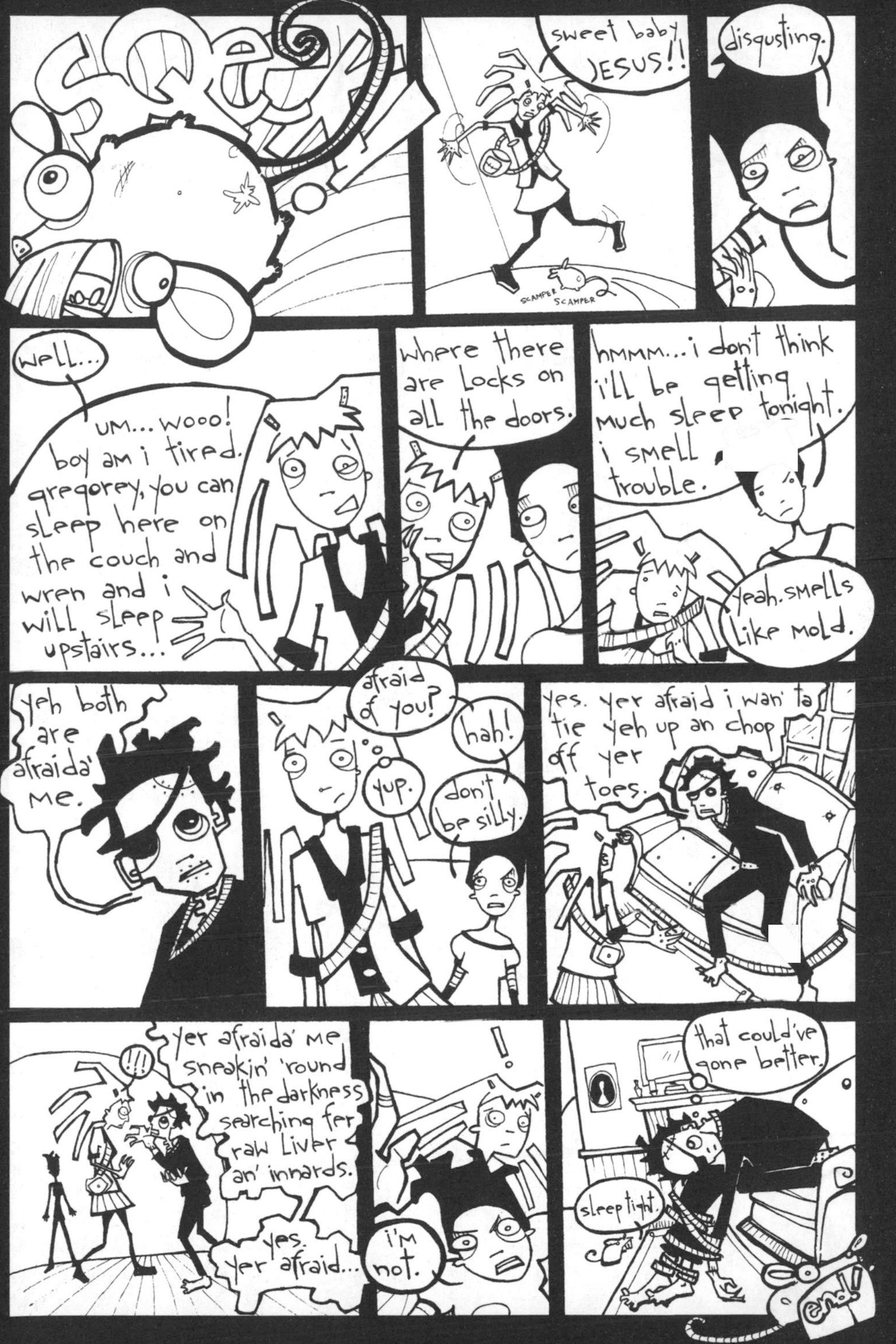

sweet baby JESUS!!
SCAMPER SCAMPER
disgusting.
well...
um... wooo! boy am i tired. gregorey, you can sleep here on the couch and wren and i will sleep upstairs...
where there are locks on all the doors.
hmmm...i don't think i'll be getting much sleep tonight. i smell trouble.
yeah. smells like mold.
yeh both are afraida' me.
afraid of you?
hah!
yup.
don't be silly.
yes. yer afraid i wan' ta tie yeh up an chop off yer toes.
!!!
yer afraida' me sneakin' 'round in the darkness searching fer raw liver an' innards.
yes. yer afraid...
!
i'm not.
that could've gone better.
sleep tight.
end!

and now, it's time for:

HORROR SCOPES

where the outlook is always grim!

ARIES

Bed bugs will soon infest your sleeping quarters, but will not account for the recent incurable rash on your nooners.

LIBRA

Your suspicions will be confirmed during your next gluttonous visit to the Magical Donut Castle. Note: stay away from the "sugar" glazed. Far, far away.

TAURUS

You fluctuate from smelling like mushroom casserole to fetid cabbage. You nauseate even the most ironclad of constitutions.

SCORPIO

Suck on three raw eggs and hide your face in dog food for two days to cure hiccups. This IS the only known medical cure.

GEMINI

Your ritualistic killings tend to lean on the sloppy side. Come on man, have some pride in your work.

SAGITTARIUS

Pay special attention to your parents' odd behavior. They are, indeed, planning on sending you to the "Nuthouse" with all the other "Fruitcakes."

CANCER

Your personal road to happiness begins and ends with Skulduggery. You have a dictionary, look it up.

CAPRICORN

Ever heard of the term "Better off dead"? Yeah. You know what I'm talking 'bout.

LEO

You may notice a negative change in those around you. Dismiss doubtfulness: It IS because you're creepy.

AQUARIUS

Your nether regions will swell up to cantalouptic* proportions.
(*That's "as big as a cantaloupe" for all you non-Ivy Leaguers.)

VIRGO

The engorged boil on your nose will soon spread to your forehead, cheeks, and chin. But, relax, it looks good on you.

PISCES

John Wayne Gacy was a Pisces. 'Nuff said.

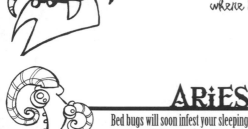

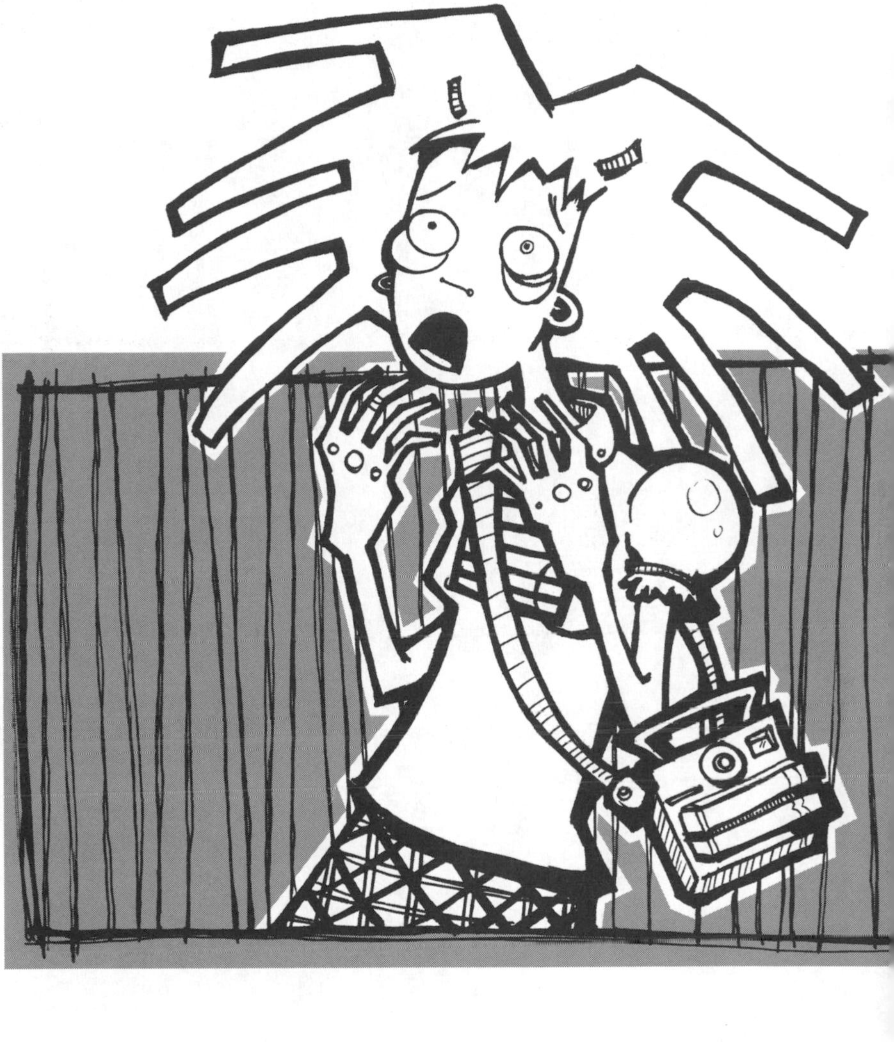

chapter five.

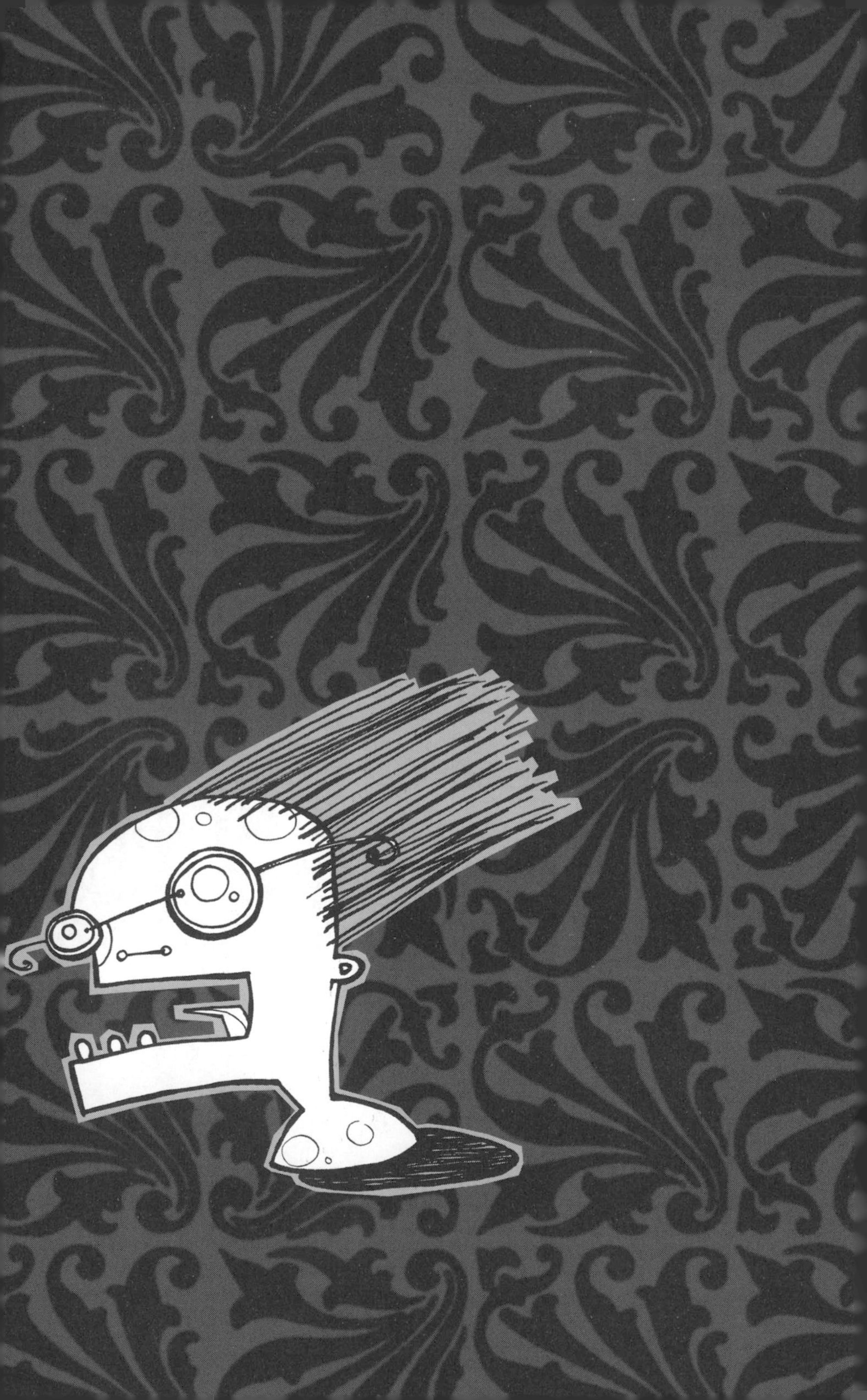

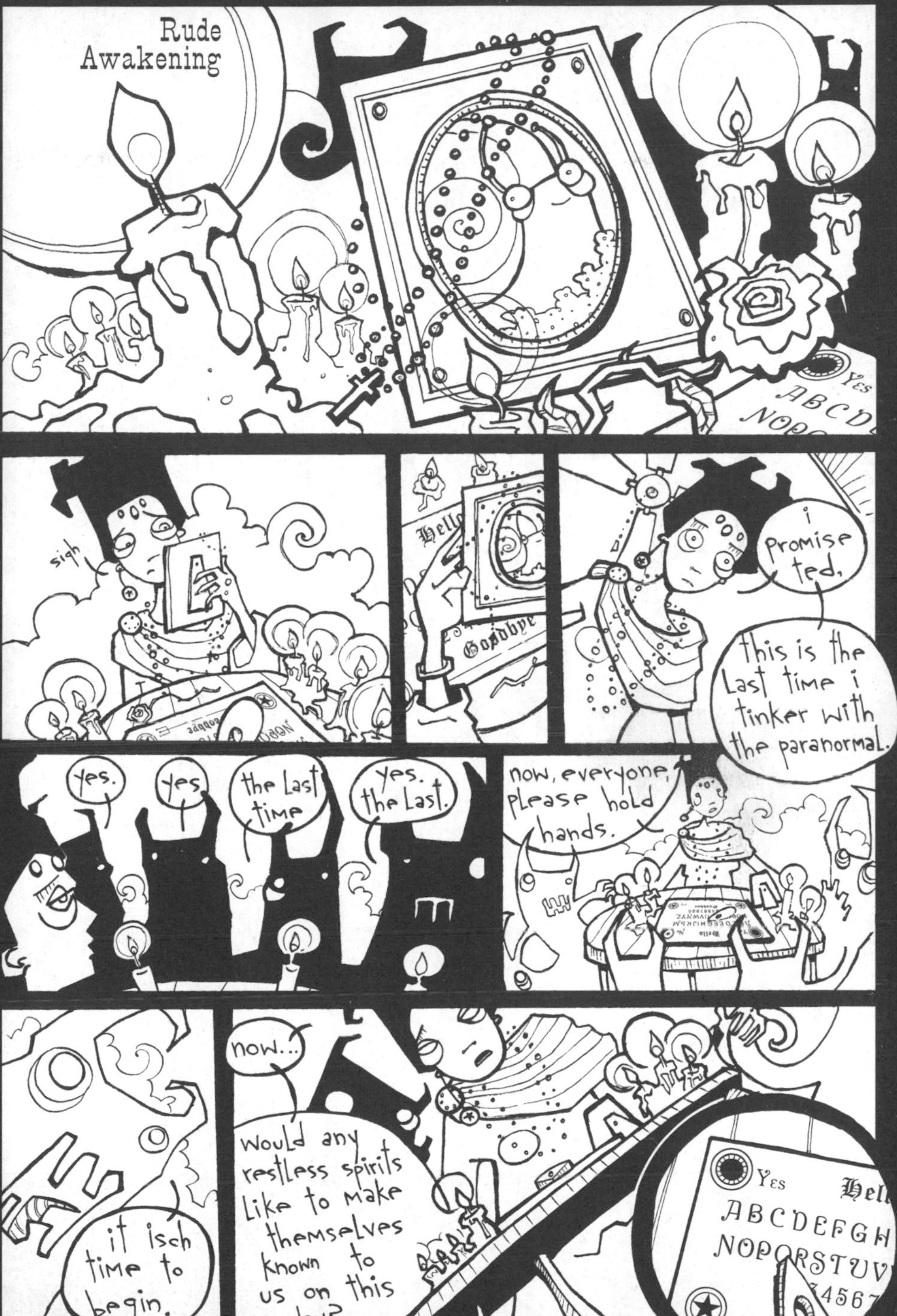
Rude Awakening
Yes
ABCD
NOP
sigh
Hell
Goodbye
i promise ted,
this is the last time i tinker with the paranormal.
yes.
yes
the last time
yes. the last.
now, everyone, please hold hands.
it isch time to begin.
now...
would any restless spirits like to make themselves known to us on this day?
Yes
Hell
ABCDEFGH
NOPQRSTUV
3 4 5 6 7

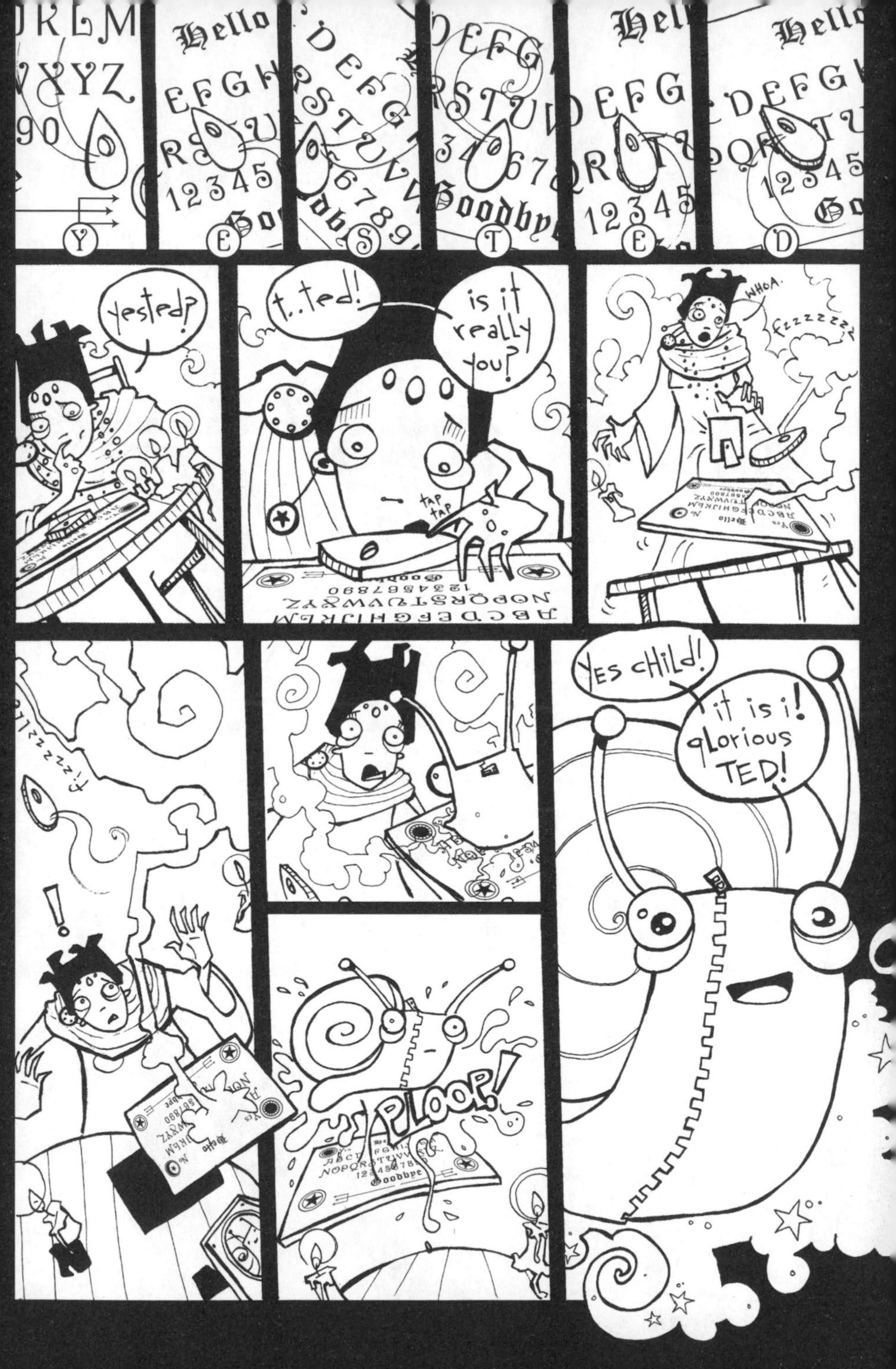

Y
E
S
T
E
D
yested?
t..ted!
is it really you?
tap tap
WHOA.
fzzzzzz
fizzzzzz
!
PLOOP!
Yes CHILD!
it is i! gLorious TED!

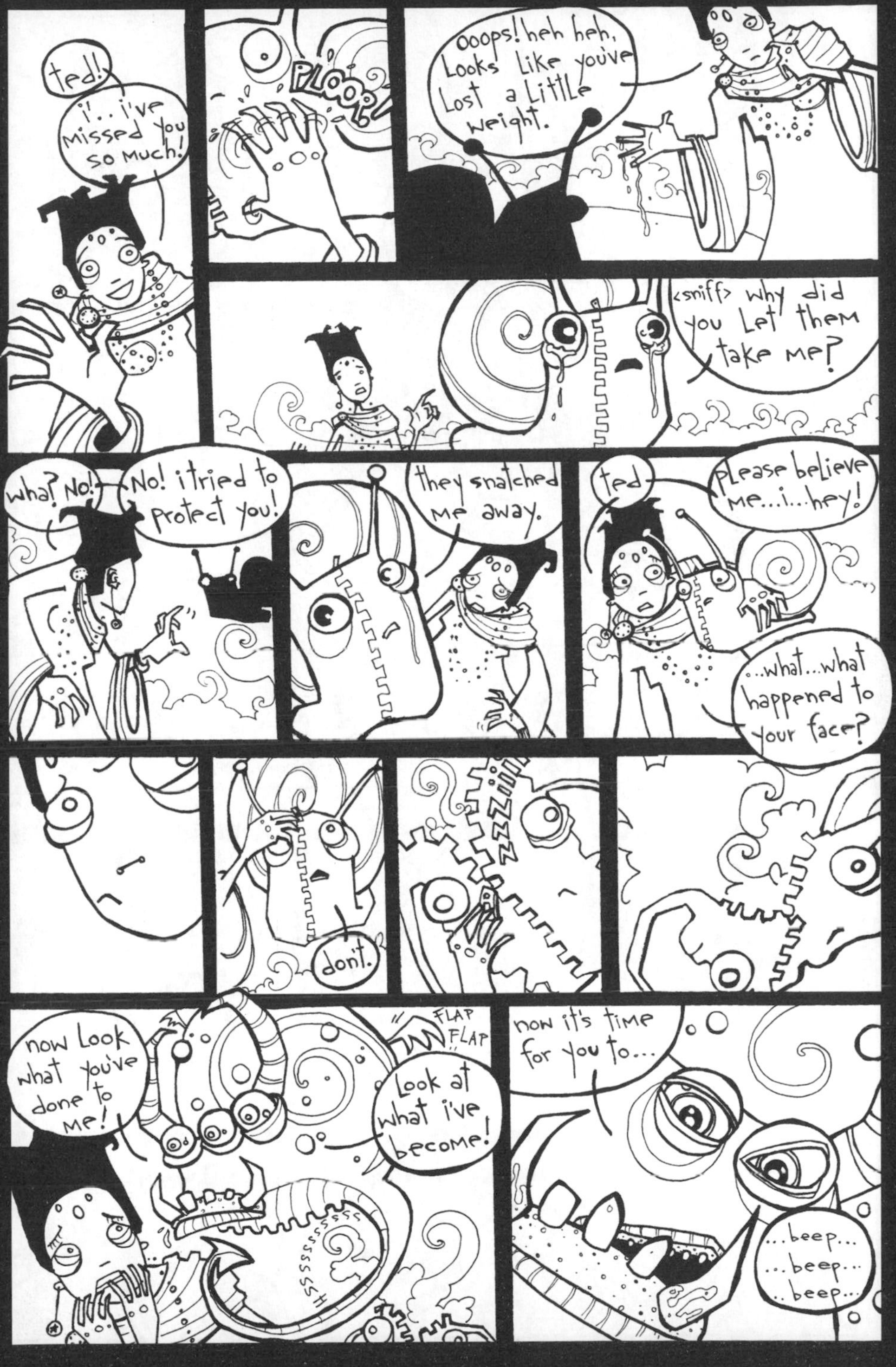
ted!
i'.. i've missed you so much!
PLOOP!
Ooops! heh heh, Looks like you've Lost a Little weight.
<sniff> why did you Let them take me?
what? No!
No! i tried to protect you!
they snatched me away.
ted
Please believe me...i...hey!
...what...what happened to your face?
don't.
ZZZiiiii
now Look what you've done to me!
FLAP FLAP
Look at what i've become!
HSSSSSSSSSSS
now it's time for you to...
...beep...
...beep...
..beep...

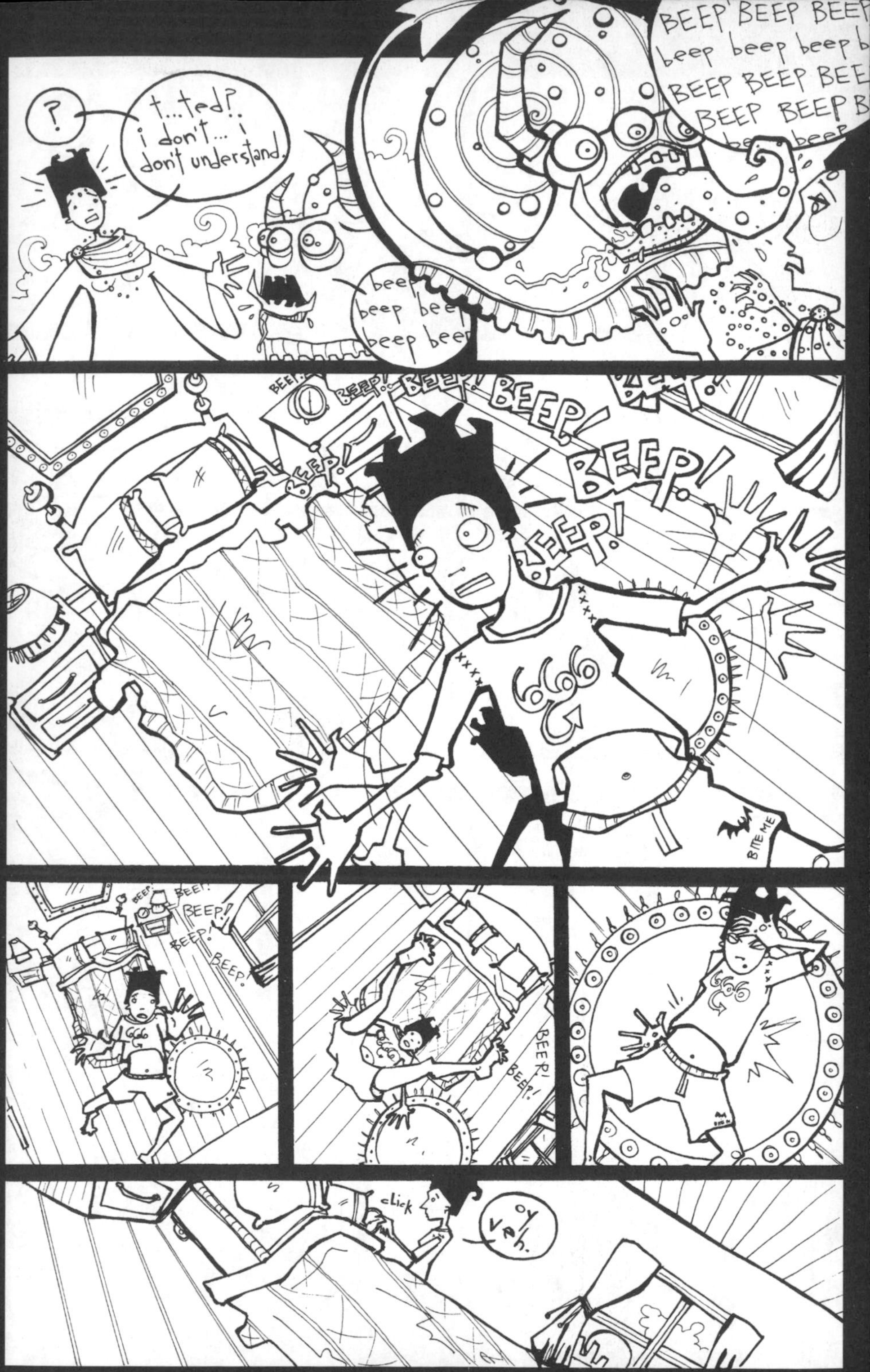
?
t...ted?.. i don't... i don't understand.
beep beep beep beep beep
BEEP BEEP BEEP beep beep beep BEEP BEEP BEE BEEP BEEP
BEEP! BEEP! BEEP! BEEP! BEEP! BEEP! BEEP!
BITE ME
BEEP! BEEP! BEEP!
BEEP! BEEP!
click
oy veh.

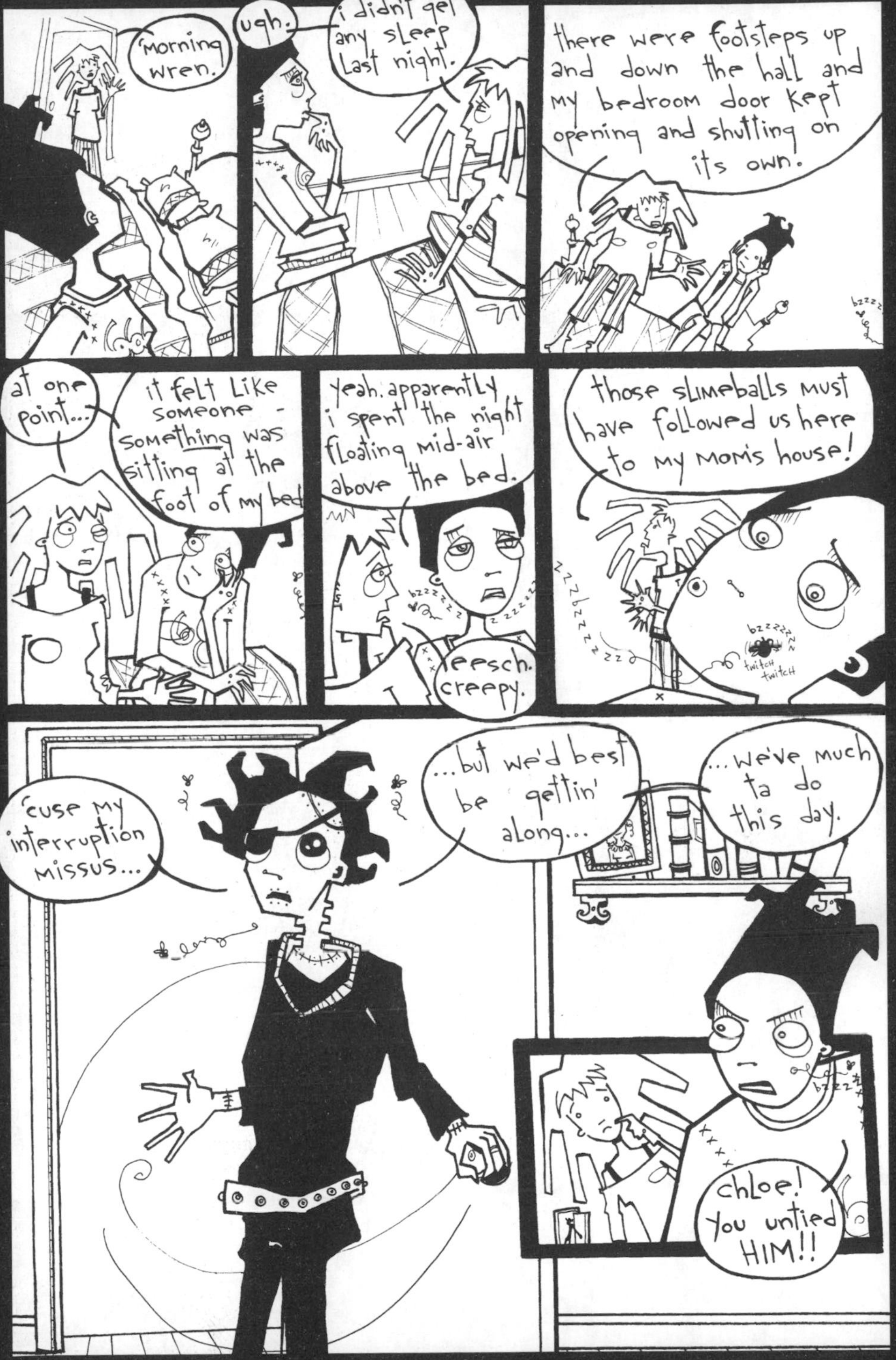
'Morning Wren.
ugh.
i didn't get any sleep last night.
there were footsteps up and down the hall and my bedroom door kept opening and shutting on its own!
bzzzz
at one point...
it felt like someone - something was sitting at the foot of my bed
yeah. apparently i spent the night floating mid-air above the bed.
bzzzzzz
zzzzzz
eesch. creepy.
those slimeballs must have followed us here to my mom's house!
zzzbzzzzzz
bzzzzz
twitch twitch
'cuse my interruption missus...
...but we'd best be gettin' along...
...we've much ta do this day.
bzzz
chloe! you untied HIM!!

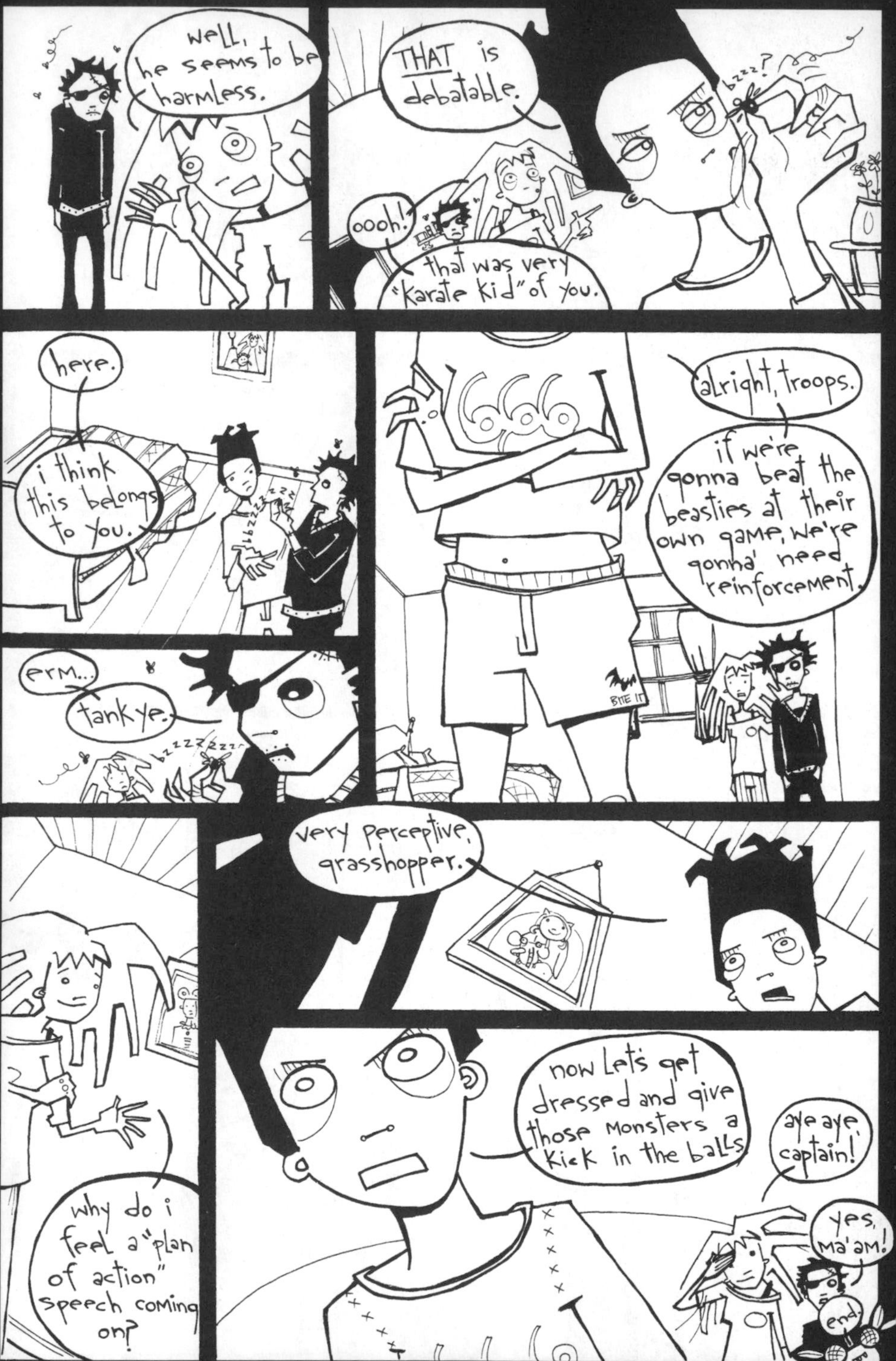
well, he seems to be harmless.
THAT is debatable.
bzzz?
oooh!
that was very "karate kid" of you.
here.
i think this belongs to you.
alright, troops.
if we're gonna beat the beasties at their own game, we're gonna' need reinforcement.
BITE IT
erm...
tank ye.
why do i feel a "plan of action" speech coming on?
very perceptive, grasshopper.
now let's get dressed and give those monsters a kick in the balls.
aye aye, captain!
yes, ma'am!
end.

lil' Toyshop of Horrors

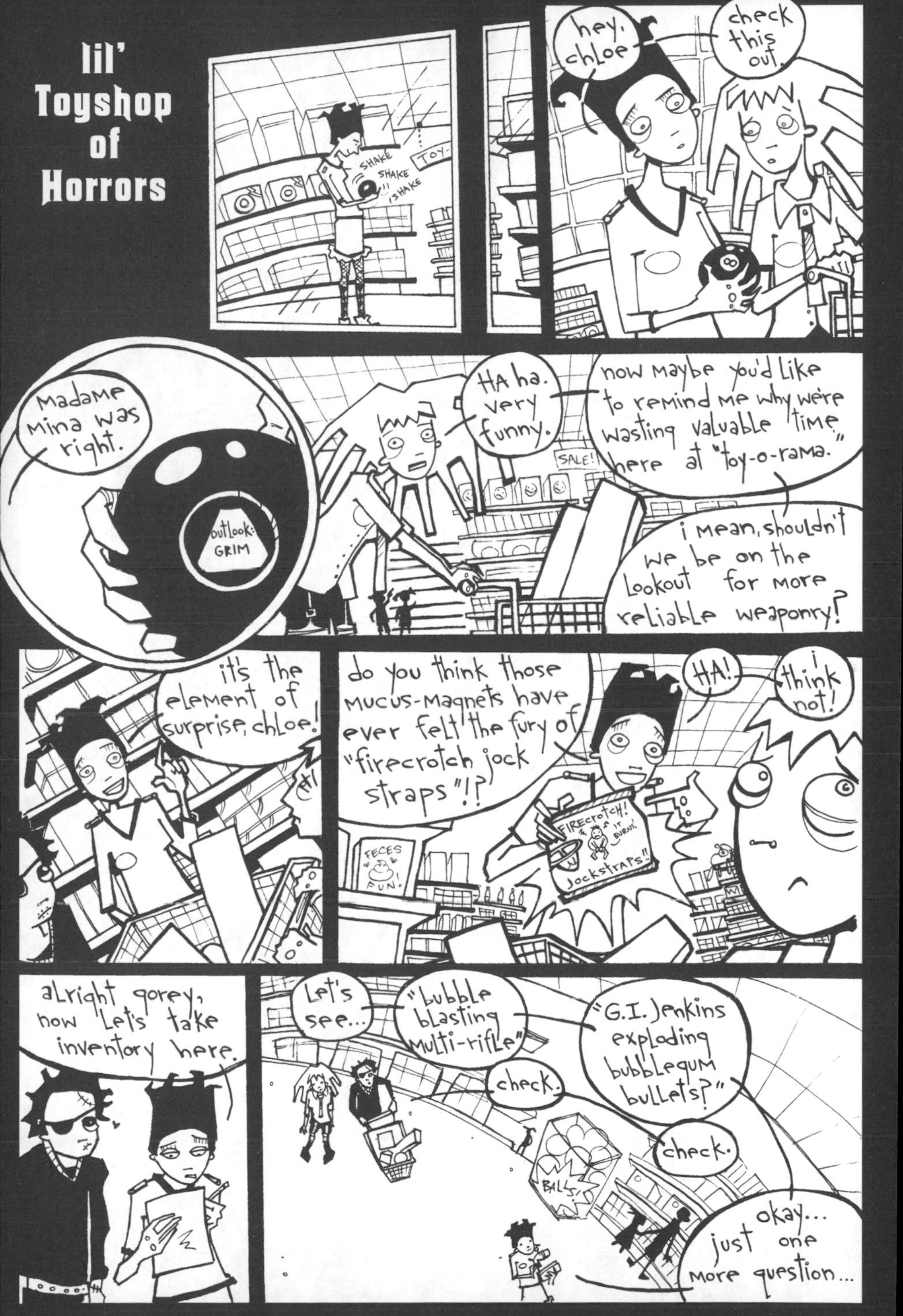
SHAKE
SHAKE
SHAKE
TOY-
hey, chloe
check this out.
Madame Mina was right.
OUTLOOK: GRIM
HA ha. very funny.
SALE!
now maybe you'd like to remind me why we're wasting valuable time here at "toy-o-rama."
i mean, shouldn't we be on the lookout for more reliable weaponry?
it's the element of surprise, chloe!
do you think those mucus-magnets have ever felt the fury of "firecrotch jock straps"!?
HA!
i think not!
FECES FUN!
FIRECROTCH! IT BURNS!
JOCKSTRAPS!!
alright gorey, now let's take inventory here.
let's see...
"bubble blasting multi-rifle"
check.
"G.I. Jenkins exploding bubblegum bullets?"
check.
BALLS
okay... just one more question...

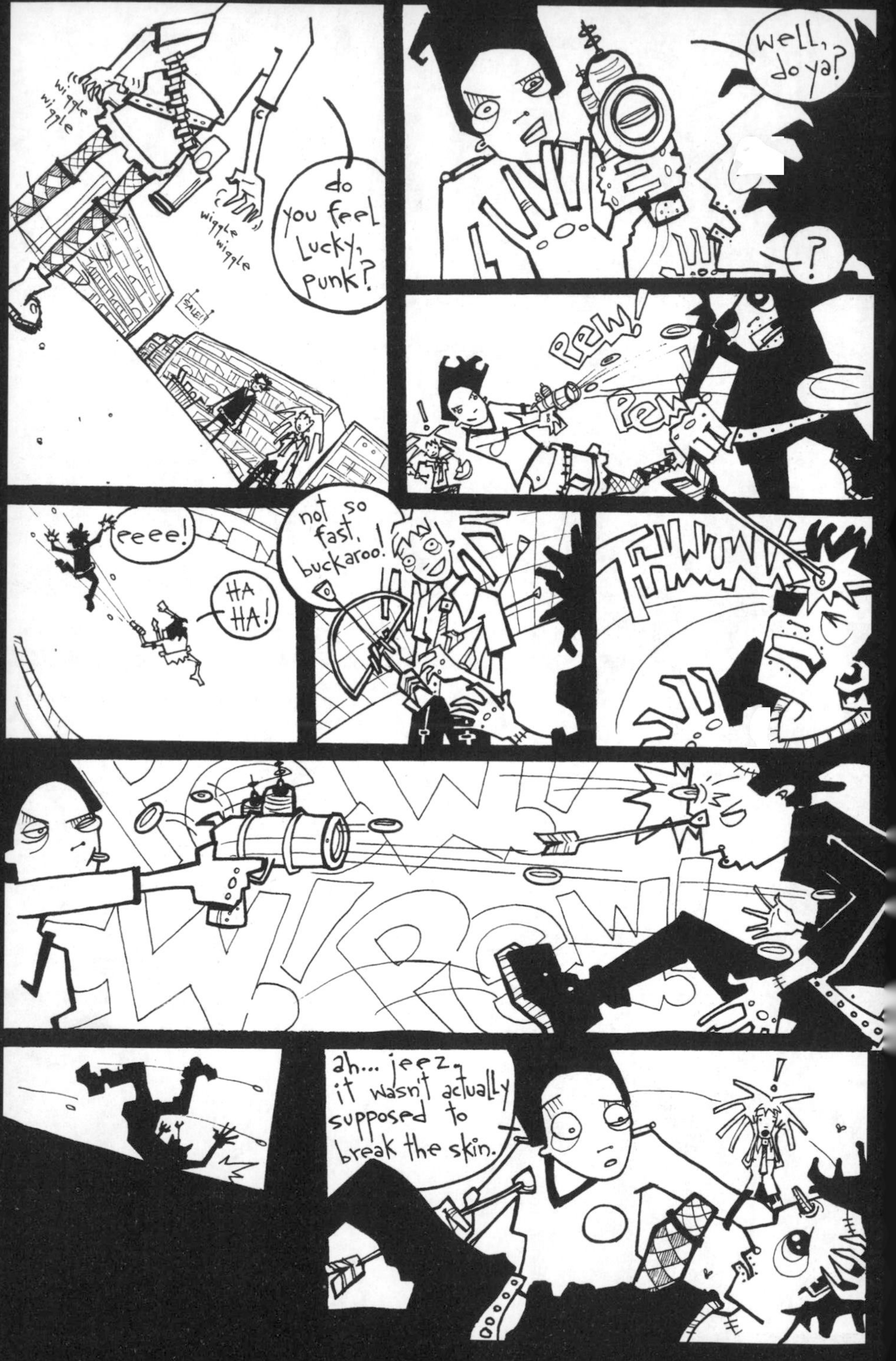
wiggle wiggle
wiggle wiggle
SALE!
do you feel Lucky, punk?
well, do ya?
?
PEW!
PEW!
!
eeee!
HA HA!
not so fast, buckaroo!
THWUNK
ah... jeez. it wasn't actually supposed to break the skin.
!

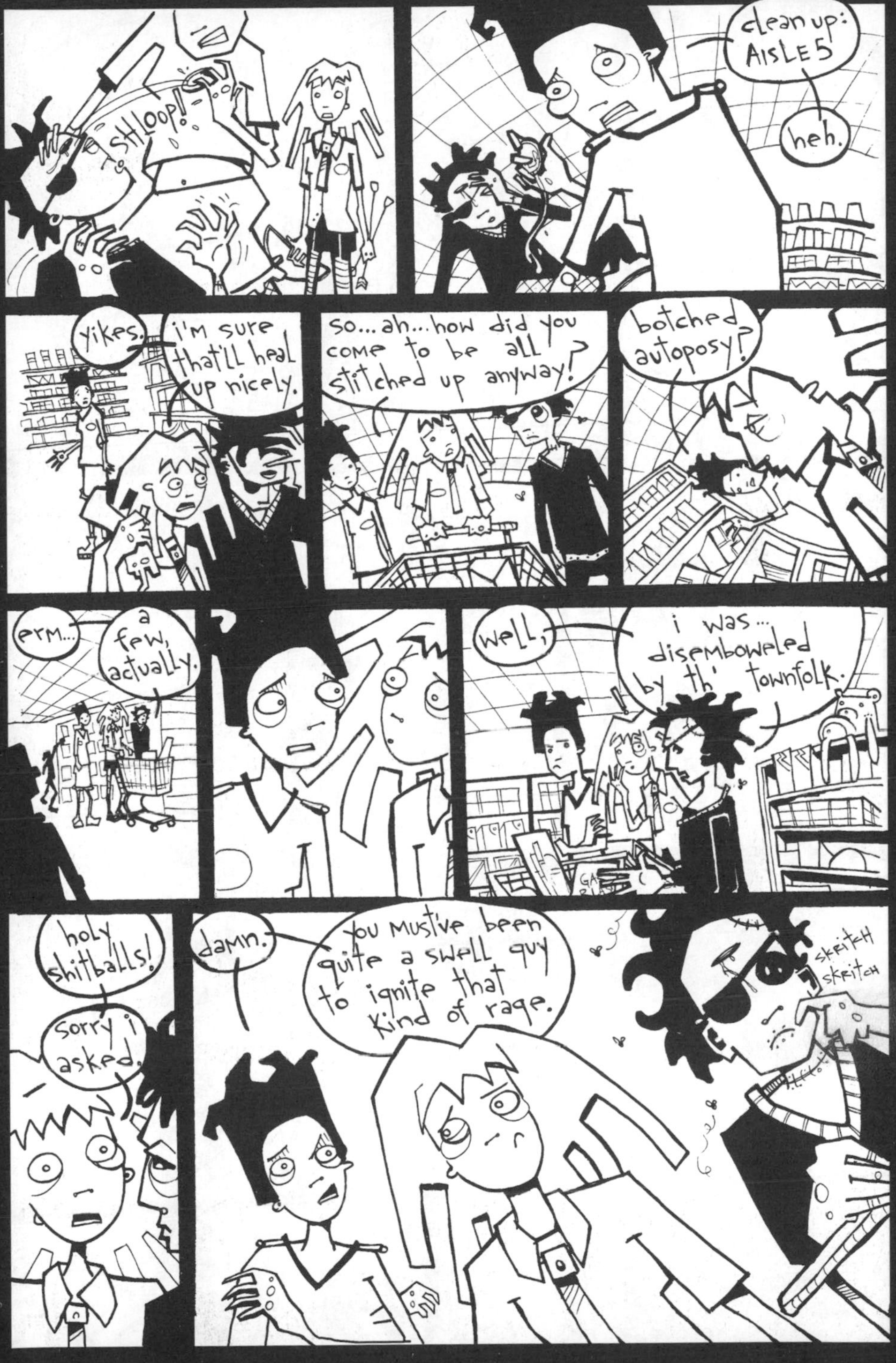
sHLOOP!
clean up: AISLE 5
heh.
yikes.
i'm sure that'll heal up nicely.
so...ah...how did you come to be all stitched up anyway?
botched autoposy?
erm...
a few, actually.
well,
i was... disemboweled by th' townfolk.
holy shitballs!
sorry i asked.
damn.
you mustve been quite a swell guy to ignite that kind of rage.
skritch skritch

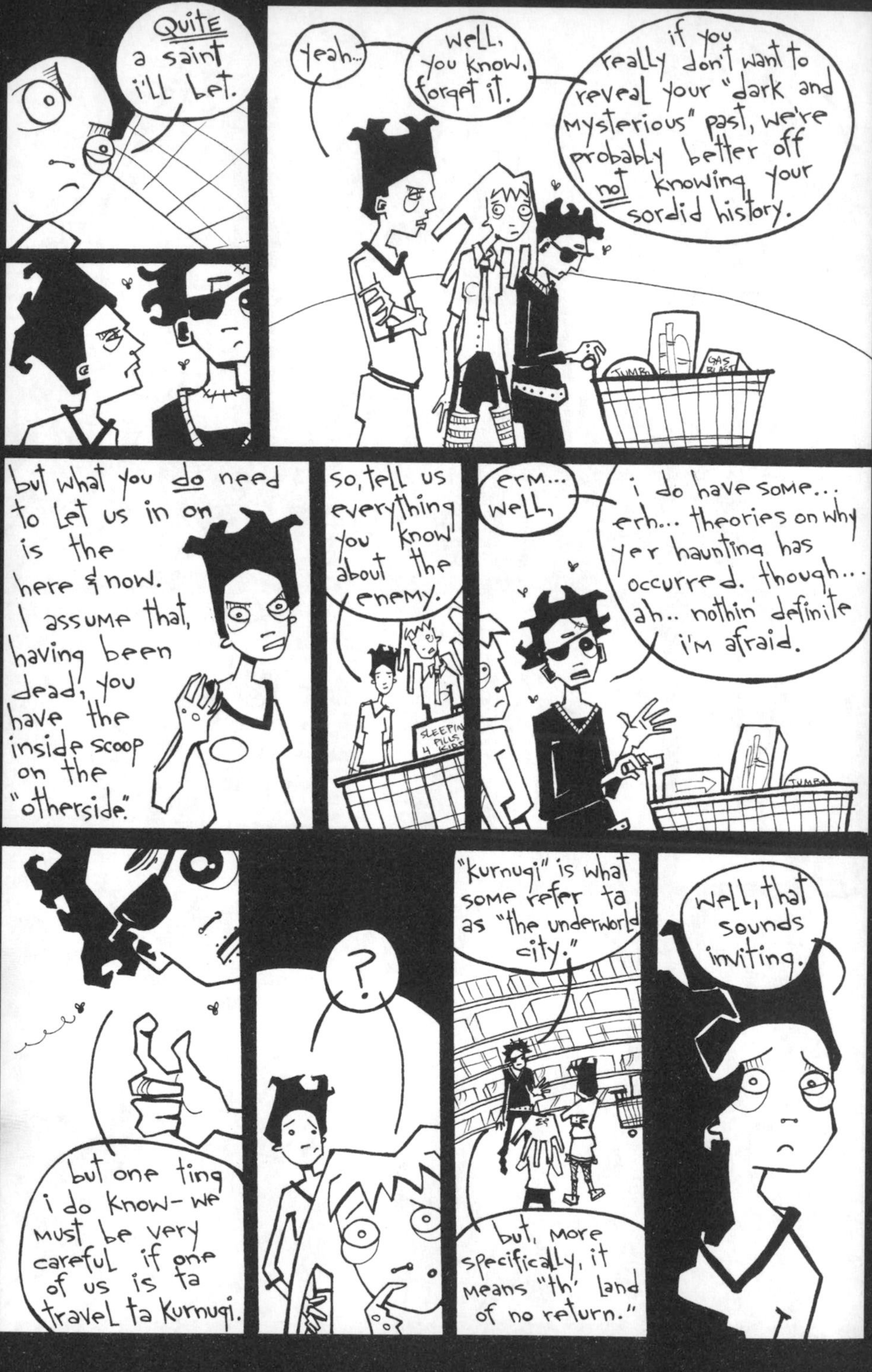
QUITE a saint i'll bet.
yeah...
well, you know, forget it.
if you really don't want to reveal your "dark and mysterious" past, we're probably better off not knowing your sordid history.
JUMBO
GAS BLAST
but what you do need to let us in on is the here & now. I assume that, having been dead, you have the inside scoop on the "otherside."
so, tell us everything you know about the enemy.
SLEEPIN PILLS 4 KIDS
erm... well,
i do have some... erh... theories on why yer haunting has occurred. though... ah.. nothin' definite i'm afraid.
JUMBO
but one ting i do know- we must be very careful if one of us is ta travel ta kurnugi.
?
"kurnugi" is what some refer ta as "the underworld city."
but, more specifically, it means "th' land of no return."
well, that sounds inviting.

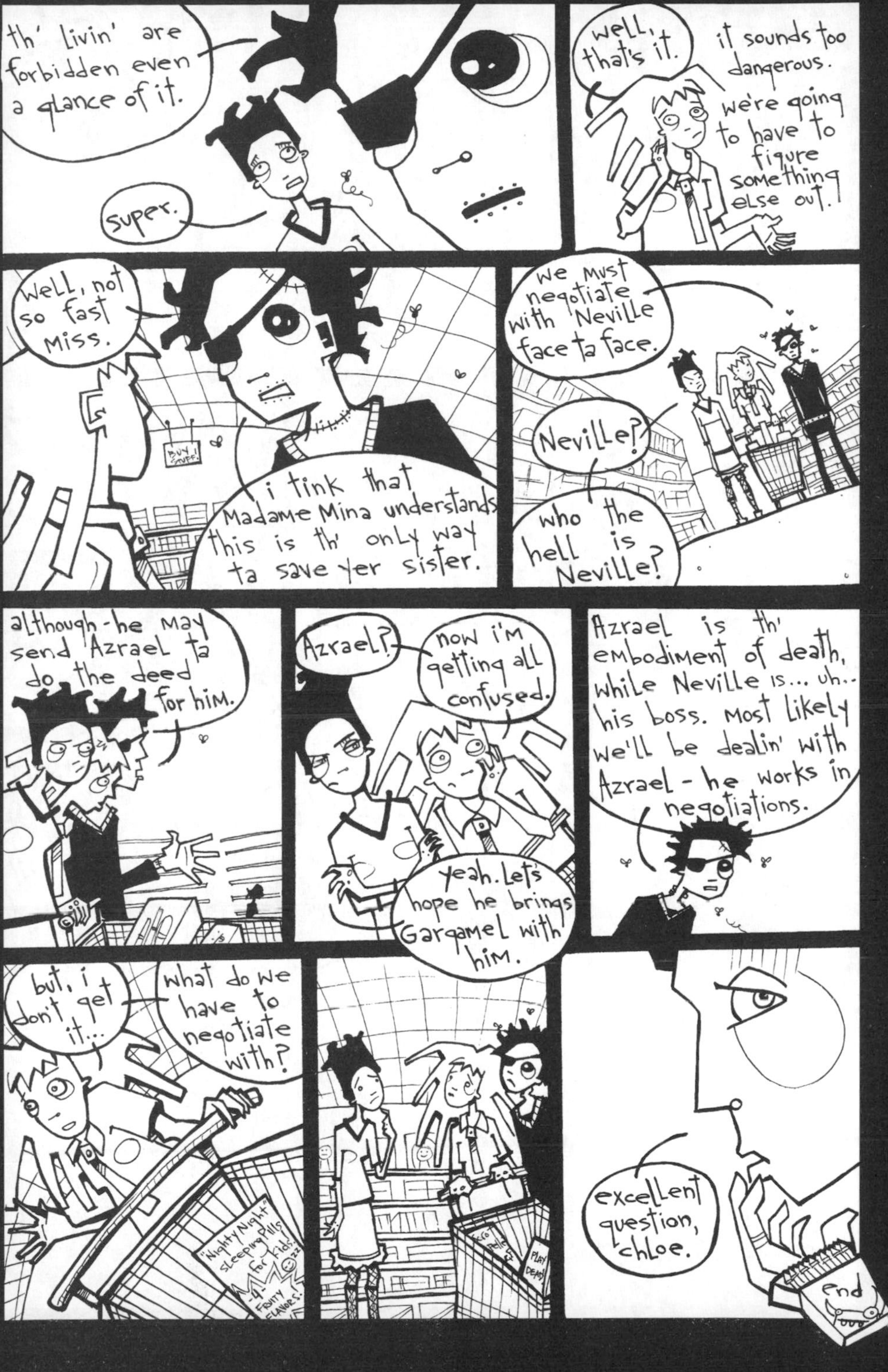
th' livin' are forbidden even a glance of it.
super.
well, that's it.
it sounds too dangerous.
we're going to have to figure something else out.
well, not so fast miss.
BUY STUFF!
i tink that Madame Mina understands this is th' only way ta save yer sister.
we must negotiate with Neville face ta face.
Neville?
who the hell is Neville?
although - he may send Azrael ta do the deed for him.
Azrael?
now i'm getting all confused.
yeah. let's hope he brings Gargamel with him.
Azrael is th' embodiment of death, while Neville is... uh.. his boss. most likely we'll be dealin' with Azrael - he works in negotiations.
but, i don't get it...
what do we have to negotiate with?
"Nighty Night" sleeping pills for kids!
FRUITY FLAVORS.
PLAY DEAD
excellent question, chloe.
end

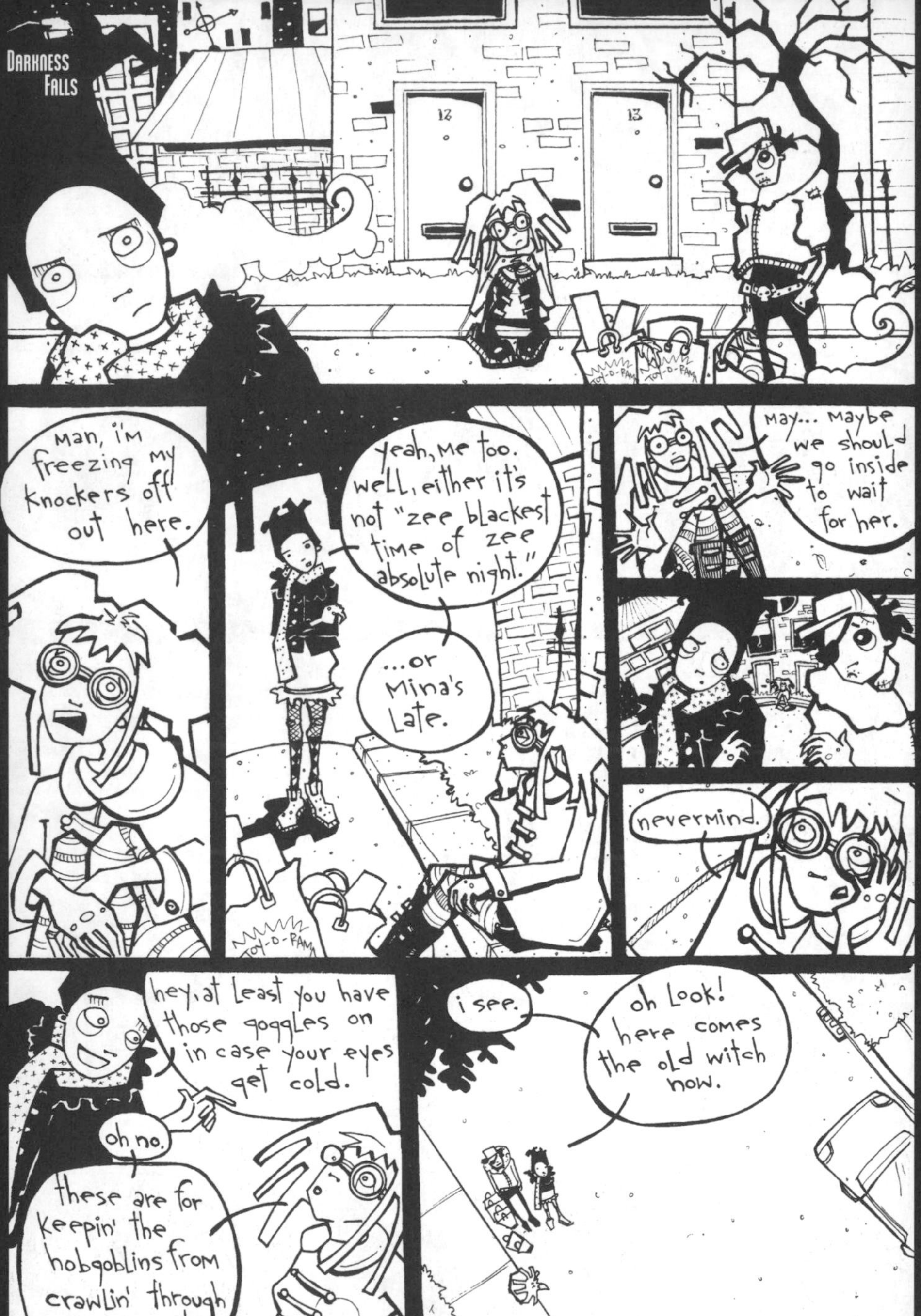
Darkness Falls
12
13
Toy-O-Rama
Toy-O-Rama
Man, i'm freezing my knockers off out here.
yeah, Me too. well, either it's not "zee blackest time of zee absolute night."
...or Mina's Late.
Toy-O-Rama
May... Maybe we should go inside to wait for her.
nevermind.
hey, at Least you have those goggles on in case your eyes get cold.
oh no.
these are for keepin' the hobgoblins from crawlin' through my eye vents.
i see.
oh Look! here comes the old witch now.

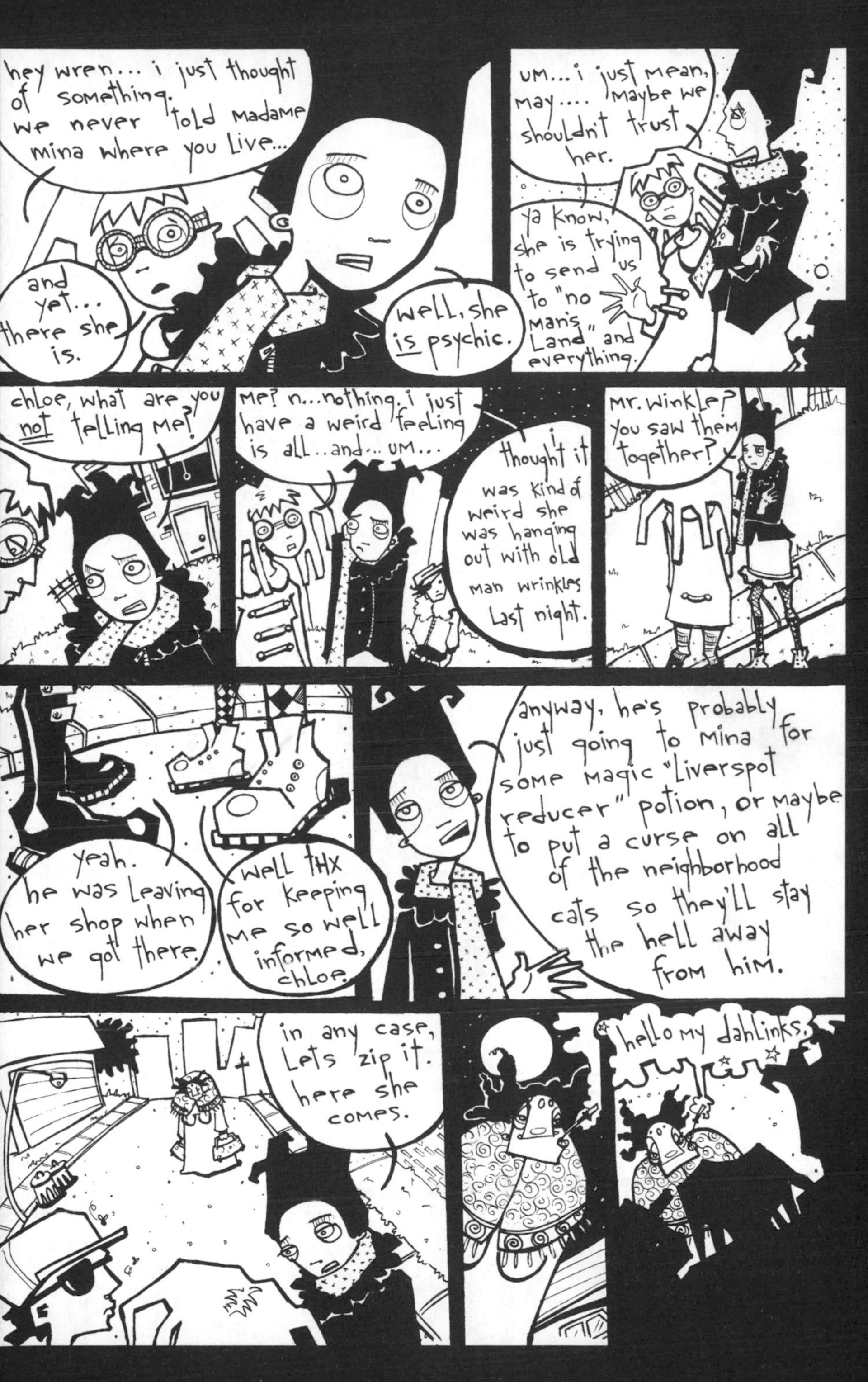
hey wren... i just thought of something. we never told madame mina where you live...
and yet... there she is.
well, she is psychic.
um... i just mean, may.... maybe we shouldn't trust her.
ya know, she is trying to send us to "no man's land" and everything.
chloe, what are you not telling me?
me? n...nothing. i just have a weird feeling is all...and... um...
i thought it was kind of weird she was hanging out with old man wrinkles last night.
mr. winkle? you saw them together?
yeah. he was leaving her shop when we got there.
well thx for keeping me so well informed, chloe.
anyway, he's probably just going to mina for some magic "liverspot reducer" potion, or maybe to put a curse on all of the neighborhood cats so they'll stay the hell away from him.
in any case, lets zip it. here she comes.
hello my dahlinks.

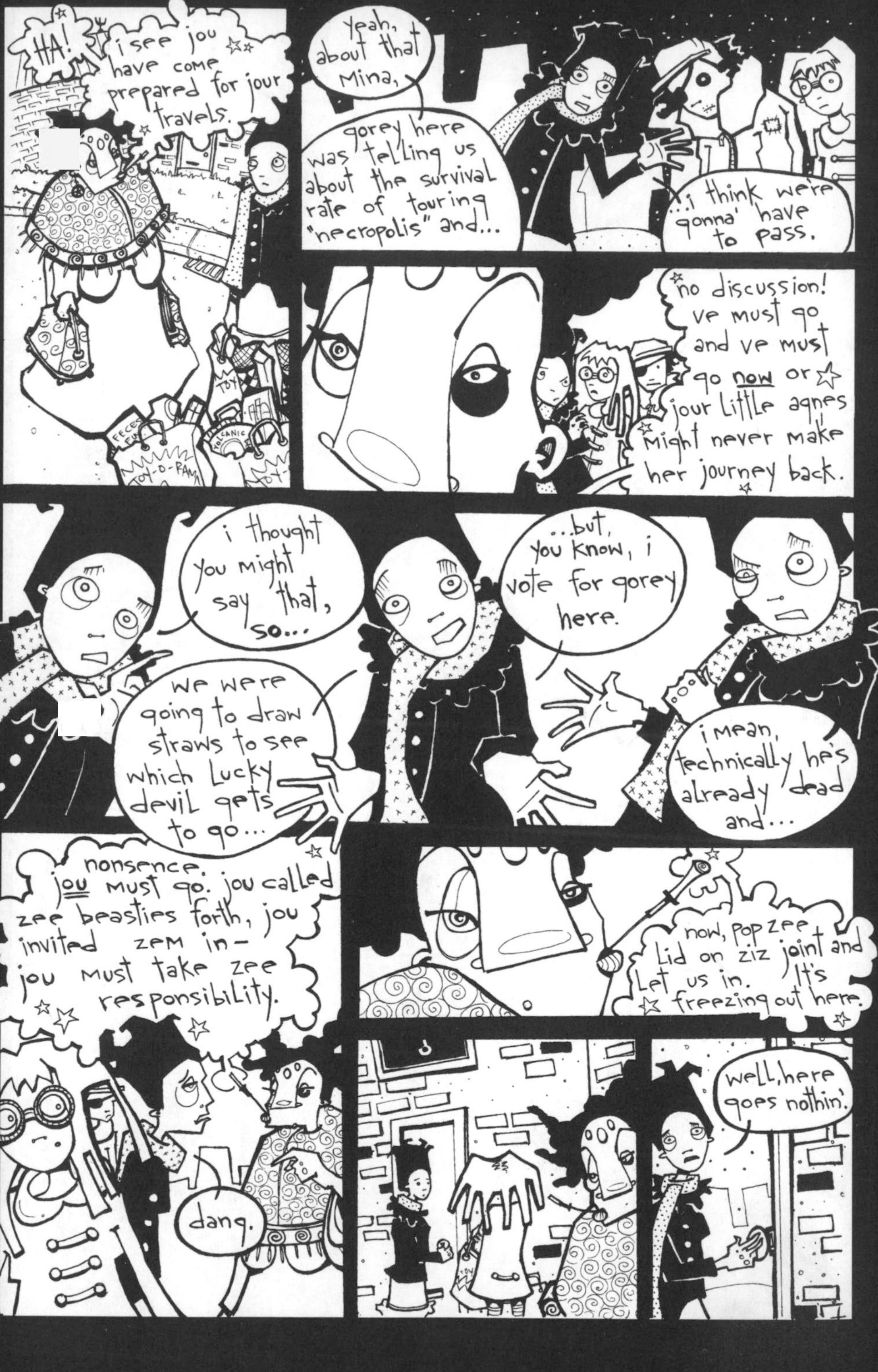
HA!
i see jou have come prepared for jour travels.
yeah, about that Mina,
gorey here was telling us about the survival rate of touring "necropolis" and...
...i think we're gonna' have to pass.
no discussion! ve must go and ve must go now or jour little agnes might never make her journey back.
i thought you might say that, so...
we were going to draw straws to see which lucky devil gets to go...
...but, you know, i vote for gorey here.
i mean, technically he's already dead and...
nonsence. jou must go. jou called zee beasties forth, jou invited zem in— jou must take zee responsibility.
dang.
now, pop zee lid on ziz joint and let us in. It's freezing out here.
well, here goes nothin'.

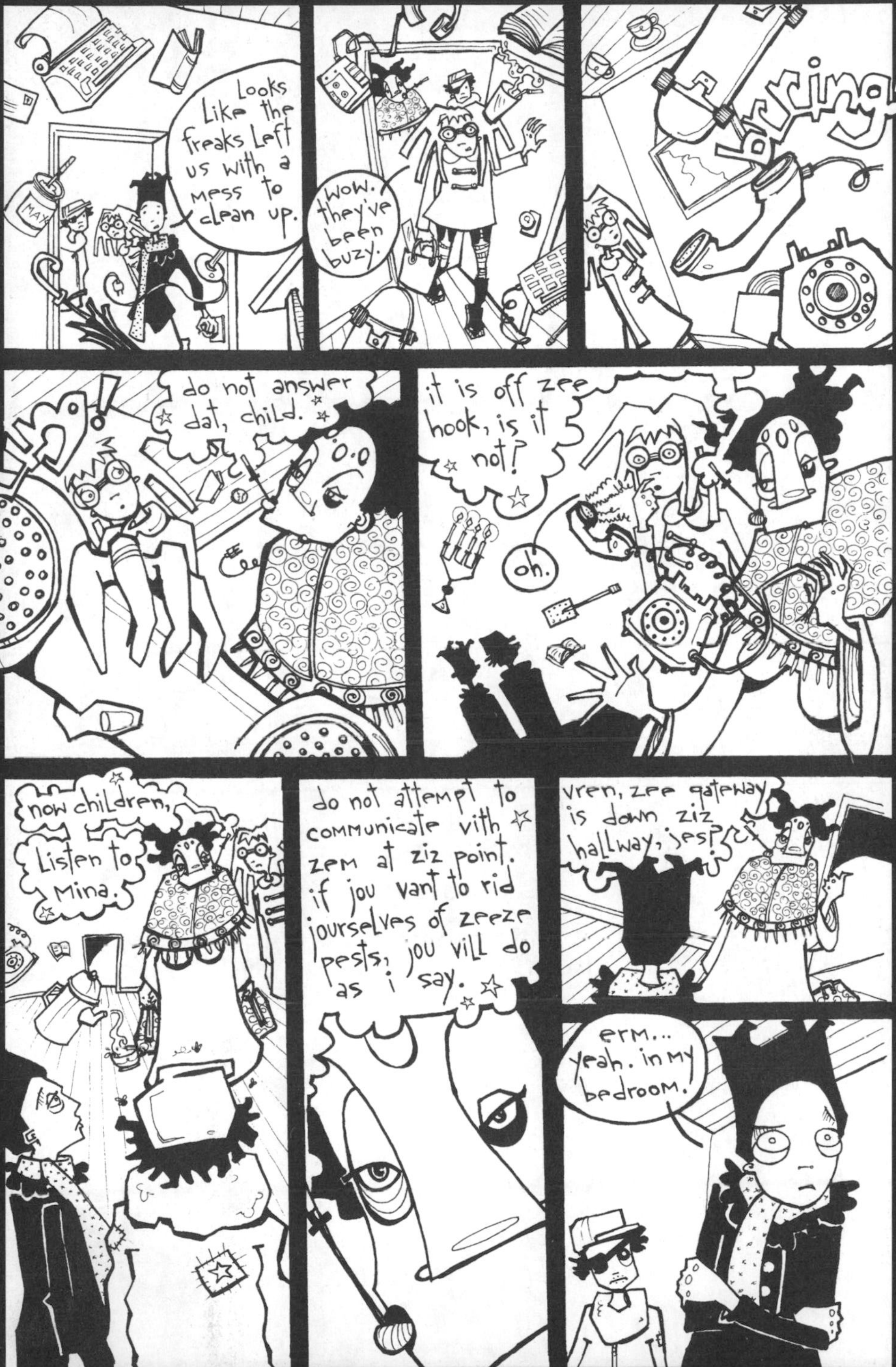
Looks Like the freaks Left us with a mess to clean up.
wow. they've been buzy.
brring!
do not answer dat, child.
it is off zee hook, is it not?
oh.
now children, Listen to Mina.
do not attempt to communicate vith zem at ziz point. if jou vant to rid jourselves of zeeze pests, jou vill do as i say.
vren, zee gateway is down ziz hallway, jes?
erm... yeah. in my bedroom.

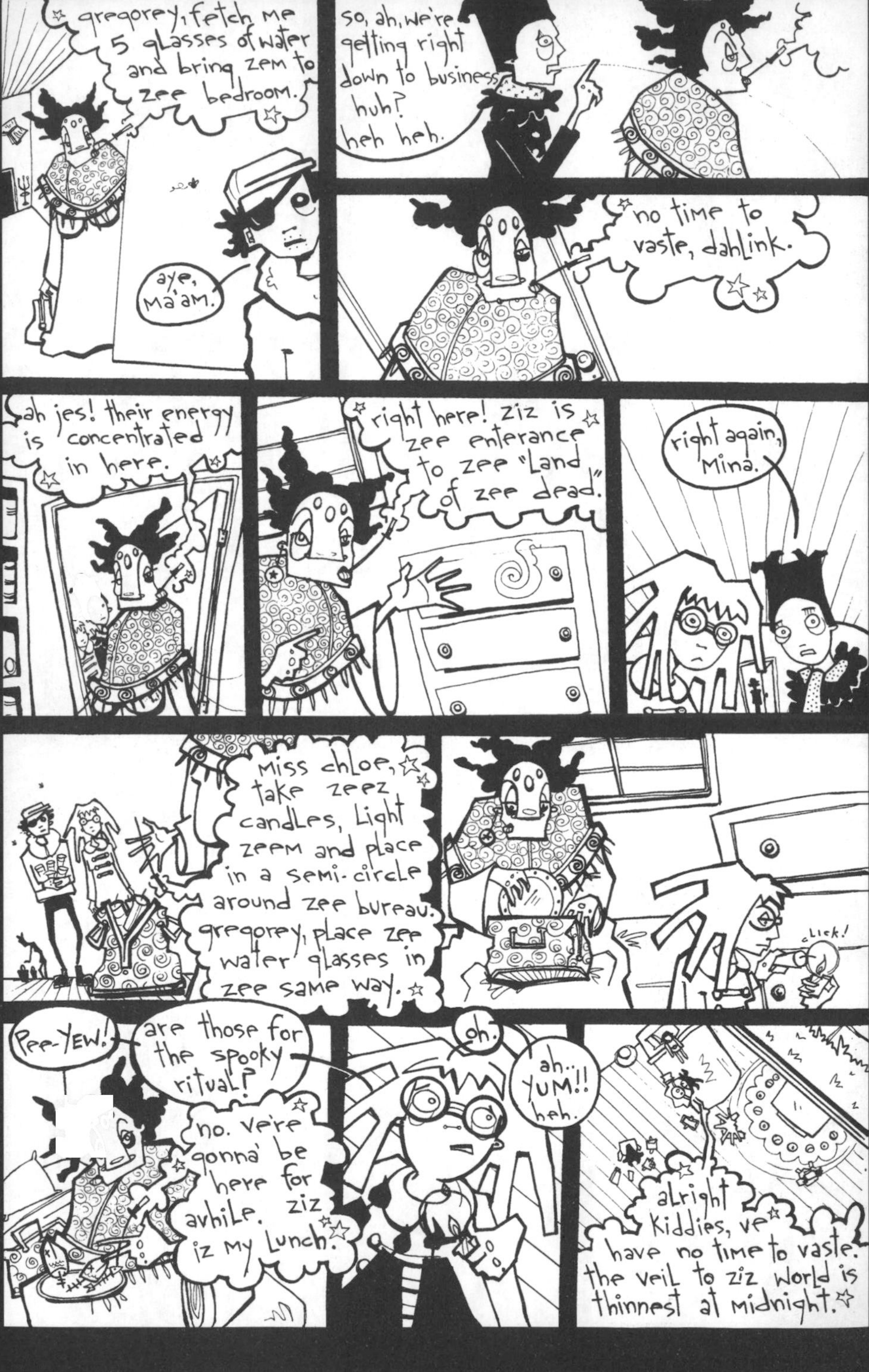
gregorey, fetch me 5 glasses of water and bring zem to zee bedroom.
aye, Ma'am.
so, ah, we're getting right down to business huh? heh heh.
no time to vaste, dahLink.
ah jes! their energy is concentrated in here.
right here! ziz is zee enterance to zee "Land of zee dead."
right again, Mina.
Miss chLoe, take zeez candLes, Light zeem and pLace in a semi-circLe around zee bureau. gregorey, pLace zee water gLasses in zee same way.
cLick!
Pee-YEW!
are those for the spooky ritual?
no. ve're gonna' be here for avhiLe. ziz iz my Lunch.
oh.
ah... YUM!! heh.
aLright kiddies, ve have no time to vaste. the veiL to ziz worLd is thinnest at midnight.

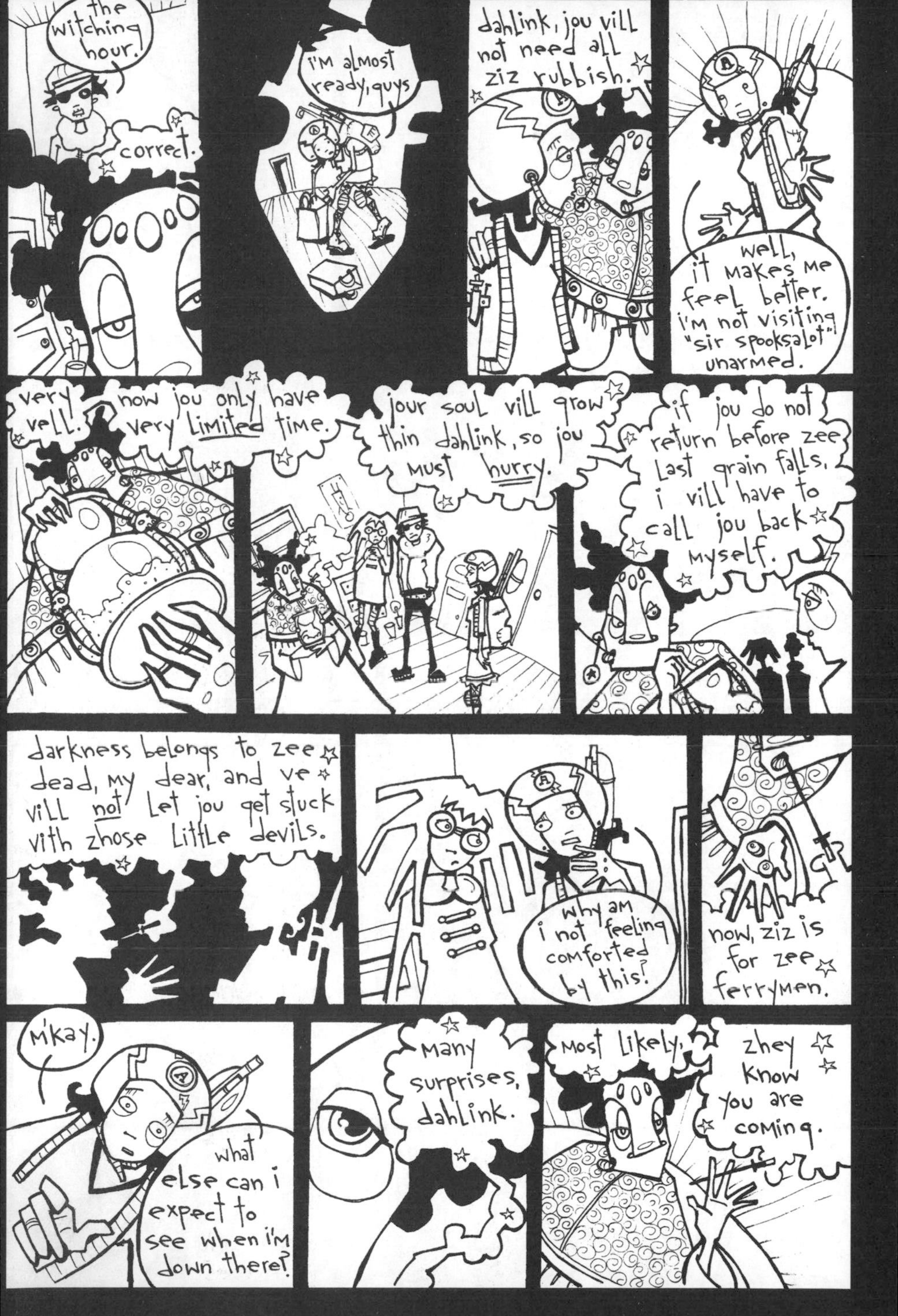
the witching hour.
correct.
i'm almost ready, guys.
dahlink, jou vill not need all ziz rubbish.
well, it makes me feel better. i'm not visiting "sir spooksalot" unarmed.
very vell.
now jou only have very limited time.
jour soul vill grow thin dahlink, so jou must hurry.
if jou do not return before zee last grain falls, i vill have to call jou back myself.
darkness belongs to zee dead, my dear, and ve vill not let jou get stuck vith zhose little devils.
why am i not feeling comforted by this?
now, ziz is for zee ferrymen.
m'kay.
what else can i expect to see when i'm down there?
many surprises, dahlink.
most likely,
zhey know you are coming.

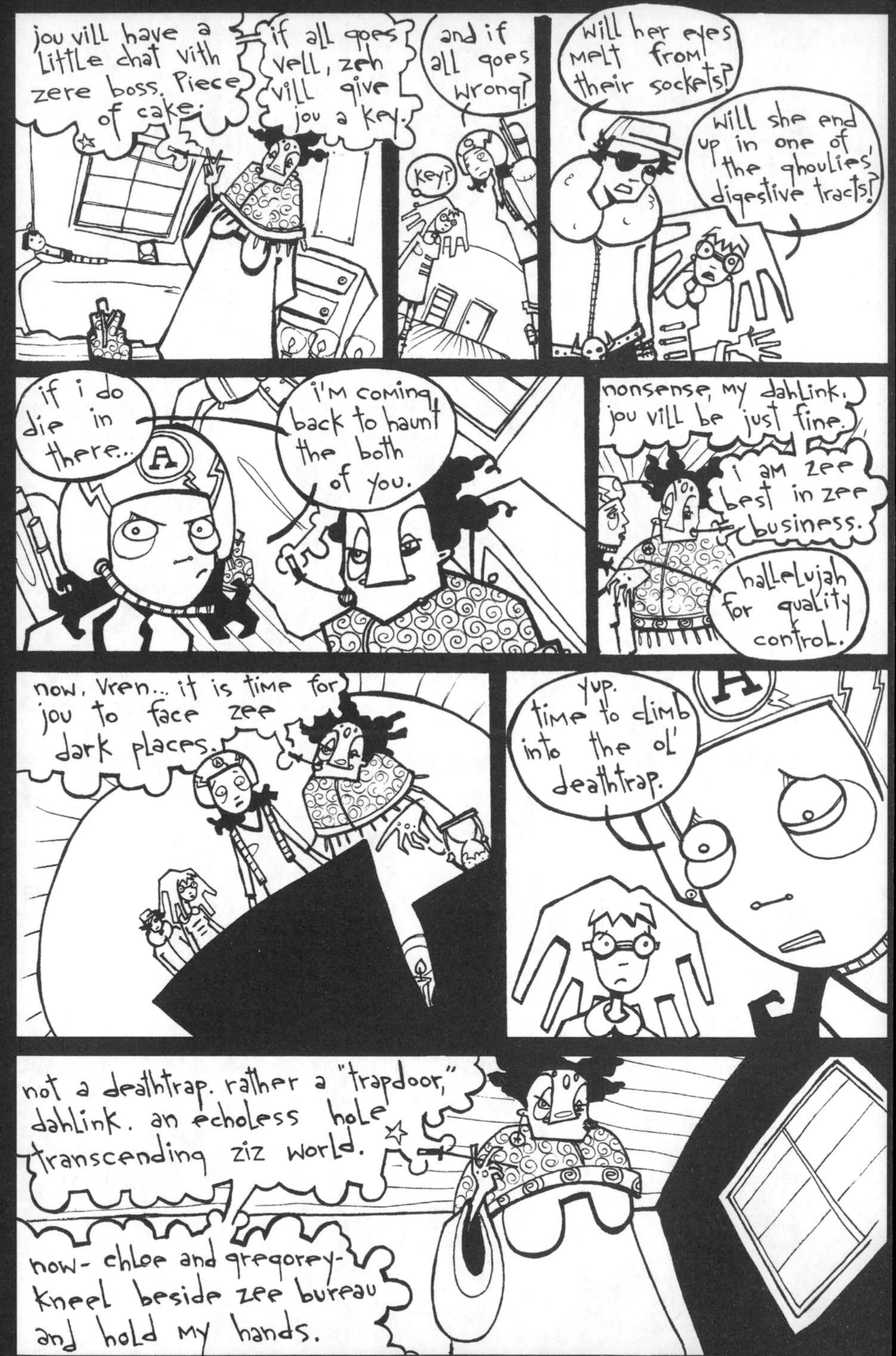
jou vill have a little chat vith zere boss. Piece of cake.
if all goes vell, zeh vill give jou a key.
and if all goes wrong?
Key?
will her eyes melt from their sockets?
will she end up in one of the ghoulies' digestive tracts?
if i do die in there...
i'm coming back to haunt the both of you.
nonsense, my dahlink. jou vill be just fine.
i am zee best in zee business.
hallelujah for quality control.
now, Vren... it is time for jou to face zee dark places.
yup. time to climb into the ol' deathtrap.
not a deathtrap. rather a "trapdoor," dahlink. an echoless hole transcending ziz world.
now- chloe and gregorey- kneel beside zee bureau and hold my hands.

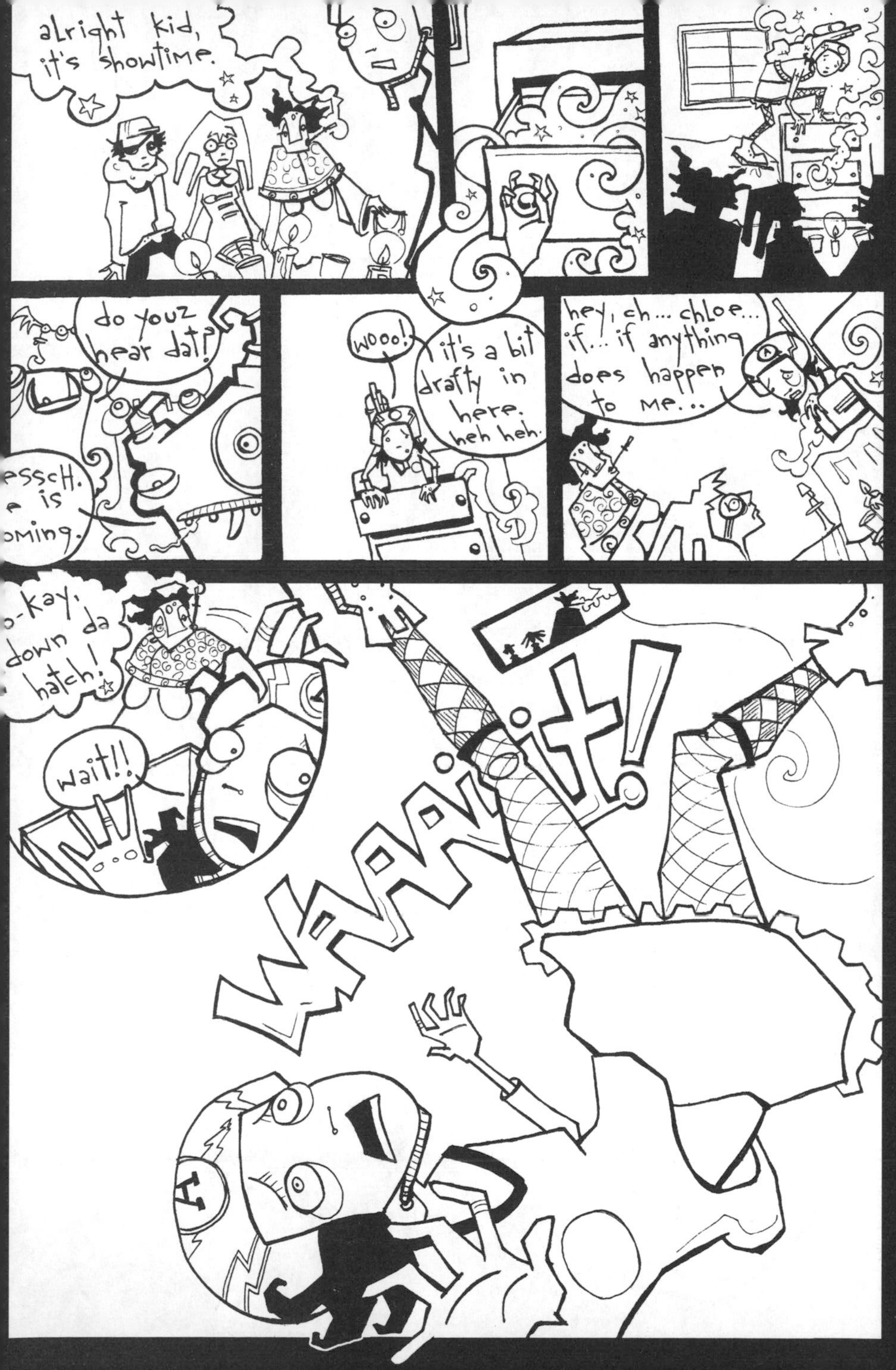
alright kid, it's showtime.
do youz hear dat?
esscH. e is oming.
wooo!
it's a bit drafty in here. heh heh.
hey, ch... chloe... if... if anything does happen to me...
o-kay, down da hatch!
wait!!
WAAAAIT!

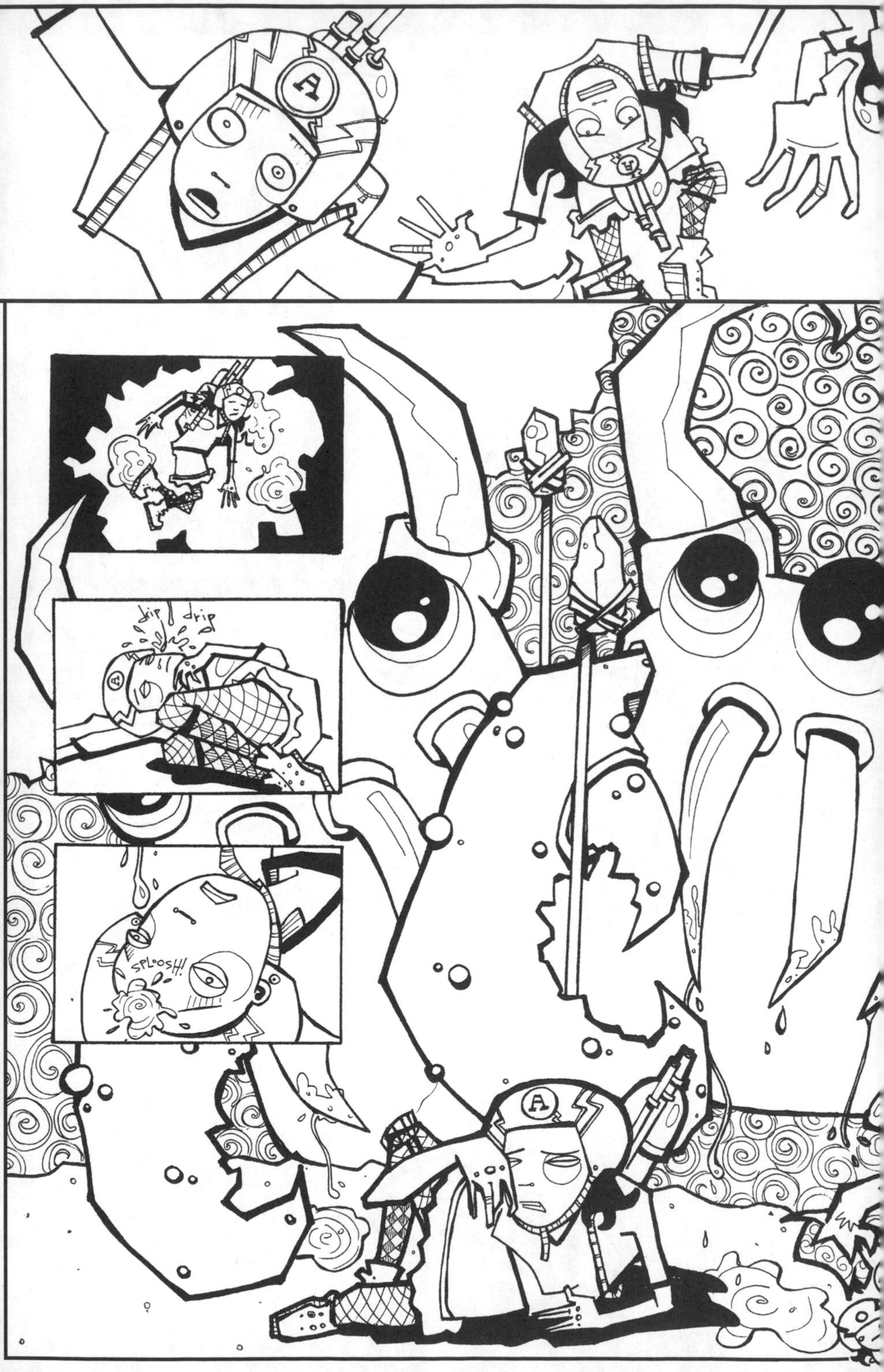

drip drip
SPLOOSH!!

chapter six.

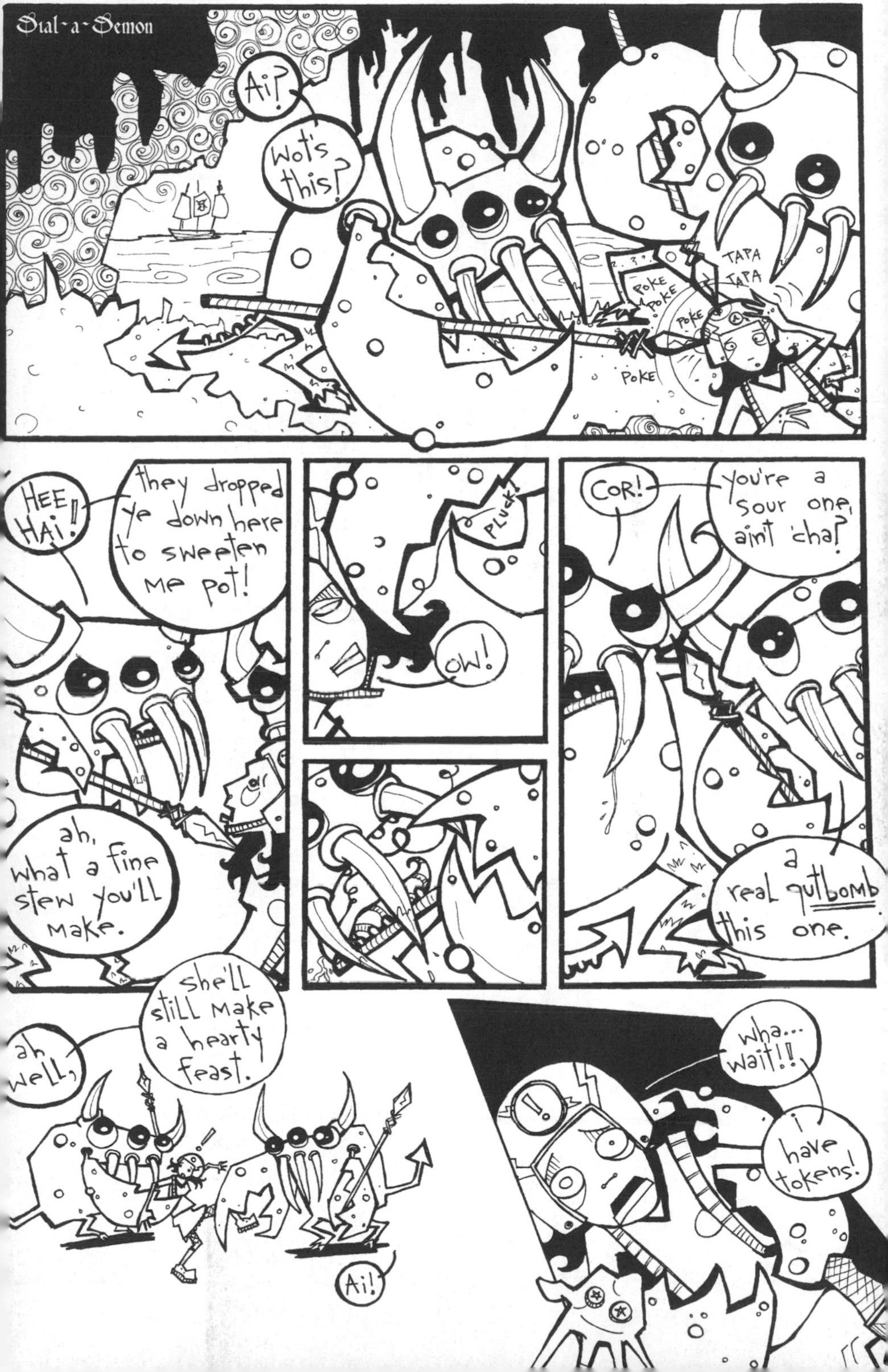
Dial-a-Demon
Ai?
Wot's this?
TAPA TAPA
POKE POKE
POKE
POKE
POKE
HEE HAI!!
they dropped ye down here to sweeten me pot!
ah, what a fine stew you'll make.
PLUCK!
OW!
COR!
you're a sour one, ain't 'cha?
a real gutbomb this one.
ah well,
she'll still make a hearty feast.
Ai!
wha... wait!!
i have tokens!

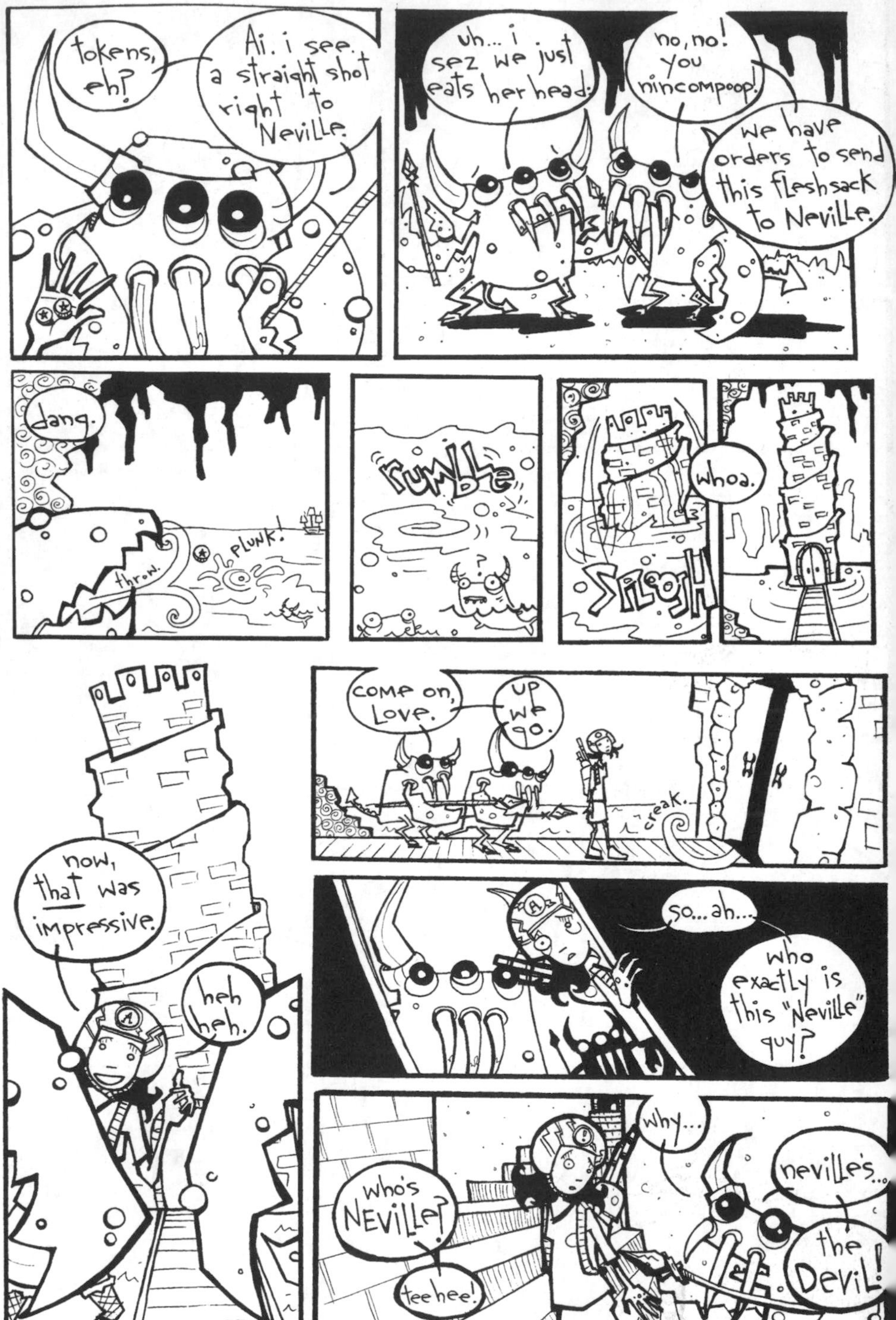
tokens, eh?
Ai. i see. a straight shot right to Neville.
uh... i sez we just eats her head.
no, no! you nincompoop!
we have orders to send this fleshsack to Neville.
dang.
throw.
PLUNK!
rumble
?
whoa.
SPLOOSH
now, that was impressive.
heh heh.
come on, Love.
up we go.
creak.
so... ah...
who exactly is this "Neville" guy?
why...
who's NEVILLE?
teehee!
neville's...
the DEVIL!

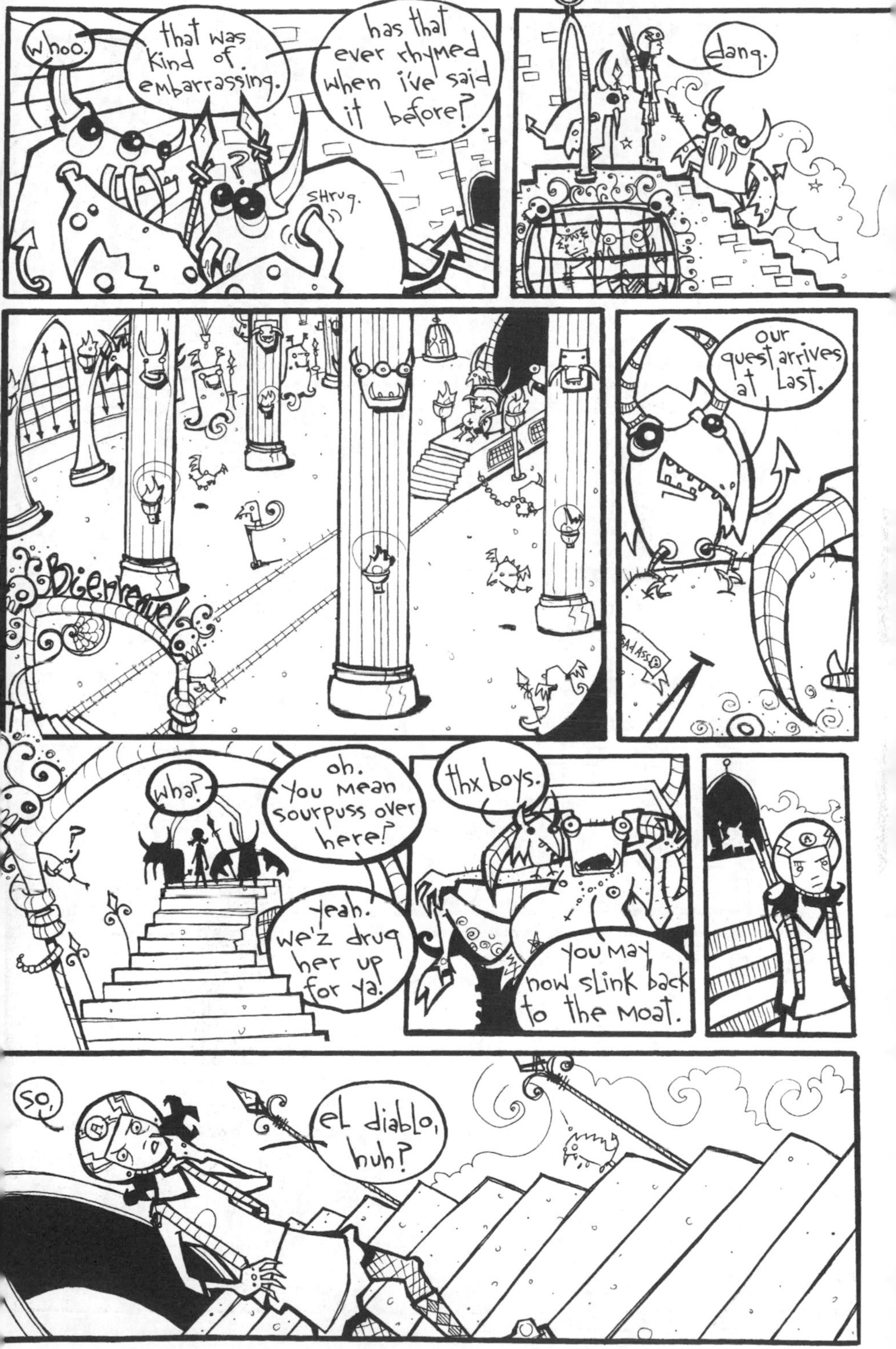
whoo.
that was kind of embarrassing.
has that ever rhymed when i've said it before?
SHrug.
dang.
Bienvenue!
our quest arrives at last.
BAdASS
what?
oh. you mean sourpuss over here?
yeah. we'z drug her up for ya!
thx boys.
you may now slink back to the moat.
so,
el diablo, huh?

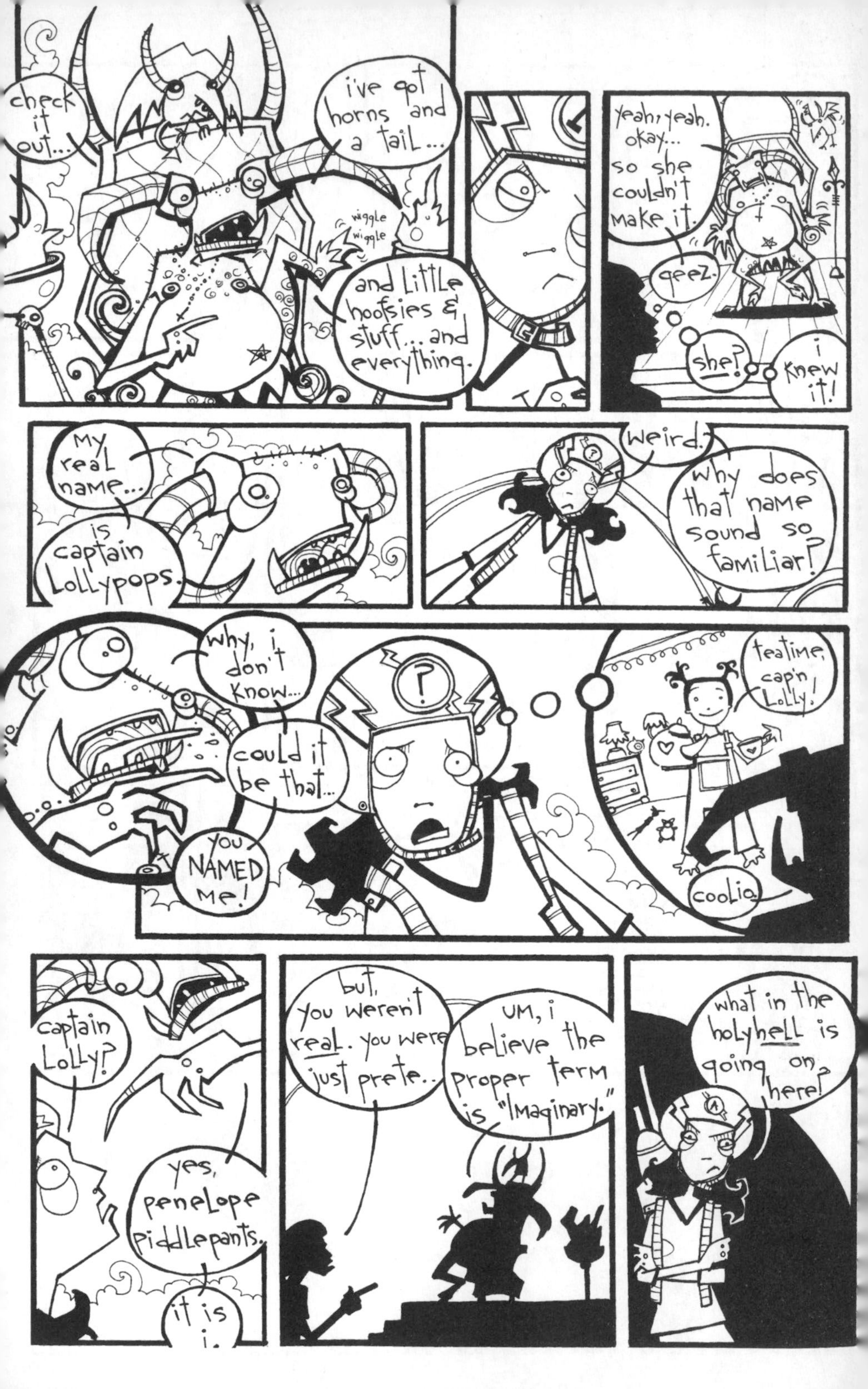
check it out...
i've got horns and a tail...
wiggle wiggle
and little hoofsies & stuff... and everything.
yeah, yeah. okay... so she couldn't make it.
geez.
she?
i knew it!
My real name...
is captain Lollypops.
weird.
why does that name sound so familiar?
why, i don't know...
could it be that...
you NAMED me!
teatime, cap'n Lolly!
coolio.
captain Lolly?
yes, penelope piddlepants.
it is i.
but, you weren't real. you were just prete..
um, i believe the proper term is "Imaginary."
what in the holy hell is going on here?

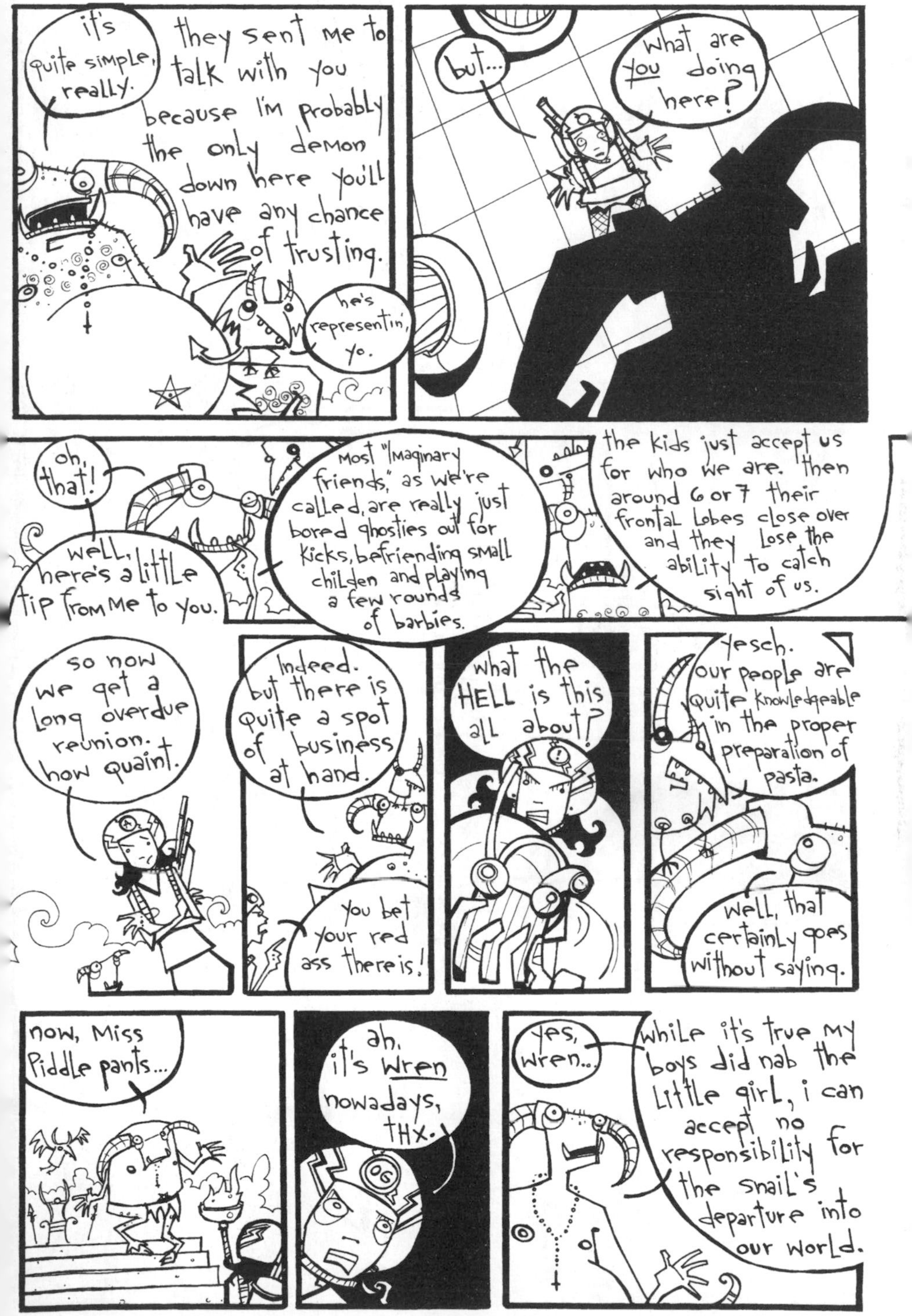
it's quite simple, really.
they sent me to talk with you because i'm probably the only demon down here you'll have any chance of trusting.
he's representin', yo.
but...
what are you doing here?
oh, that!
well, here's a little tip from me to you.
Most "Imaginary friends," as we're called, are really just bored ghosties out for kicks, befriending small childen and playing a few rounds of barbies.
the kids just accept us for who we are. then around 6 or 7 their frontal lobes close over and they lose the ability to catch sight of us.
so now we get a long overdue reunion. how quaint.
Indeed. but there is quite a spot of business at hand.
you bet your red ass there is!
what the HELL is this all about?
yesch. our people are quite knowledgeable in the proper preparation of pasta.
well, that certainly goes without saying.
now, Miss Piddle pants...
ah. it's wren nowadays, THX.
yes, wren...
while it's true my boys did nab the little girl, i can accept no responsibility for the snail's departure into our world.

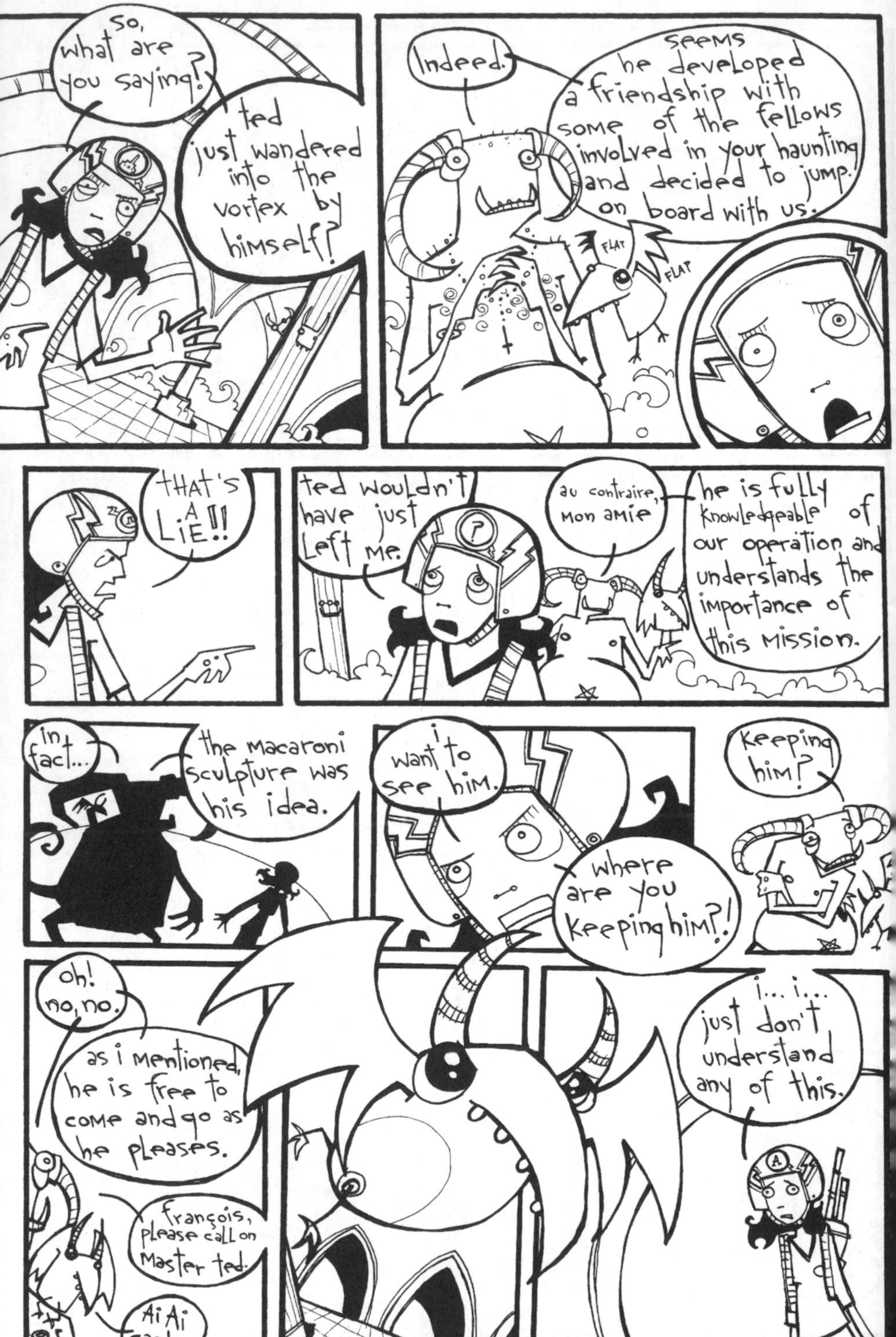
so, what are you saying?
ted just wandered into the vortex by himself?
Indeed.
seems he developed a friendship with some of the fellows involved in your haunting and decided to jump on board with us.
FLAT
FLAP
THAT'S A LIE!!
ted wouldn't have just left me.
au contraire, mon amie
he is fully knowledgeable of our operation and understands the importance of this mission.
in fact...
the macaroni sculpture was his idea.
i want to see him.
where are you keeping him?!
keeping him?
oh! no, no.
as i mentioned, he is free to come and go as he pleases.
françois, please call on master ted.
Ai Ai cap'n.
i... i... just don't understand any of this.

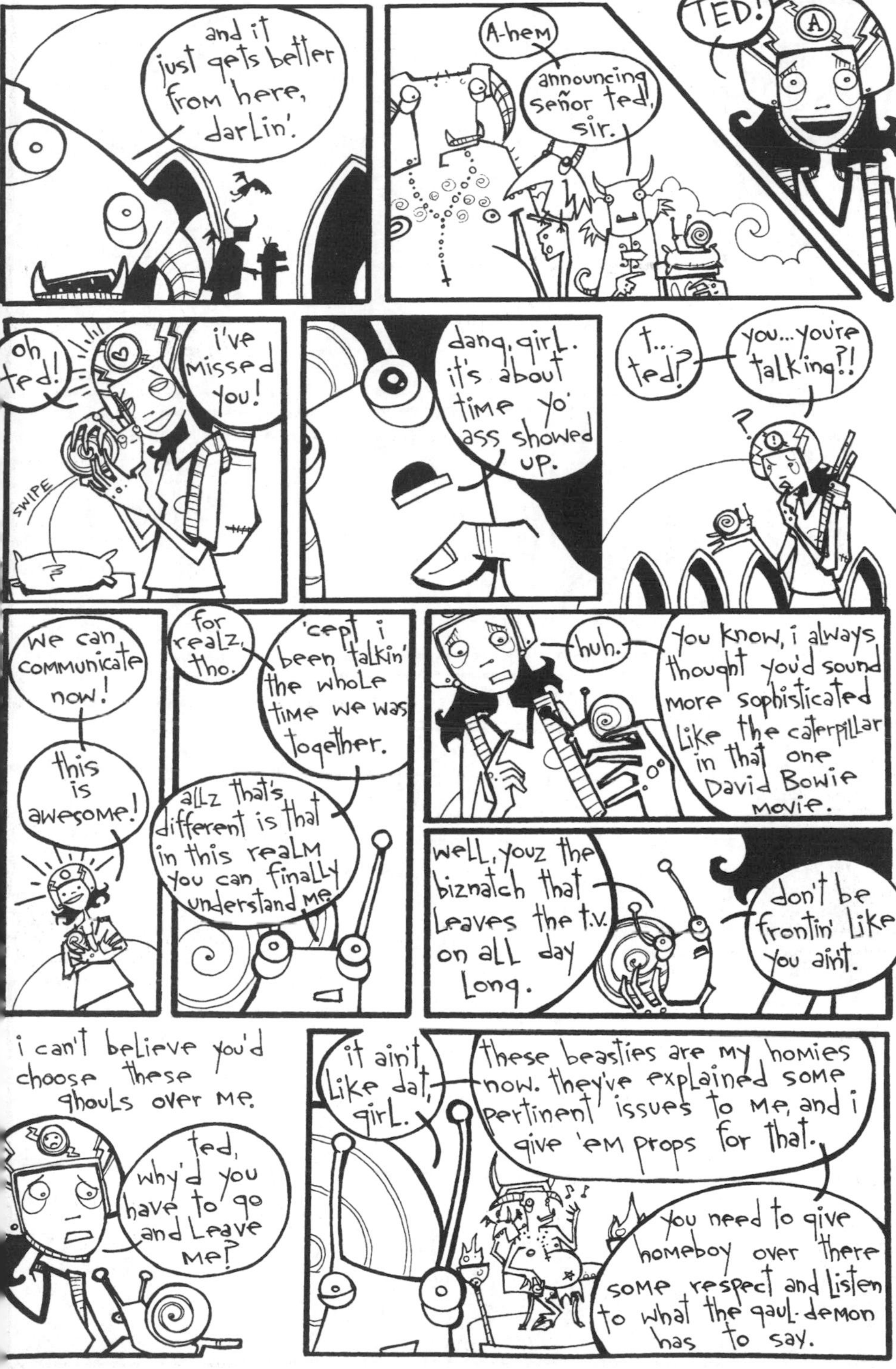
and it just gets better from here, darlin'.
A-hem
announcing señor ted, sir.
TED!
oh ted!
i've missed you!
SWIPE
dang, girl. it's about time yo' ass showed up.
t... ted?
you... you're talking?!
we can communicate now!
this is awesome!
for realz, tho.
'cept i been talkin' the whole time we was together.
allz that's different is that in this realm you can finally understand me.
huh.
you know, i always thought you'd sound more sophisticated like the caterpillar in that one David Bowie movie.
well, youz the biznatch that leaves the t.v. on all day long.
don't be frontin' like you aint.
i can't believe you'd choose these ghouls over me.
ted, why'd you have to go and leave me?
it ain't like dat, girl.
these beasties are my homies now. they've explained some pertinent issues to me, and i give 'em props for that.
you need to give homeboy over there some respect and listen to what the gaul-demon has to say.

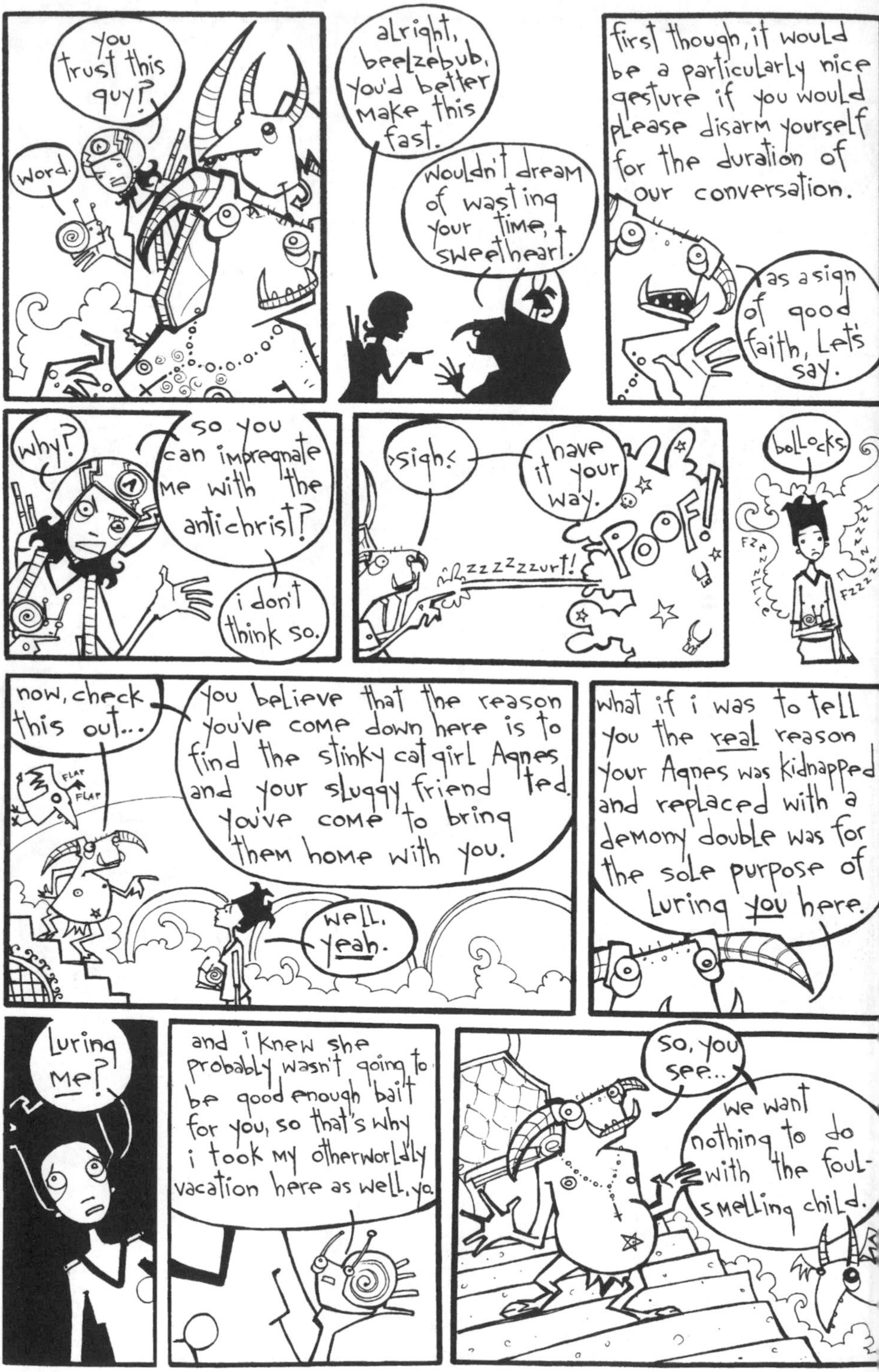
you trust this guy?
word.
alright, beelzebub, you'd better make this fast.
wouldn't dream of wasting your time, sweetheart.
first though, it would be a particularly nice gesture if you would please disarm yourself for the duration of our conversation.
as a sign of good faith, let's say.
why?
so you can impregnate me with the antichrist?
i don't think so.
>sigh<
have it your way.
zzzzzzzurt!
POOF!
bollocks.
now, check this out...
you believe that the reason you've come down here is to find the stinky catgirl Agnes and your sluggy friend ted. you've come to bring them home with you.
FLAP FLAP
well, yeah.
what if i was to tell you the real reason your Agnes was kidnapped and replaced with a demony double was for the sole purpose of luring you here.
luring me?
and i knew she probably wasn't going to be good enough bait for you, so that's why i took my otherworldly vacation here as well, yo.
so, you see...
we want nothing to do with the foul-smelling child.

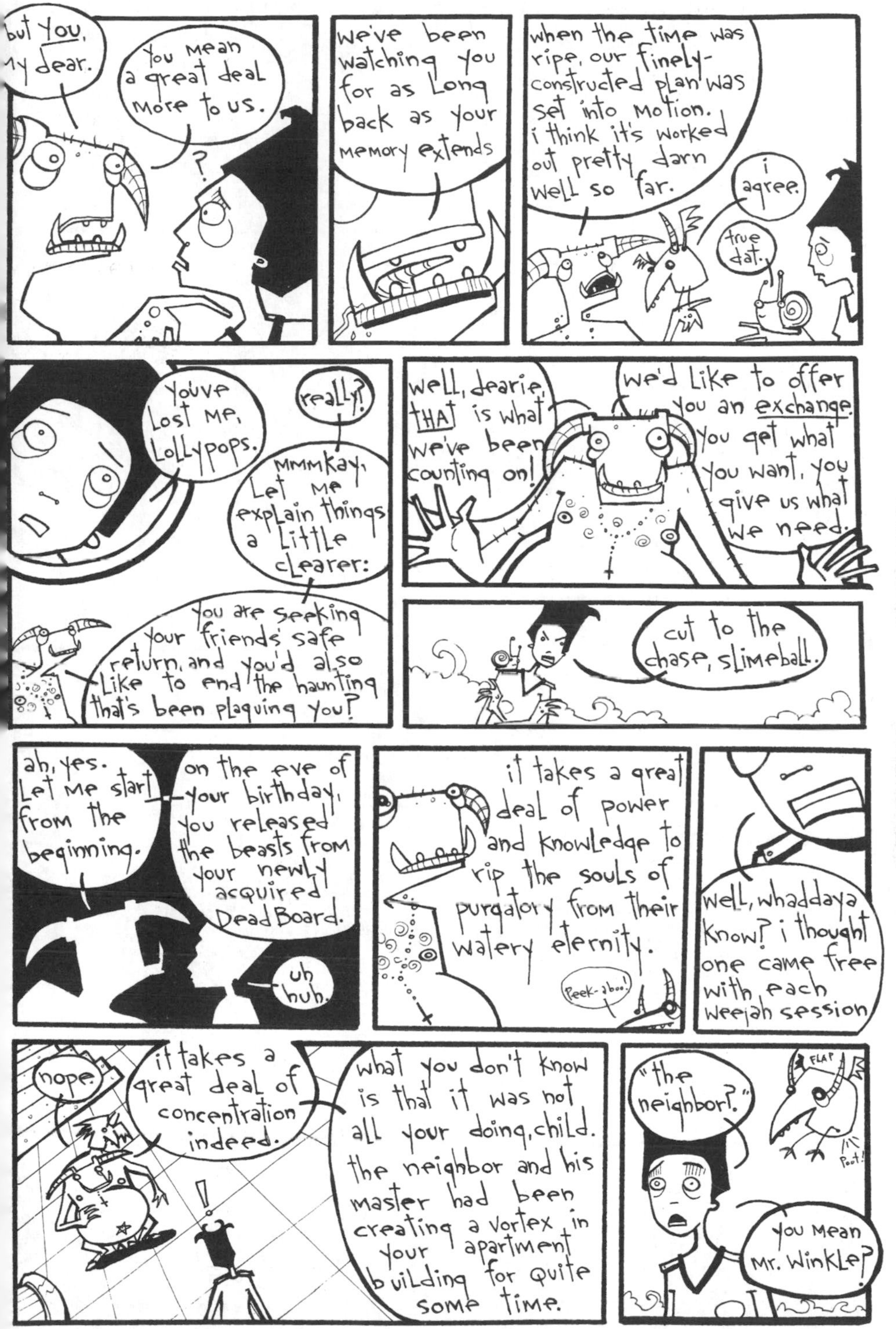
but YOU, my dear.
You mean a great deal more to us.
?
we've been watching you for as long back as your memory extends
when the time was ripe, our finely-constructed plan was set into motion. i think it's worked out pretty darn well so far.
i agree.
true dat.
You've lost me, Lollypops.
really?
Mmmkay, let me explain things a little clearer:
You are seeking your friends' safe return, and you'd also like to end the haunting that's been plaguing you?
well, dearie, THAT is what we've been counting on!
we'd like to offer you an exchange. You get what you want, you give us what we need.
cut to the chase, slimeball.
ah, yes. let me start from the beginning.
on the eve of your birthday, you released the beasts from your newly acquired DeadBoard.
uh huh.
it takes a great deal of power and knowledge to rip the souls of purgatory from their watery eternity.
Peek-a-boo!
well, whaddaya know? i thought one came free with each weejah session
nope.
it takes a great deal of concentration indeed.
!
what you don't know is that it was not all your doing, child. the neighbor and his master had been creating a vortex in your apartment building for quite some time.
"the neighbor?"
FLAP
Poot!
you mean Mr. Winkle?

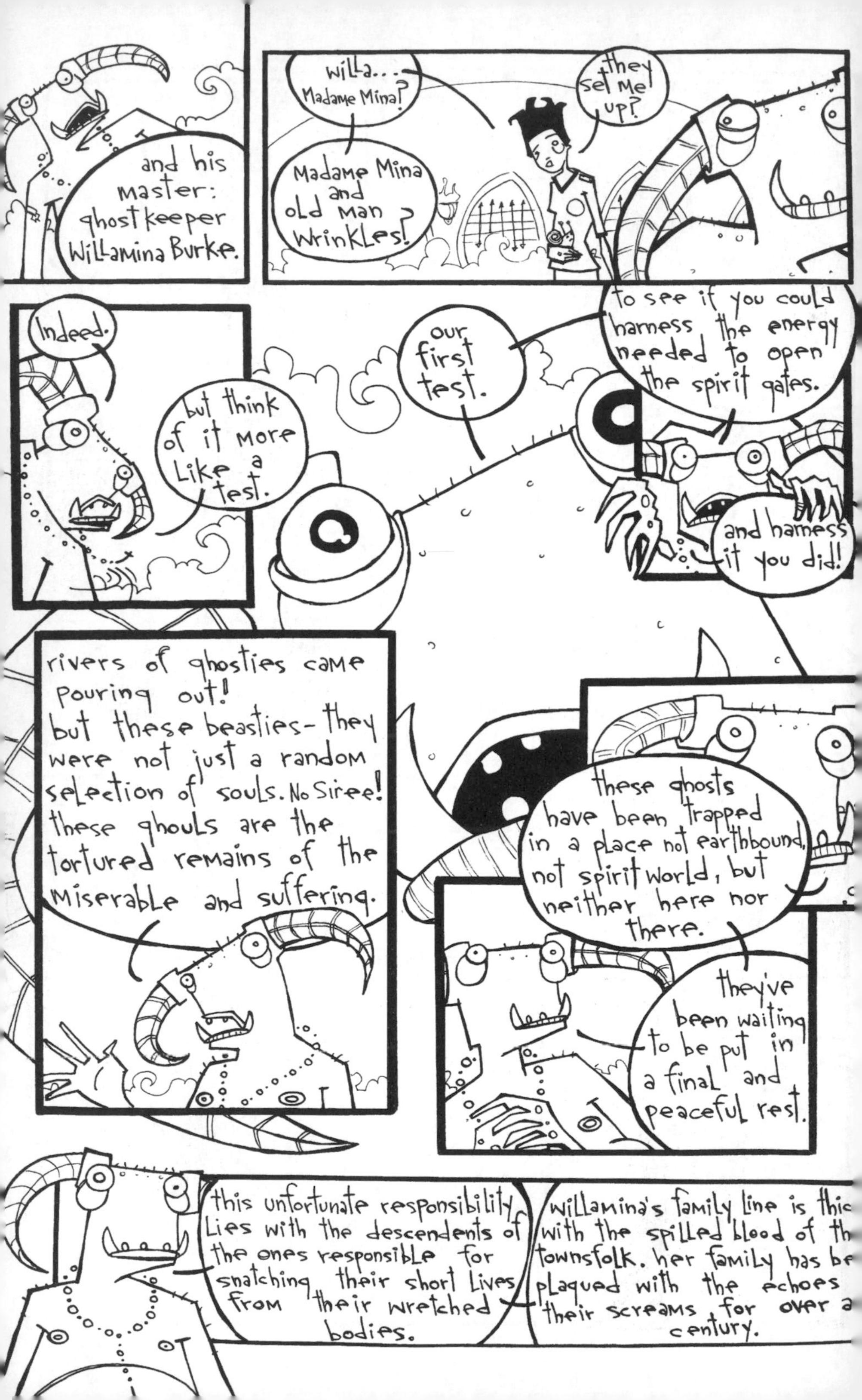

and his master: ghostkeeper Willamina Burke.
Willa... Madame Mina?
Madame Mina and Old Man Wrinkles!
they set me up?
Indeed.
but think of it more like a test.
our first test.
to see if you could harness the energy needed to open the spirit gates.
and harness it you did!
rivers of ghosties came pouring out! but these beasties- they were not just a random selection of souls. No Siree! these ghouls are the tortured remains of the miserable and suffering.
these ghosts have been trapped in a place not earthbound, not spirit world, but neither here nor there.
they've been waiting to be put in a final and peaceful rest.
this unfortunate responsibility lies with the descendents of the ones responsible for snatching their short lives from their wretched bodies.
willamina's family line is thic with the spilled blood of th townsfolk. her family has be plagued with the echoes their screams for over a century.

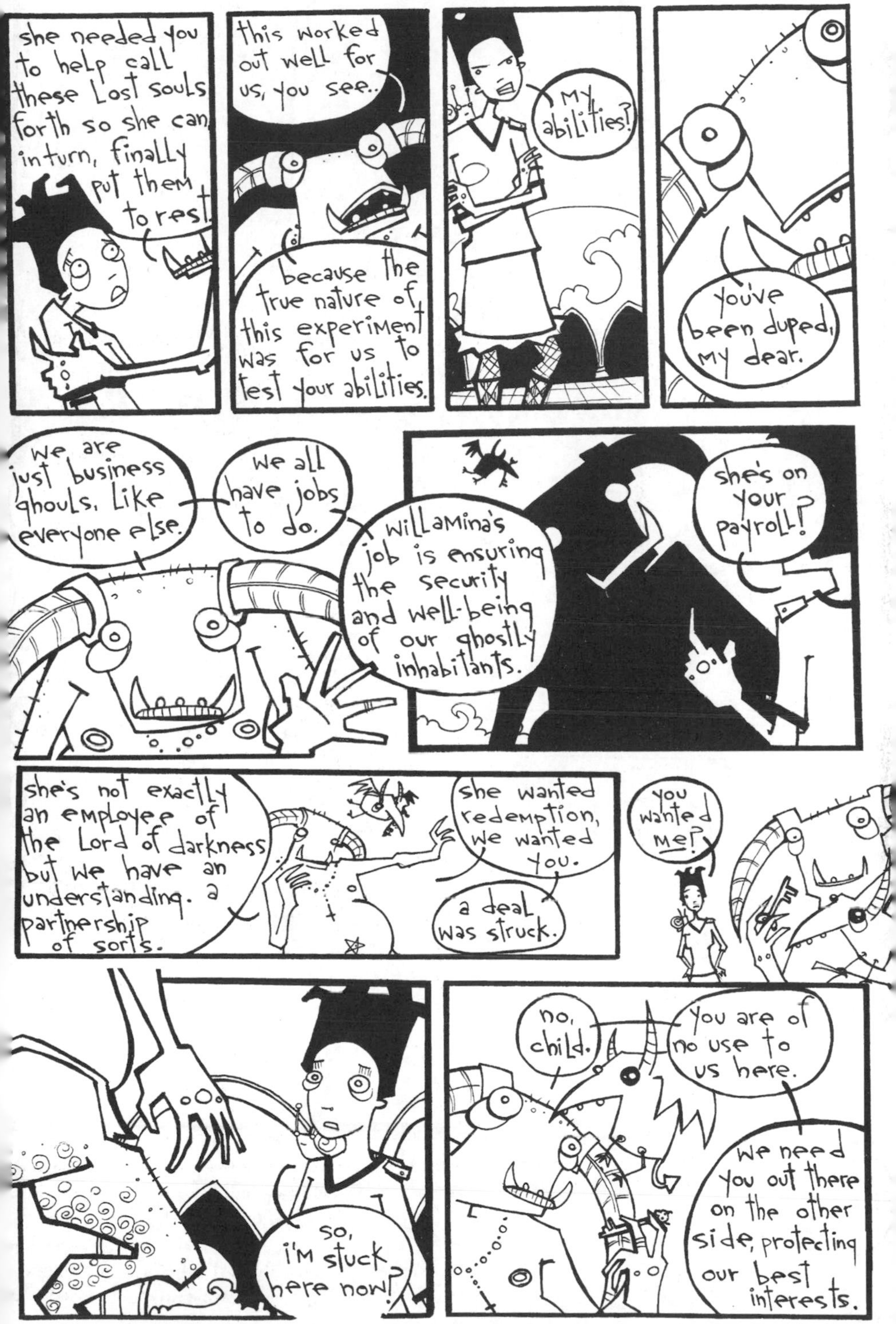
she needed you to help call these Lost souls forth so she can, in turn, finally put them to rest.
this worked out well for us, you see..
because the true nature of this experiment was for us to test your abilities.
My abilities?
you've been duped, my dear.
we are just business ghouls, like everyone else.
we all have jobs to do.
willamina's job is ensuring the security and well-being of our ghostly inhabitants.
she's on your payroll?
she's not exactly an employee of the Lord of darkness but we have an understanding. a partnership of sorts.
she wanted redemption, we wanted you.
a deal was struck.
you wanted me?
so, i'm stuck here now?
no, child.
you are of no use to us here.
we need you out there on the other side, protecting our best interests.

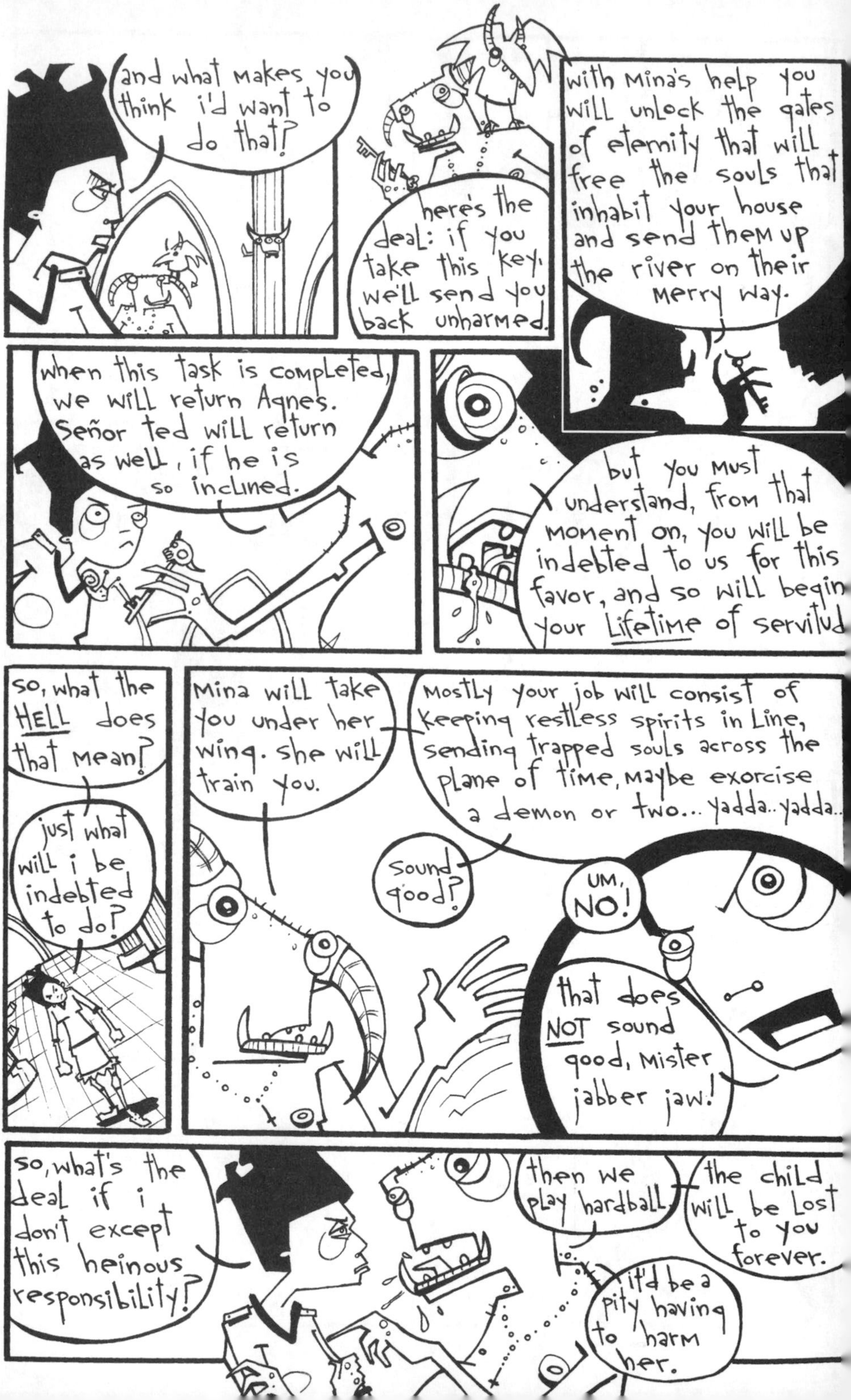
and what makes you think i'd want to do that?
here's the deal: if you take this key, we'll send you back unharmed.
with Mina's help you will unlock the gates of eternity that will free the souls that inhabit your house and send them up the river on their merry way.
when this task is completed, we will return Agnes. Señor ted will return as well, if he is so inclined.
but you must understand, from that moment on, you will be indebted to us for this favor, and so will begin your lifetime of servitud
so, what the HELL does that mean?
just what will i be indebted to do?
Mina will take you under her wing. she will train you.
mostly your job will consist of keeping restless spirits in line, sending trapped souls across the plane of time, maybe exorcise a demon or two... yadda.. yadda..
sound good?
UM, NO!
that does NOT sound good, Mister jabber jaw!
so, what's the deal if i don't except this heinous responsibility?
then we play hardball.
the child will be lost to you forever.
it'd be a pity having to harm her.

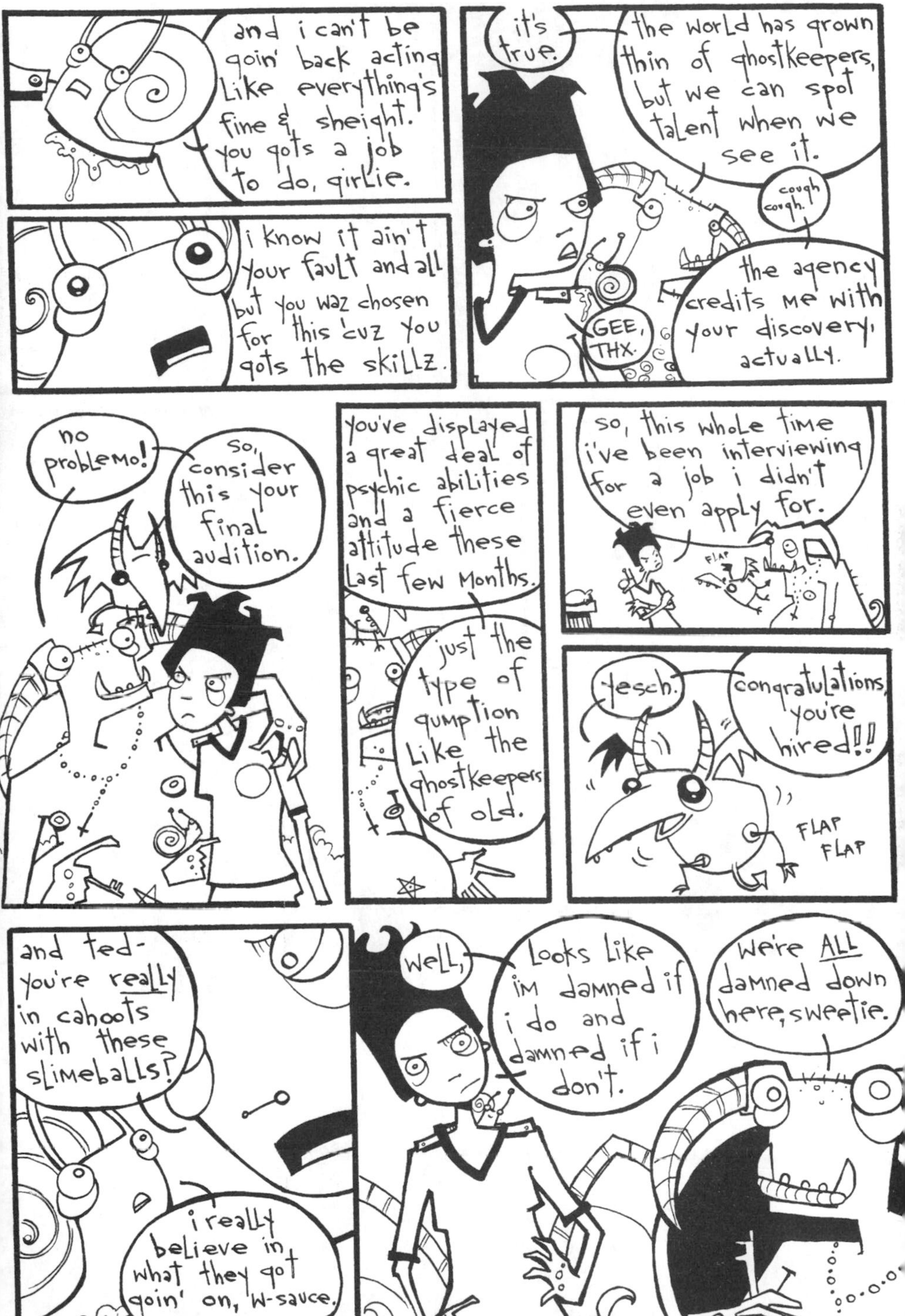

and i can't be goin' back acting like everything's fine & sheight. you gots a job to do, girlie.
i know it ain't your fault and all but you waz chosen for this 'cuz you gots the skillz.
it's true.
the world has grown thin of ghostkeepers, but we can spot talent when we see it.
cough cough.
the agency credits me with your discovery, actually.
GEE, THX.
no problemo!
so, consider this your final audition.
you've displayed a great deal of psychic abilities and a fierce attitude these last few months.
just the type of gumption like the ghostkeepers of old.
so, this whole time i've been interviewing for a job i didn't even apply for.
FLAP
yesch.
congratulations, you're hired!!
FLAP FLAP
and ted- you're really in cahoots with these slimeballs?
i really believe in what they got goin' on, w-sauce.
well,
looks like im damned if i do and damned if i don't.
we're ALL damned down here, sweetie.

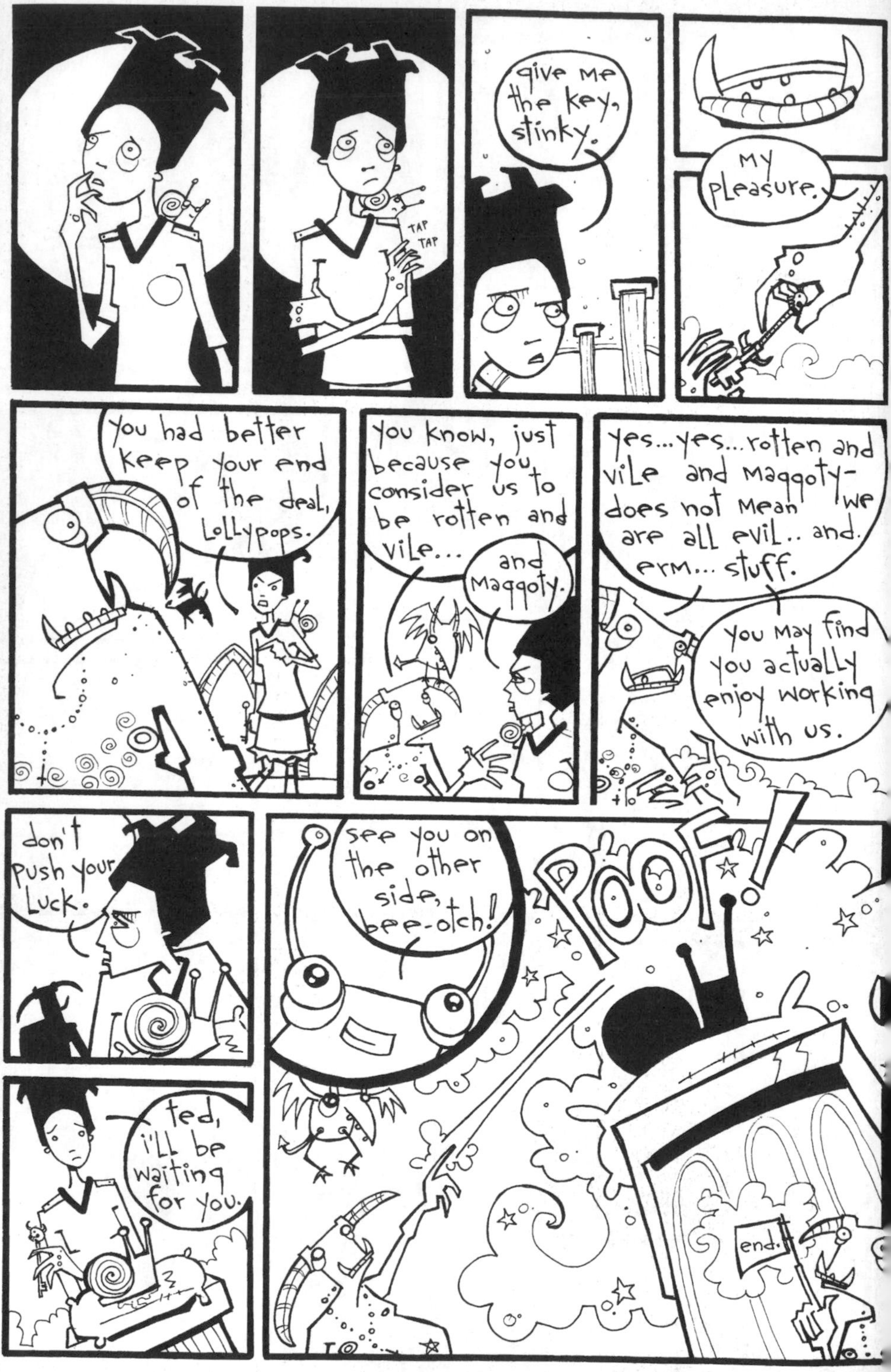
TAP TAP
give me the key, stinky.
My pleasure.
you had better keep your end of the deal, Lollypops.
you know, just because you consider us to be rotten and vile...
and maggoty.
yes...yes...rotten and vile and maggoty- does not mean we are all evil.. and. erm... stuff.
you may find you actually enjoy working with us.
don't push your luck.
ted, i'll be waiting for you.
see you on the other side, bee-otch!
POOF!
end.

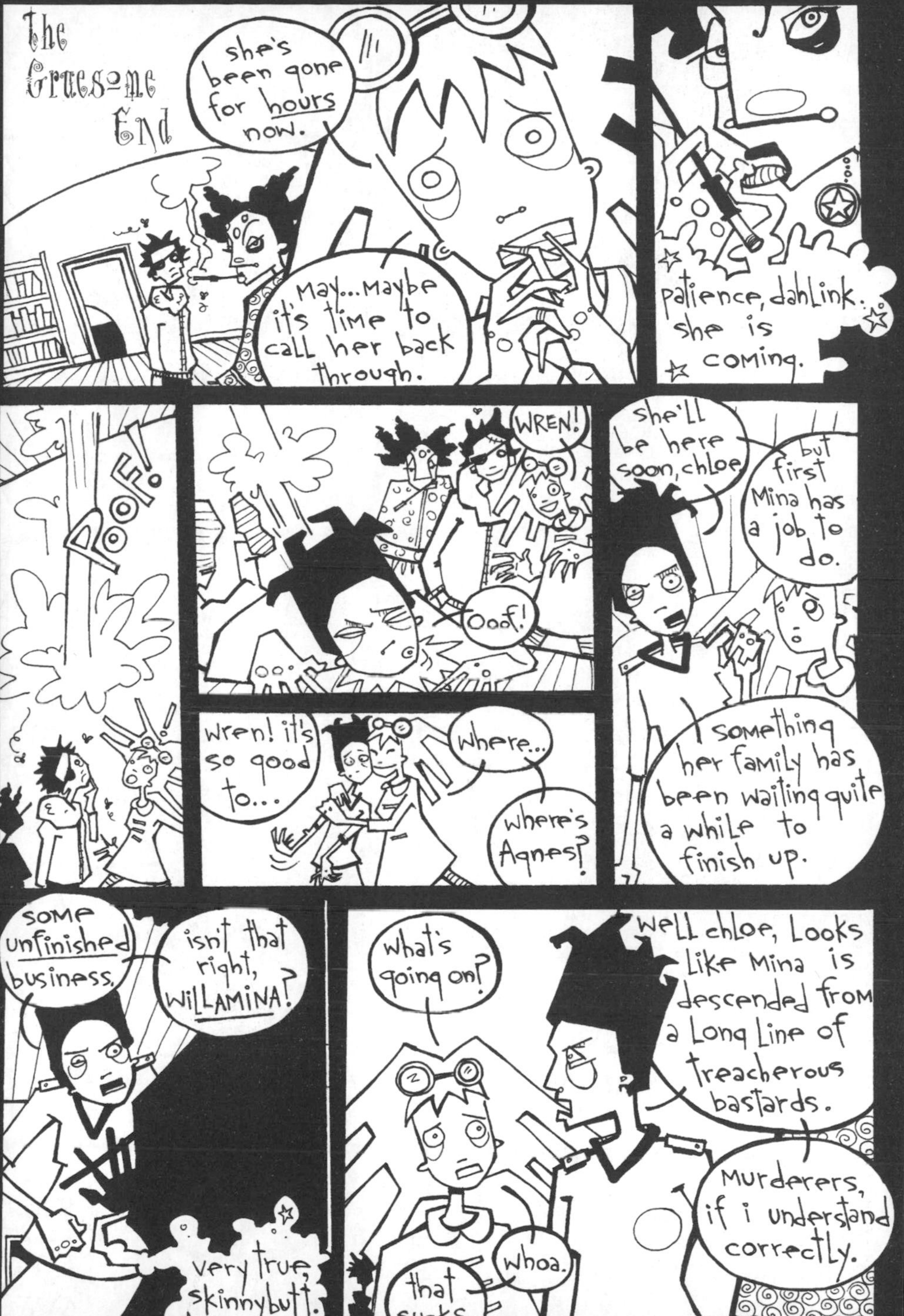
The Gruesome End
she's been gone for hours now.
May... Maybe it's time to call her back through.
patience, dahLink.. she is coming.
POOF!
WREN!
Ooof!
wren! it's so good to...
where...
where's Agnes?
she'LL be here soon, chLoe.
but first Mina has a job to do.
something her family has been waiting quite a whiLe to finish up.
some unfinished business.
isn't that right, WILLAMINA?
very true, skinnybutt.
what's going on?
weLL chLoe, Looks Like Mina is descended from a Long Line of treacherous bastards.
Murderers, if i understand correctLy.
whoa.
that sucks.

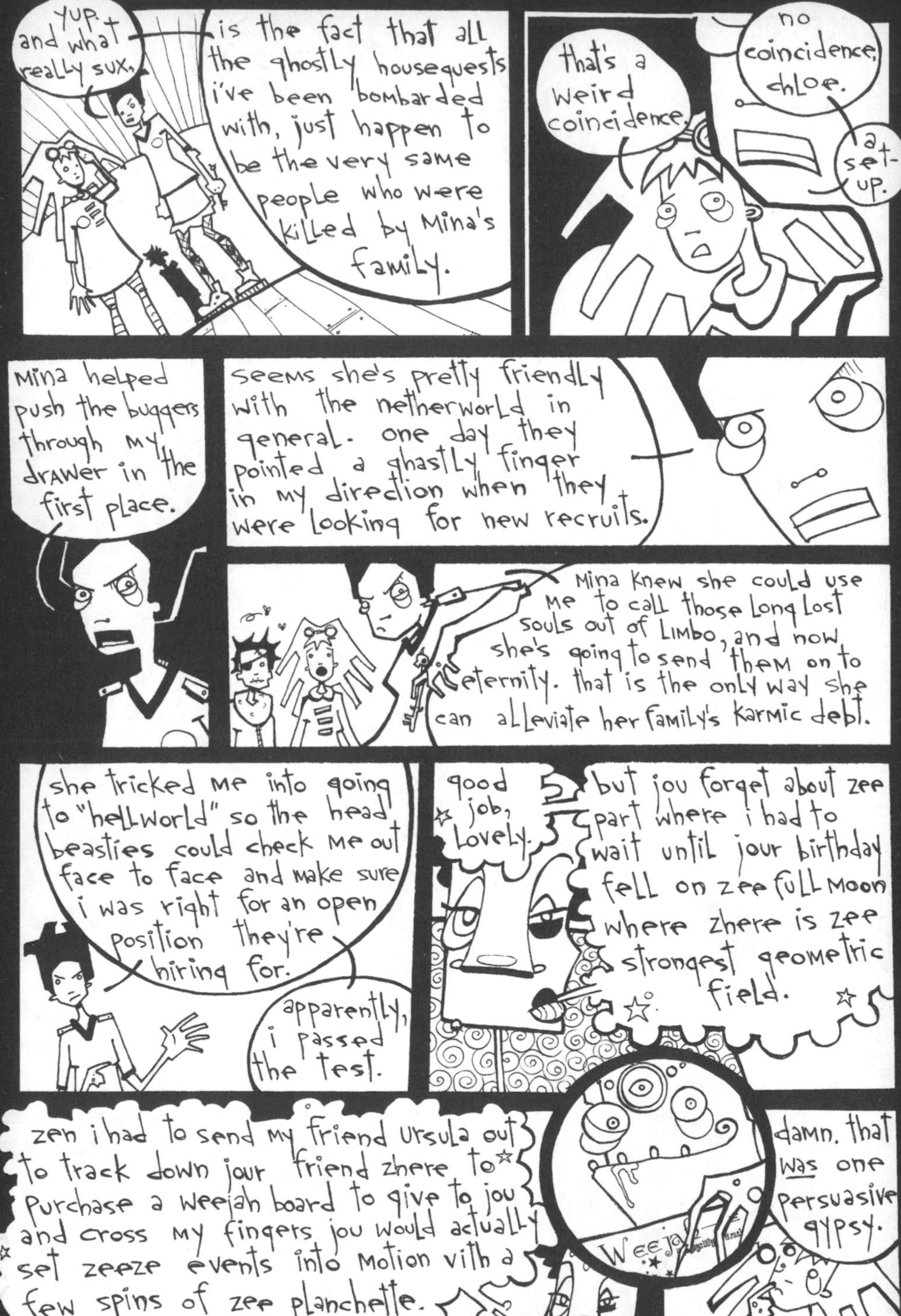

yup. and what really sux,
is the fact that all the ghostly houseguests i've been bombarded with, just happen to be the very same people who were killed by Mina's family.
that's a weird coincidence.
no coincidence, chloe.
a set-up.
Mina helped push the buggers through my drawer in the first place.
seems she's pretty friendly with the netherworld in general. one day they pointed a ghastly finger in my direction when they were looking for new recruits.
Mina knew she could use me to call those long lost souls out of limbo, and now she's going to send them on to eternity. that is the only way she can alleviate her family's karmic debt.
she tricked me into going to "hellworld" so the head beasties could check me out face to face and make sure i was right for an open position they're hiring for.
apparently, i passed the test.
good job, lovely.
but jou forget about zee part where i had to wait until jour birthday fell on zee full moon where zhere is zee strongest geometric field.
zen i had to send my friend ursula out to track down jour friend zhere to purchase a weejah board to give to jou and cross my fingers jou would actually set zeeze events into motion vith a few spins of zee planchette.
damn. that was one persuasive gypsy.

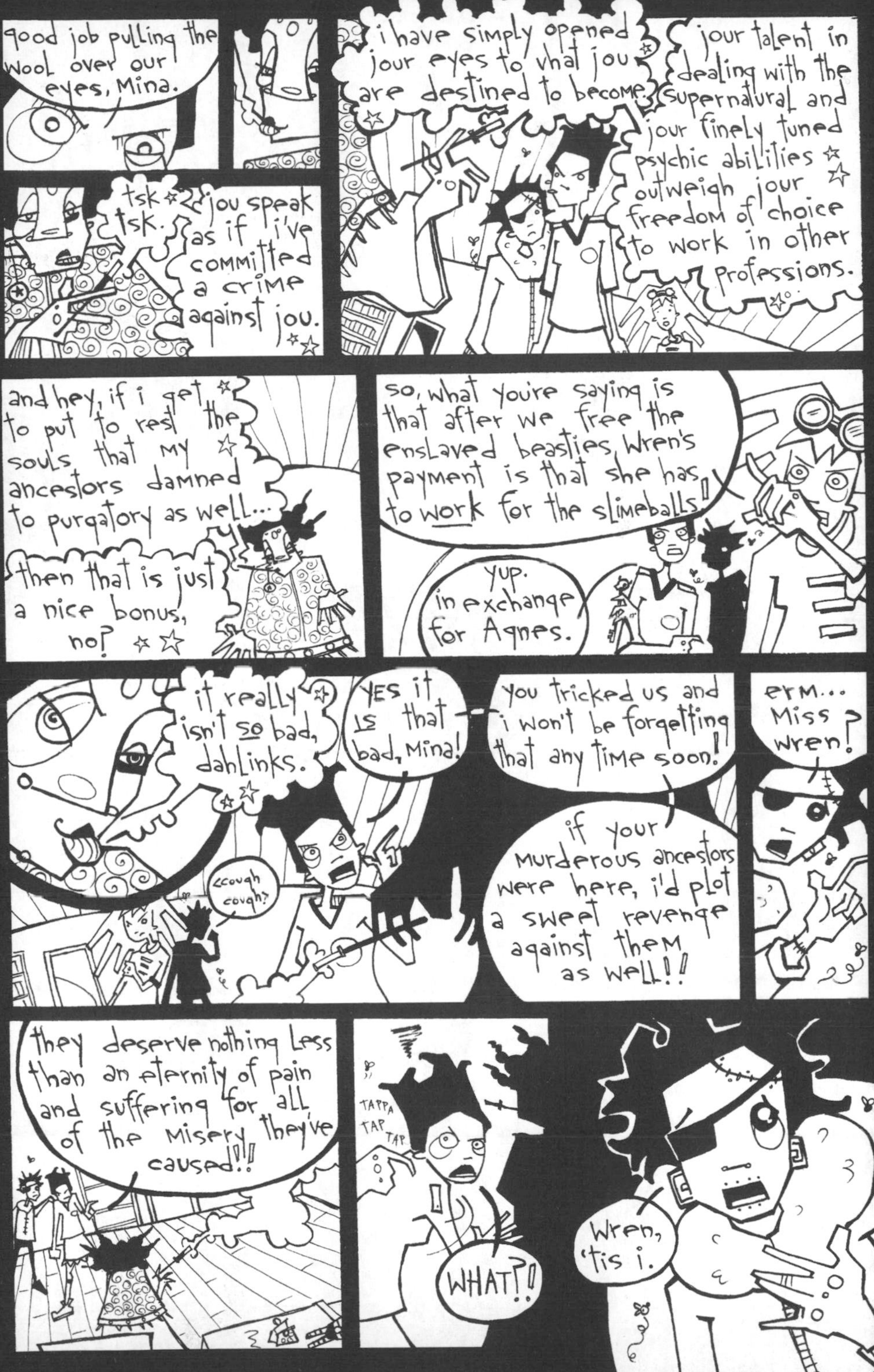
good job pulling the wool over our eyes, Mina.
tsk tsk.
jou speak as if i've committed a crime against jou.
i have simply opened jour eyes to vhat jou are destined to become.
jour talent in dealing with the supernatural and jour finely tuned psychic abilities outweigh jour freedom of choice to work in other professions.
and hey, if i get to put to rest the souls that my ancestors damned to purgatory as well...
then that is just a nice bonus, no?
so, what you're saying is that after we free the enslaved beasties, Wren's payment is that she has to work for the slimeballs!
yup. in exchange for Agnes.
it really isn't so bad, dahlinks.
<cough cough>
yes it is that bad, Mina!
you tricked us and i won't be forgetting that any time soon!
if your murderous ancestors were here, i'd plot a sweet revenge against them as well!!
erm... Miss Wren!
they deserve nothing less than an eternity of pain and suffering for all of the misery they've caused!!!
TAPPA TAP TAP
WHAT?!
Wren, 'tis i.

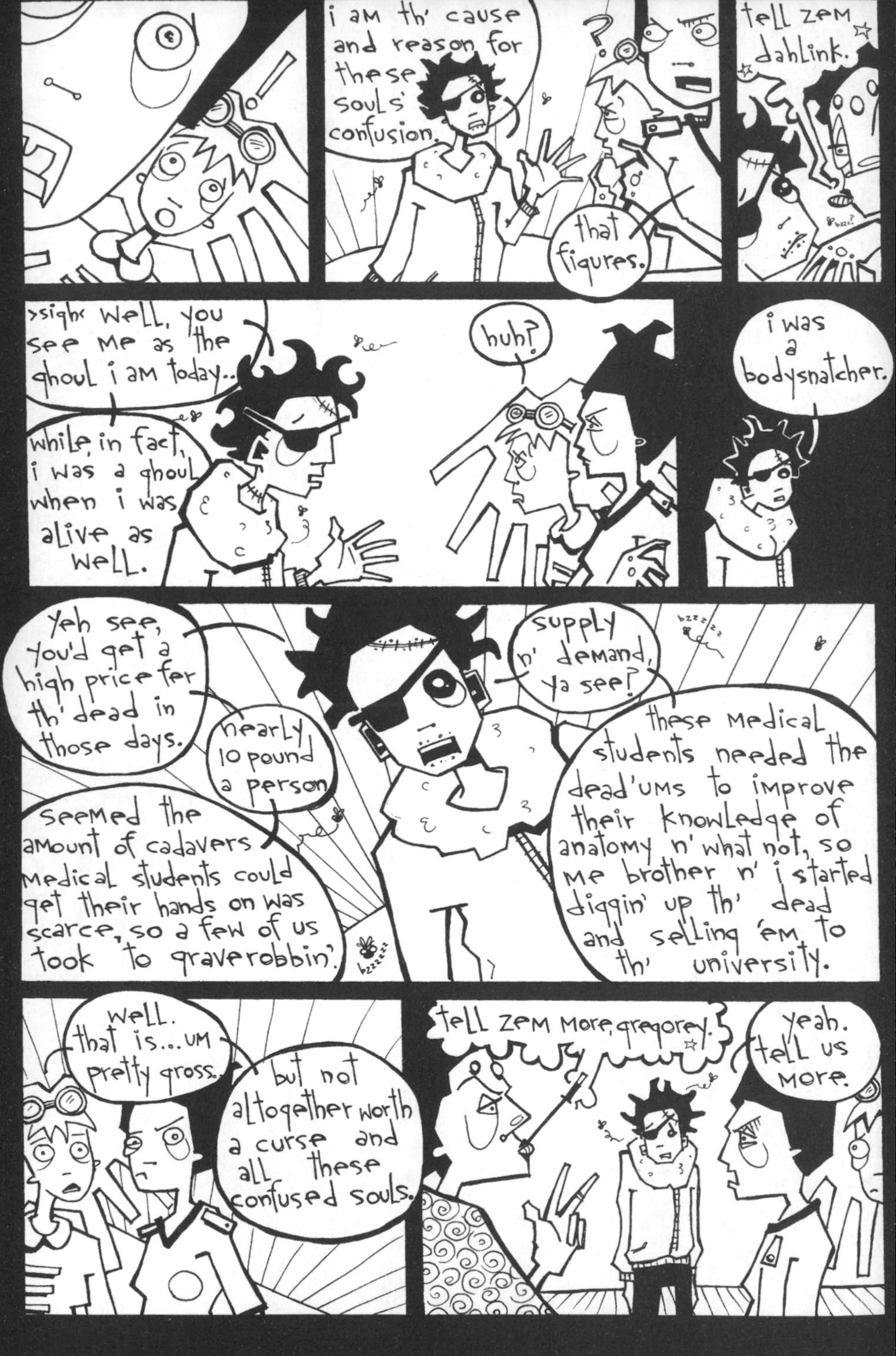

!
i am th' cause and reason for these souls' confusion.
?
that figures.
tell zem dahlink.
bzzz?
>sigh< well, you see me as the ghoul i am today..
while, in fact, i was a ghoul when i was alive as well.
huh?
i was a bodysnatcher.
Yeh see, you'd get a high price fer th' dead in those days.
nearly 10 pound a person
seemed the amount of cadavers medical students could get their hands on was scarce, so a few of us took to graverobbin'.
bzzzzzz
supply n' demand, ya see?
bzzzzz
these medical students needed the dead'ums to improve their knowledge of anatomy n' what not, so me brother n' i started diggin' up th' dead and selling 'em to th' university.
well. that is... um pretty gross.
but not altogether worth a curse and all these confused souls.
tell zem more, gregorey.
yeah. tell us more.

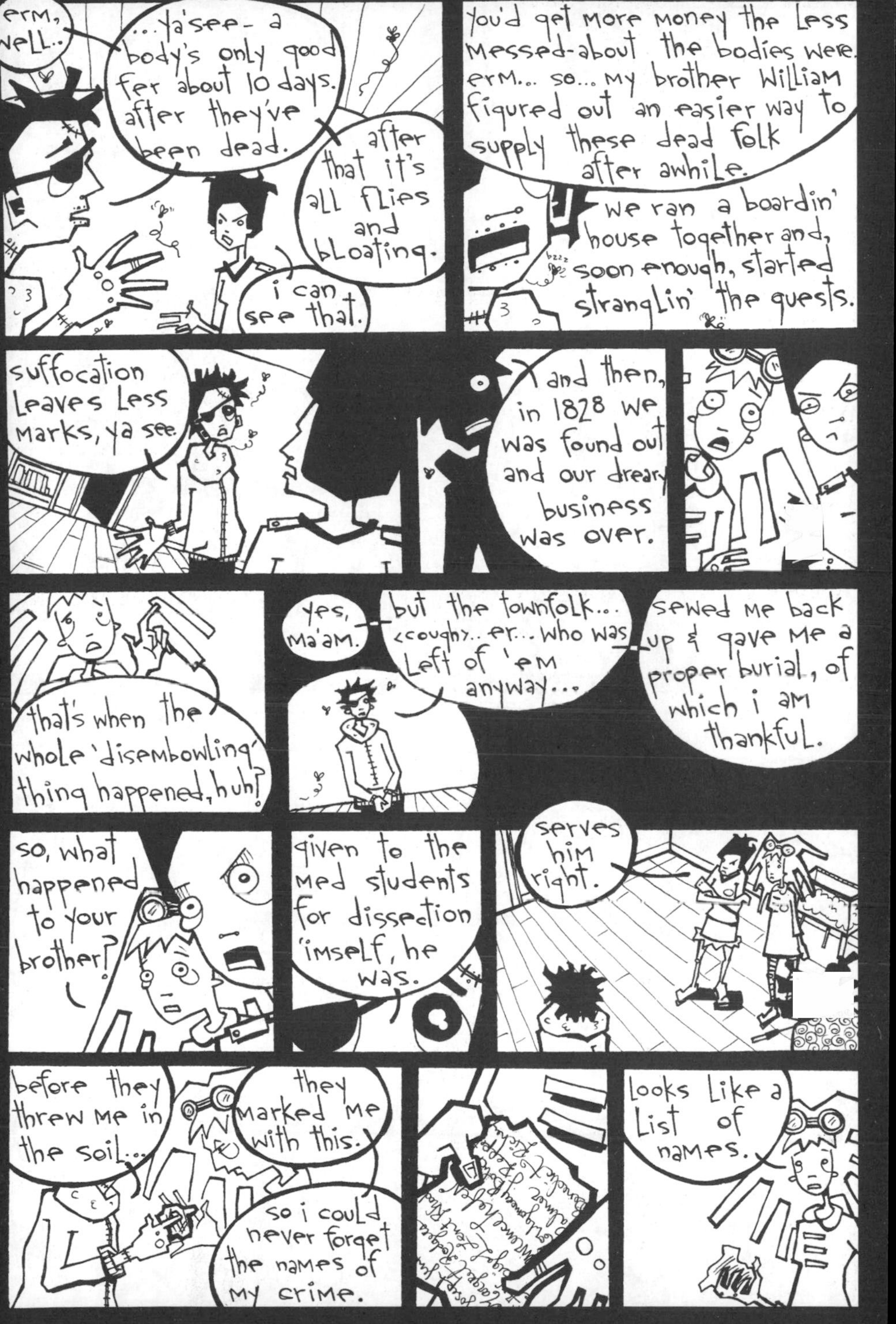
erm, well..
...ya'see- a body's only good fer about 10 days. after they've been dead.
after that it's all flies and bloating.
i can see that.
you'd get more money the less messed-about the bodies were. erm... so... my brother William figured out an easier way to supply these dead folk after awhile.
we ran a boardin' house together and, soon enough, started stranglin' the guests.
bzzz
suffocation leaves less marks, ya see.
and then, in 1828 we was found out and our dreary business was over.
that's when the whole 'disembowling' thing happened, huh?
yes, ma'am.
but the townfolk... <cough>.. er... who was left of 'em anyway...
sewed me back up & gave me a proper burial, of which i am thankful.
so, what happened to your brother?
given to the med students for dissection 'imself, he was.
serves him right.
before they threw me in the soil...
they marked me with this.
so i could never forget the names of my crime.
looks like a list of names.

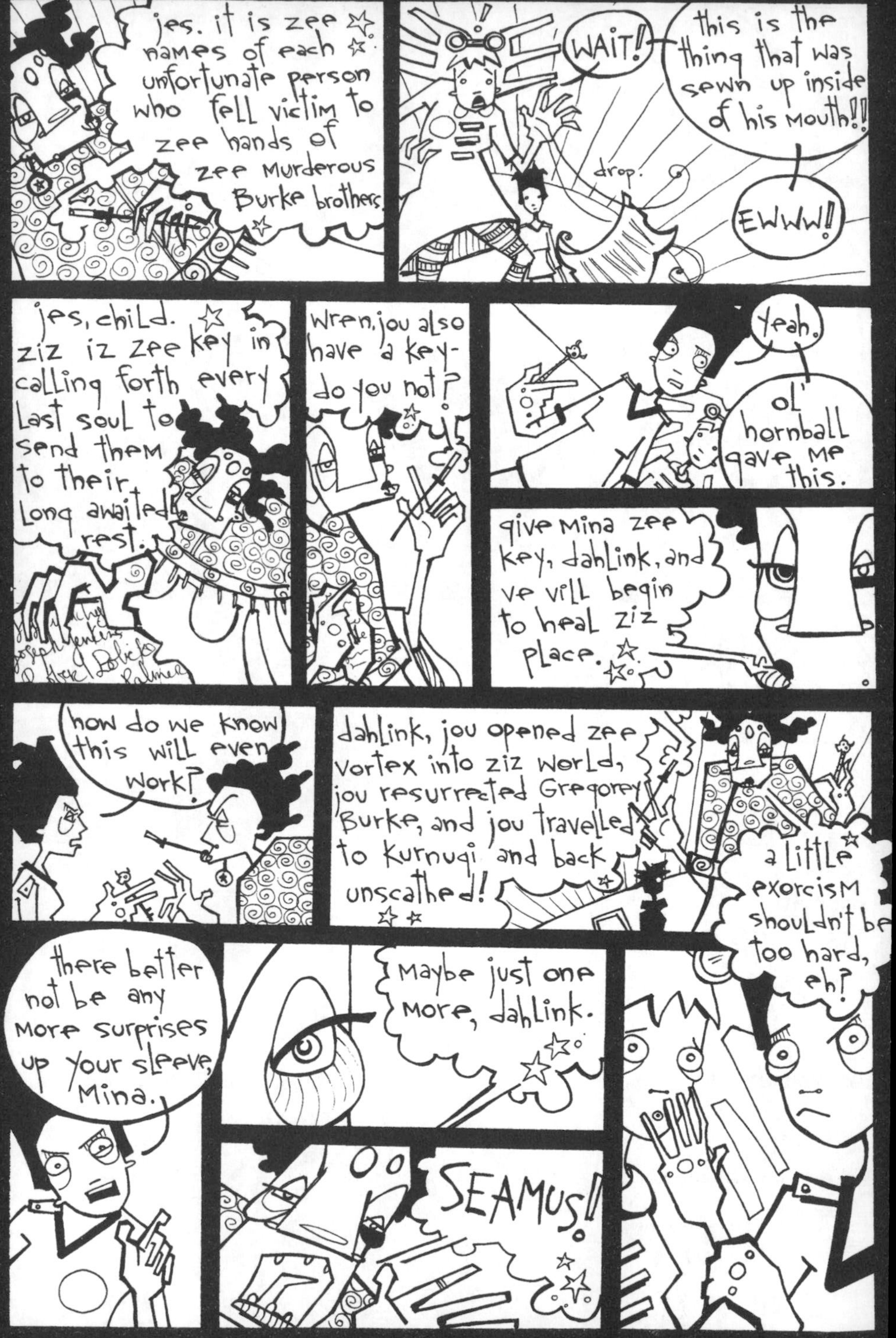

jes. it is zee names of each unfortunate person who fell victim to zee hands of zee Murderous Burke brothers.
WAIT!
this is the thing that was sewn up inside of his mouth!!
drop.
EWWW!
jes, child. ziz iz zee key in calling forth every last soul to send them to their long awaited rest.
Wren, jou also have a key- do you not?
Yeah.
ol' hornball gave me this.
give Mina zee key, dahLink, and ve vill begin to heal ziz place.
how do we know this will even work?
dahLink, jou opened zee vortex into ziz world, jou resurrected Gregorey Burke, and jou travelled to Kurnugi and back unscathed!
a little exorcism shouldn't be too hard, eh?
there better not be any more surprises up your sleeve, Mina.
Maybe just one more, dahLink.
SEAMUS!!

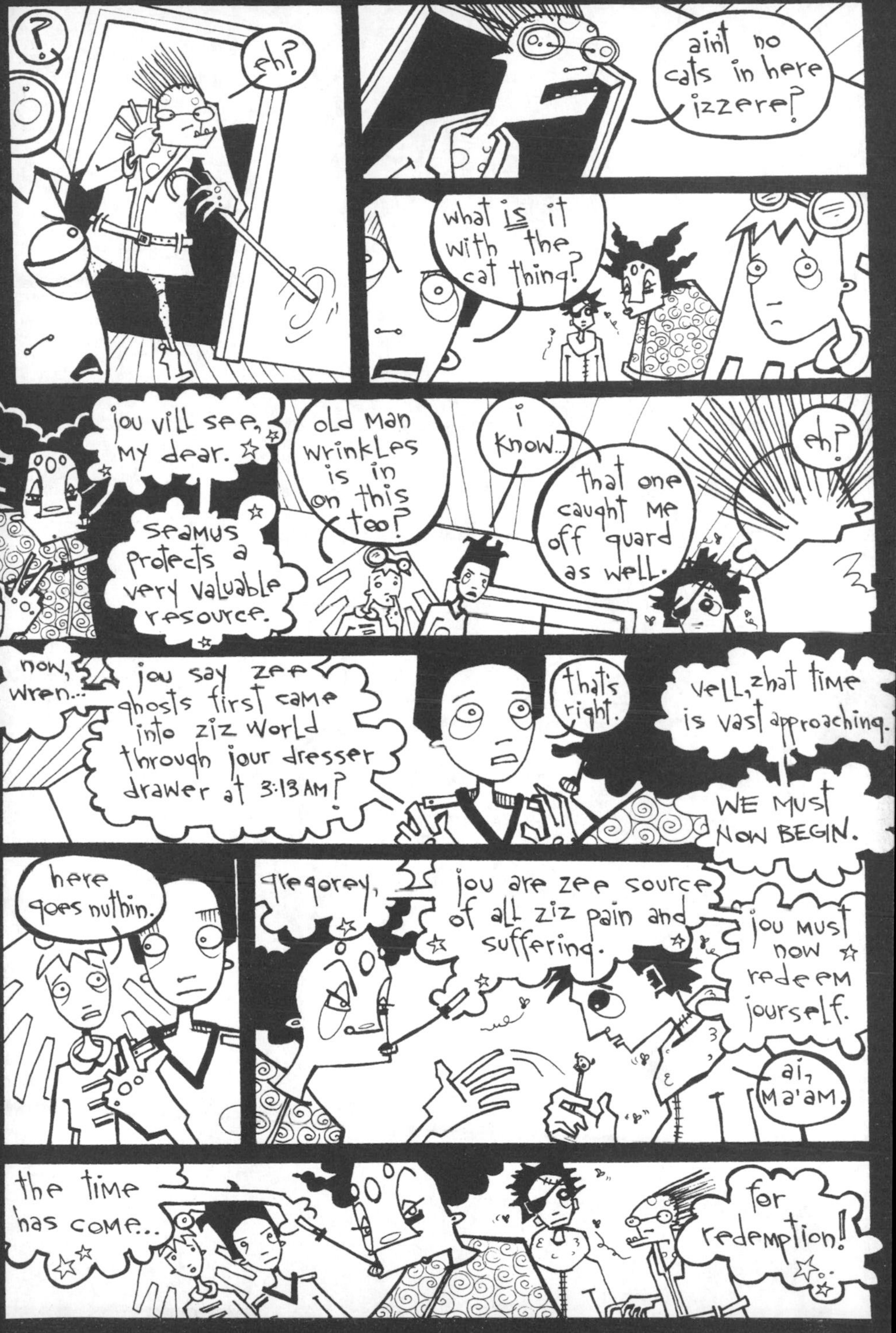
?
eh?
aint no cats in here izzere?
what IS it with the cat thing?
jou vill see, my dear.
seamus protects a very valuable resource.
old man wrinkles is in on this too?
i know...
that one caught me off guard as well.
eh?
now, wren...
jou say zee ghosts first came into ziz world through jour dresser drawer at 3:13AM?
that's right.
vell, zhat time is vast approaching.
WE MUST NOW BEGIN.
here goes nuthin.
gregorey,
jou are zee source of all ziz pain and suffering.
jou must now redeem jourself.
ai, ma'am.
the time has come...
for redemption!

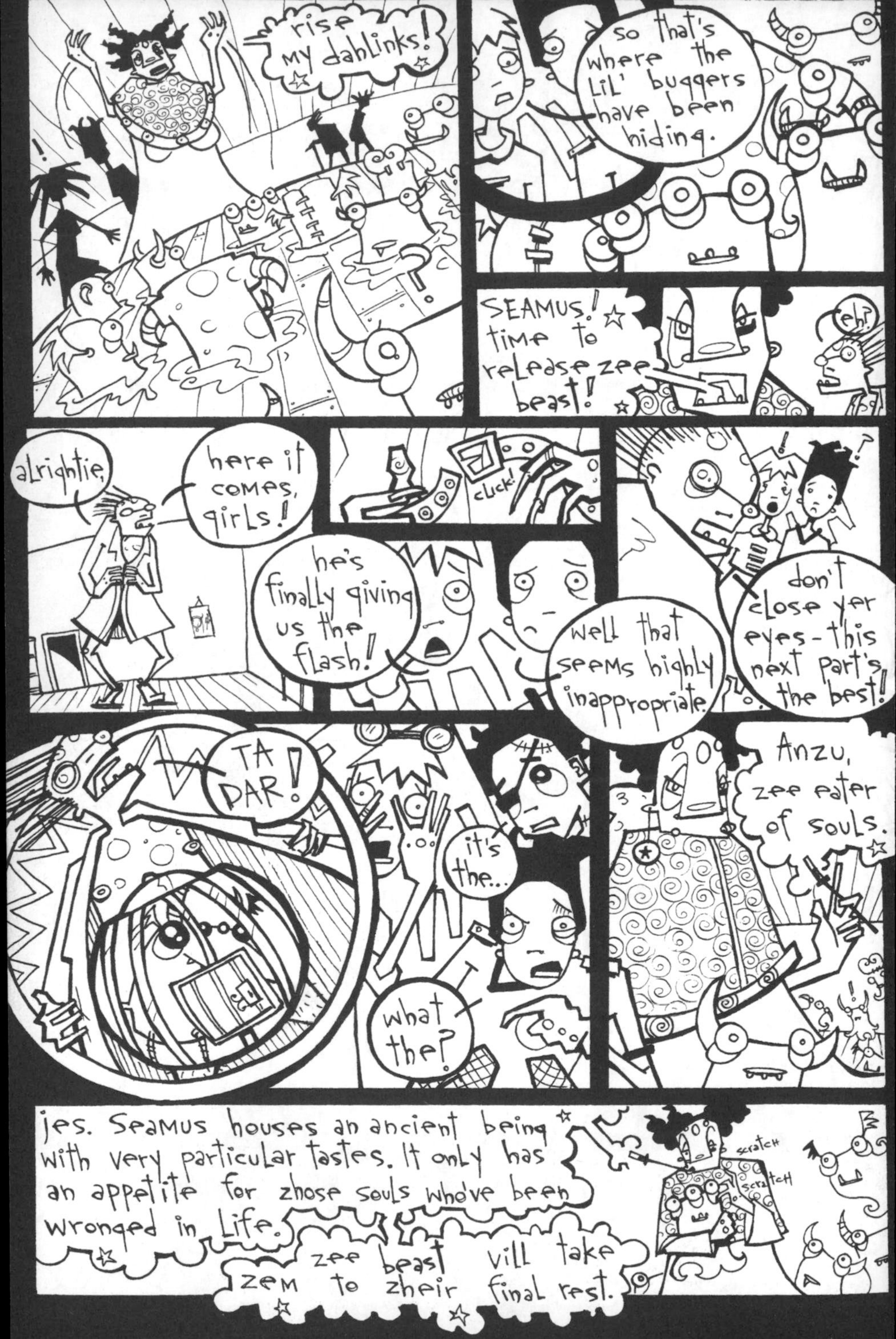
rise my dahlinks!
!
so that's where the lil' buggers have been hiding.
SEAMUS! time to release zee beast!
eh?
alrightie,
here it comes, girls!
click!
!
?
he's finally giving us the flash!
well that seems highly inappropriate.
don't close yer eyes - this next part's the best!
TA DAR!
it's the...
what the?
Anzu, zee eater of souls.
jes. Seamus houses an ancient being with very particular tastes. It only has an appetite for zhose souls who've been wronged in life.
scratch
scratch
zee beast vill take zem to zheir final rest.

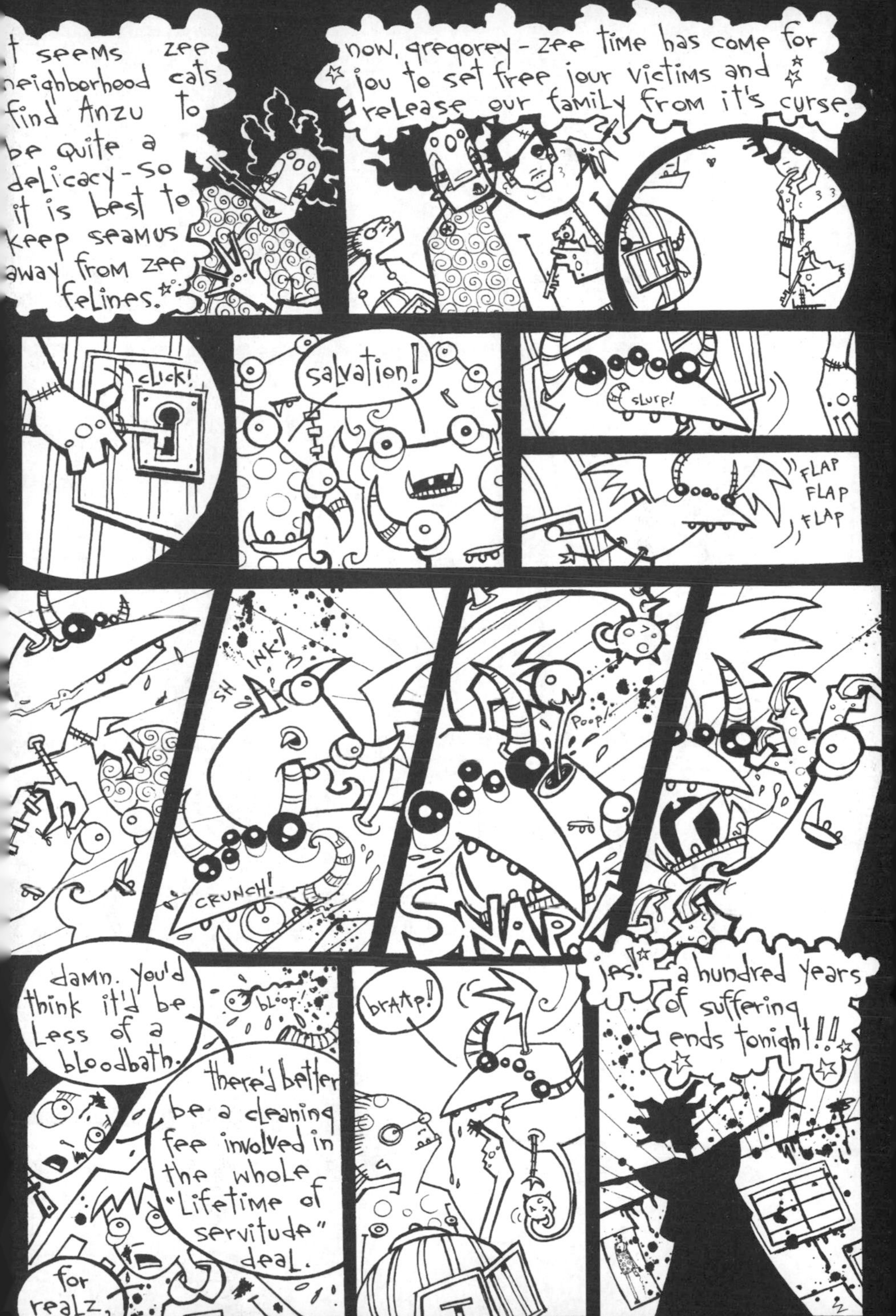

t seems zee neighborhood cats find Anzu to be quite a deLicacy - so it is best to keep seamus away from zee feLines.
now, gregorey - zee time has come for jou to set free jour victims and reLease our famiLy from it's curse.
cLick!
salvation!
sLurp!
FLAP FLAP FLAP
SHINK!
CRUNCH!
Poop!
SNAP!
damn. You'd think it'd be Less of a bLoodbath.
bLoop!
there'd better be a cLeaning fee involved in the whole "Lifetime of servitude" deaL.
for reaLz, tho.
braap!
jes! a hundred years of suffering ends tonight!!

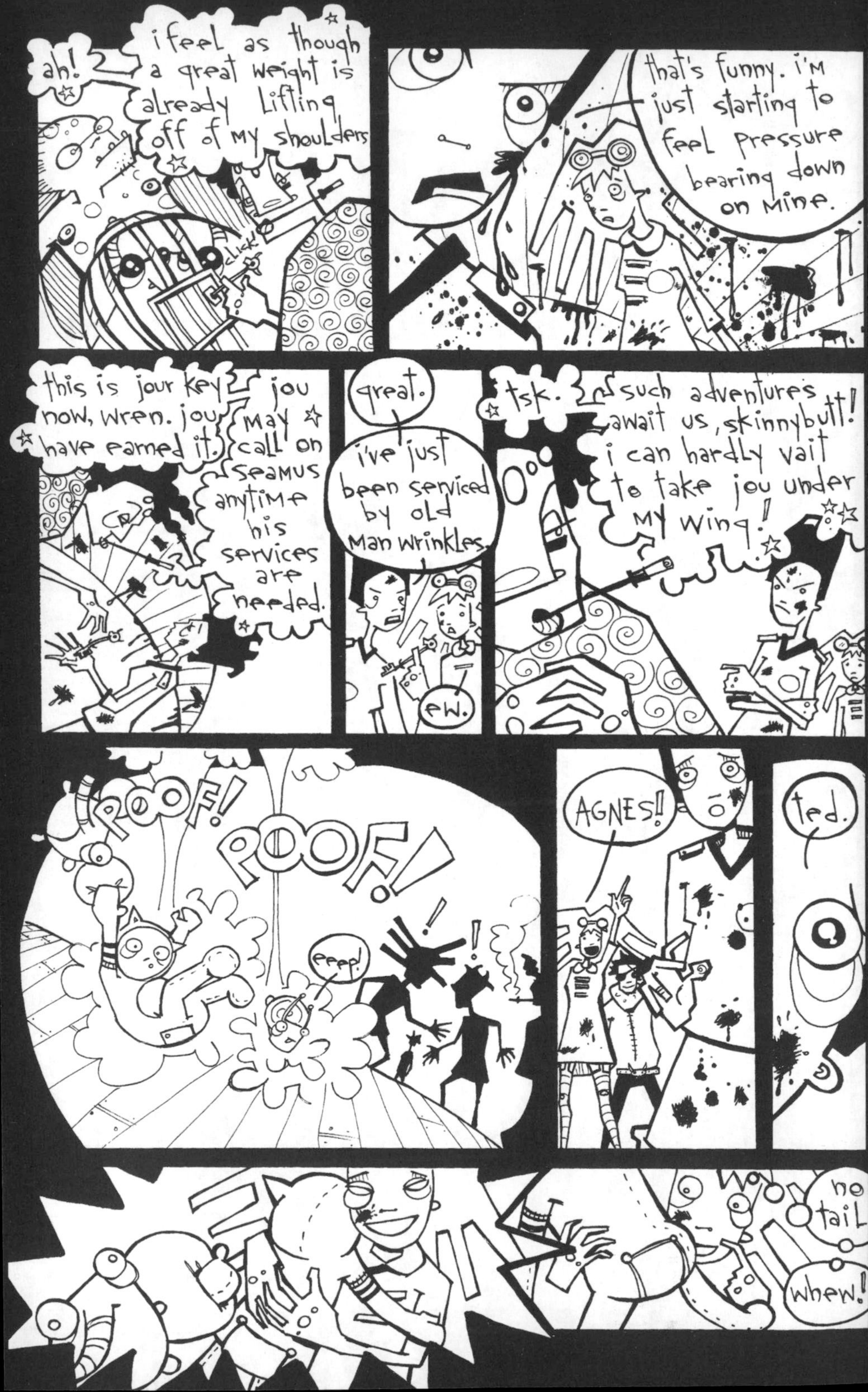
ah!
i feel as though a great weight is already lifting off of my shoulders
that's funny. i'm just starting to feel pressure bearing down on mine.
this is jour key now, wren. jou have earned it.
jou may call on seamus anytime his services are needed.
great.
i've just been serviced by old man wrinkles.
ew.
tsk.
such adventures await us, skinnybutt! i can hardly vait to take jou under my wing!
POOF!
POOF!
eeep!
!
!
AGNES!
ted.
no tail
whew!

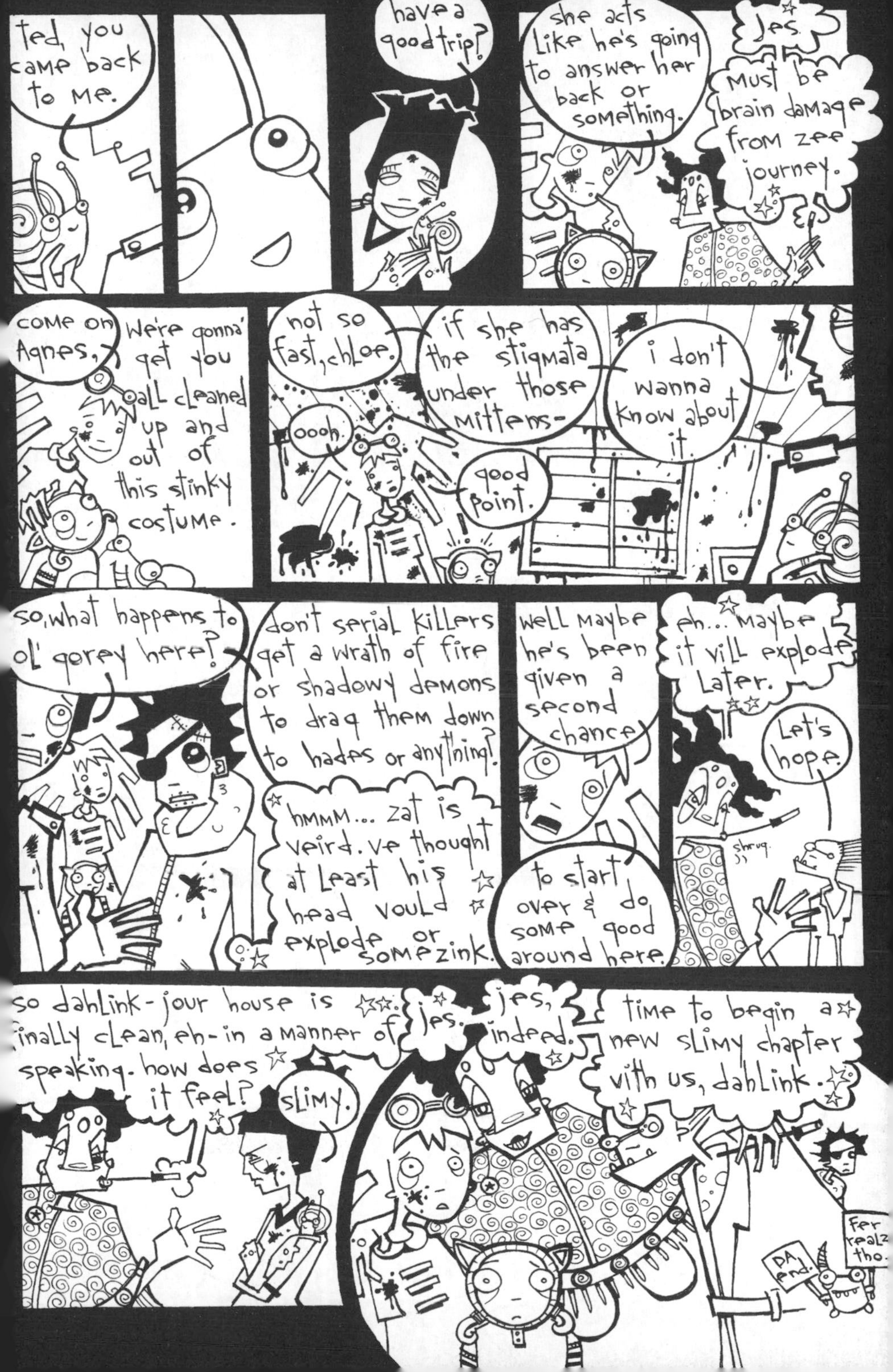
ted, you came back to me.
have a good trip?
she acts like he's going to answer her back or something.
jes. Must be brain damage from zee journey.
come on Agnes,
we're gonna' get you all cleaned up and out of this stinky costume.
not so fast, chloe.
if she has the stigmata under those mittens-
i don't wanna know about it.
oooh.
good point.
so, what happens to ol' gorey here?
don't serial killers get a wrath of fire or shadowy demons to drag them down to hades or anything?
hmmm... zat is veird. ve thought at least his head vould explode or somezink.
well maybe he's been given a second chance
to start over & do some good around here.
eh... maybe it vill explode later.
Let's hope.
shrug.
so dahlink - jour house is finally clean, eh - in a manner of speaking. how does it feel?
slimy.
jes.
jes, indeed.
time to begin a new slimy chapter with us, dahlink.
DA end.
Fer realz tho.

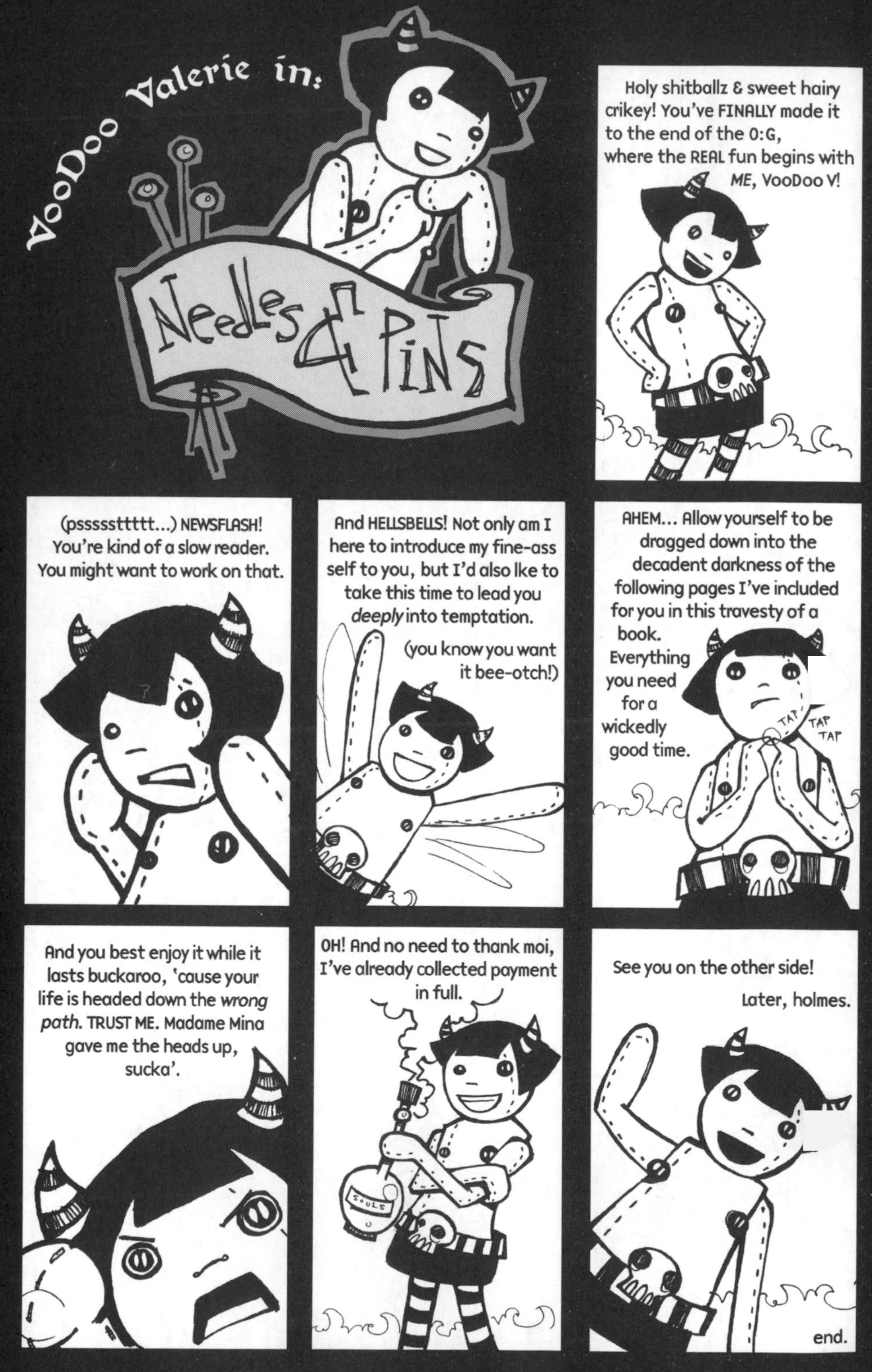
VooDoo Valerie in:
Needles & Pins
Holy shitballz & sweet hairy crikey! You've FINALLY made it to the end of the O:G, where the REAL fun begins with ME, VooDoo V!
(psssssttttt...) NEWSFLASH! You're kind of a slow reader. You might want to work on that.
And HELLSBELLS! Not only am I here to introduce my fine-ass self to you, but I'd also lke to take this time to lead you deeply into temptation.
(you know you want it bee-otch!)
AHEM... Allow yourself to be dragged down into the decadent darkness of the following pages I've included for you in this travesty of a book. Everything you need for a wickedly good time.
TAP TAP TAP
And you best enjoy it while it lasts buckaroo, 'cause your life is headed down the wrong path. TRUST ME. Madame Mina gave me the heads up, sucka'.
OH! And no need to thank moi, I've already collected payment in full.
SOULS
See you on the other side!
Later, holmes.
end.

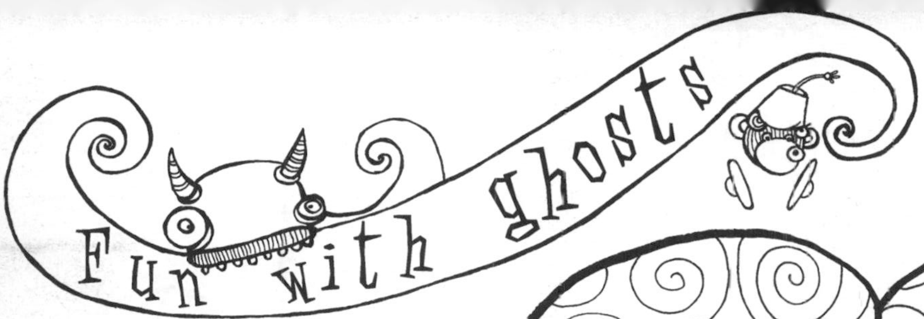
Fun with ghosts

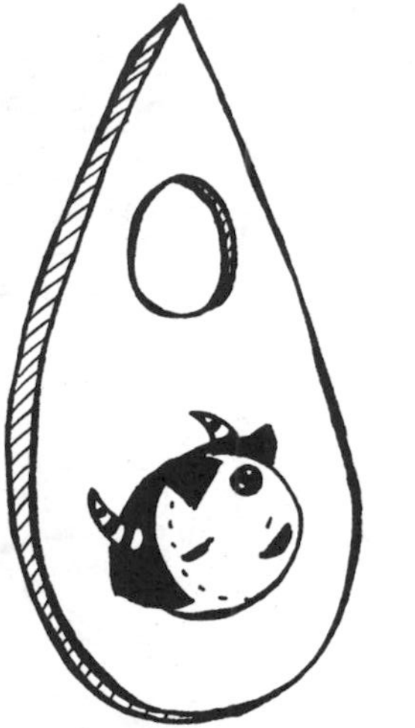

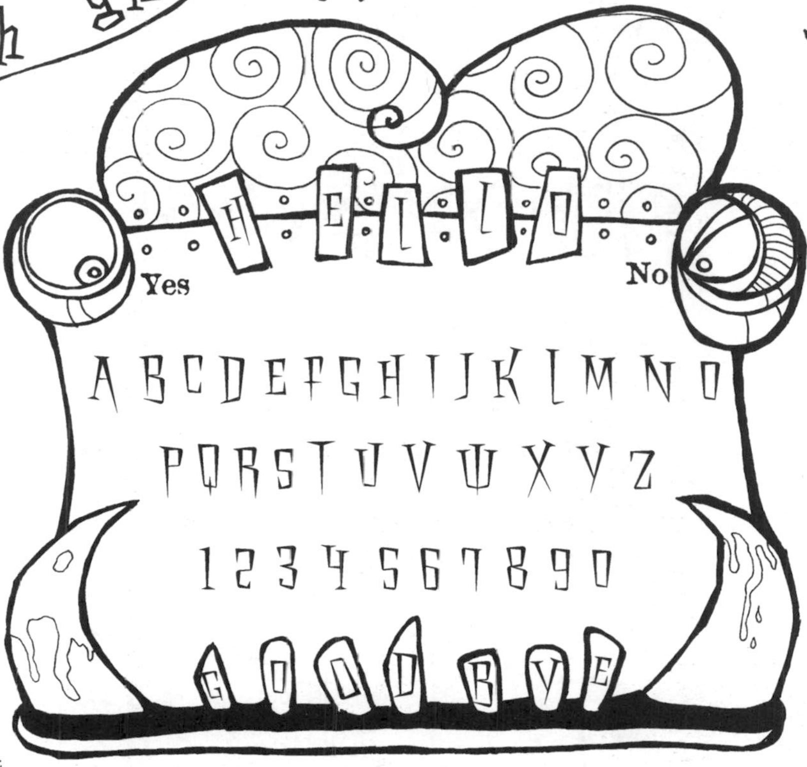
HELLO
Yes
No
A B C D E F G H I J K L M N O
P Q R S T U V W X Y Z
1 2 3 4 5 6 7 8 9 0
GOODBYE

Instructions

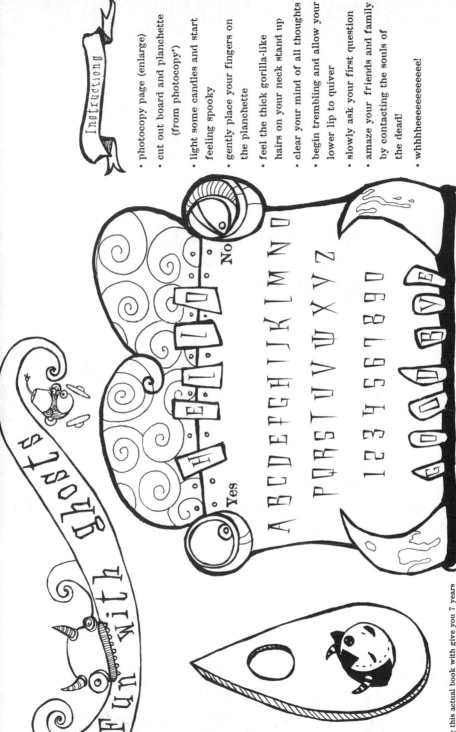

- photocopy page (enlarge)
- cut out board and planchette (from photocopy*)
- light some candles and start feeling spooky
- gently place your fingers on the planchette
- feel the thick gorilla-like hairs on your neck stand up
- clear your mind of all thoughts
- begin trembling and allow your lower lip to quiver
- slowly ask your first question
- amaze your friends and family by contacting the souls of the dead!
- whhhheeeeeeeeeee!

* Cutting this actual book with give you 7 years of bad luck. It also means you are completely incompetent and deserve a large eyeball papercut

The Secret Secret Letter Writing Club

Ingredients

lemon juice
white paper
Lamp
q-tips or pen quill

Instructions

1. Dip the pen quill or q-tip into the lemon juice and scribe your poison pen letter onto the paper.

2. Let your ghastly message dry.

3. When ready to disclose your top secret secret letter, place the paper over a hot light bulb (careful not to touch the letter, you pyro) and gasp in horror as your message magically appears.

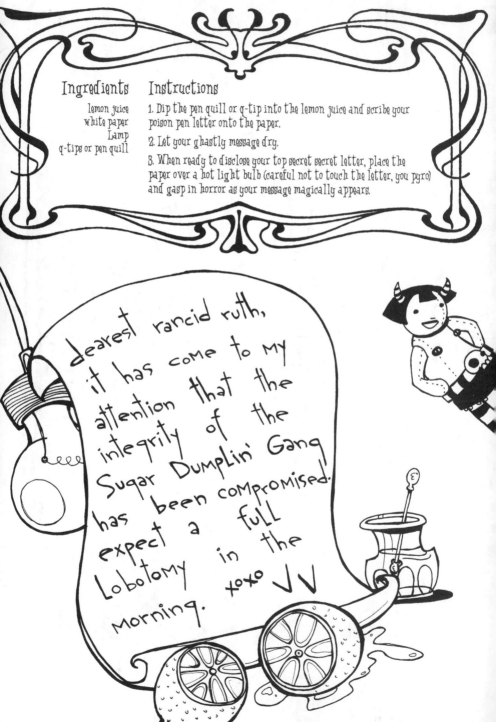

dearest rancid ruth,
it has come to my attention that the integrity of the Sugar Dumplin' Gang has been compromised! expect a full lobotomy in the morning. xoxo ∨∨

Instructions

How To Make Your Own Voo Doo Doll

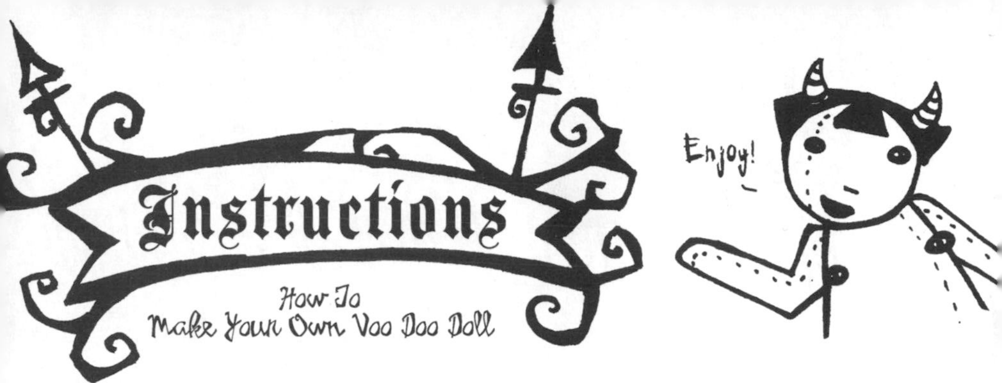
Enjoy!

. Photocopy page on heavy card stock. (**Enlarge**)
. Cut out front and back of doll.
. Grab the needle and thread you keep handy.
finally a use for it!)
. Use the sewing technique Gramsy taught you
nd sew the front and the back together.
Only sew up half way).

5. Pick a special stuffing material of your choosing.
6. Pretend she is a Thanksgiving Turkey. Stuff her up!
7. Sew up the rest of her spooky body.
8. Laugh mischievously.
9. Grab some straight pins from Mumsy
and have a wickedly fun time.

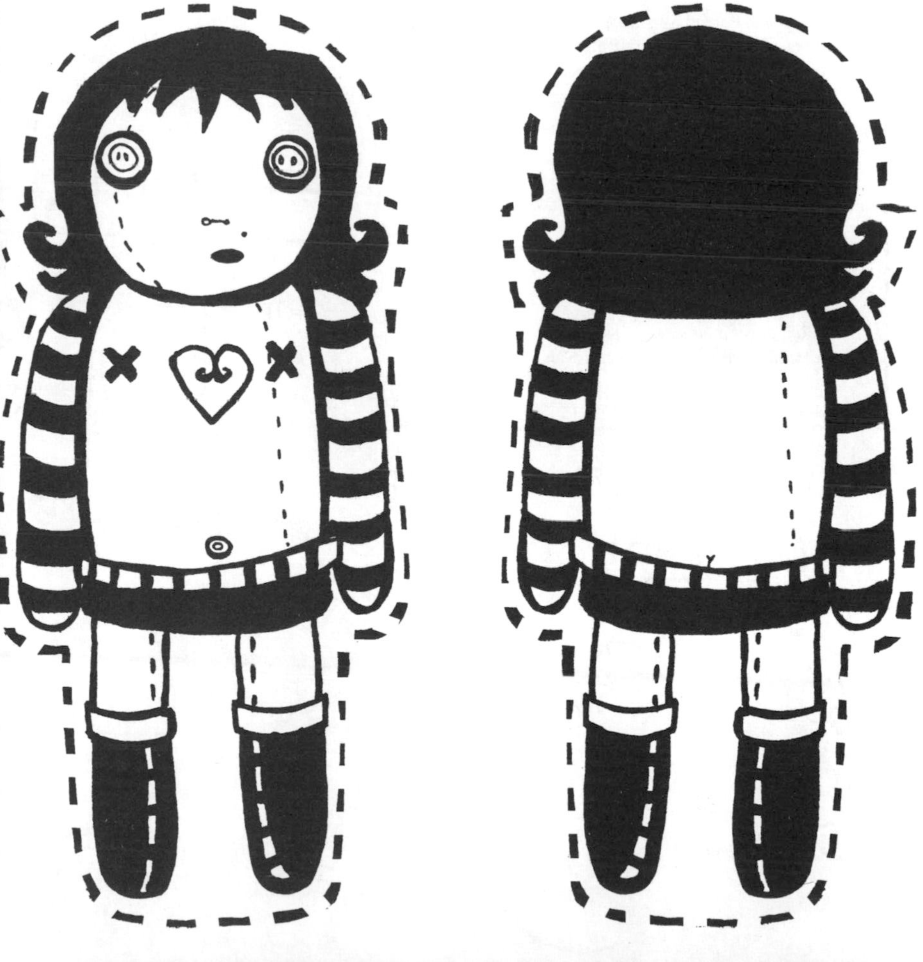

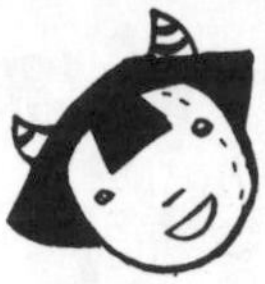
— Well hot damn, you found it!
This here's a lil' somefin' I call:

Pin The Tail On The Demon

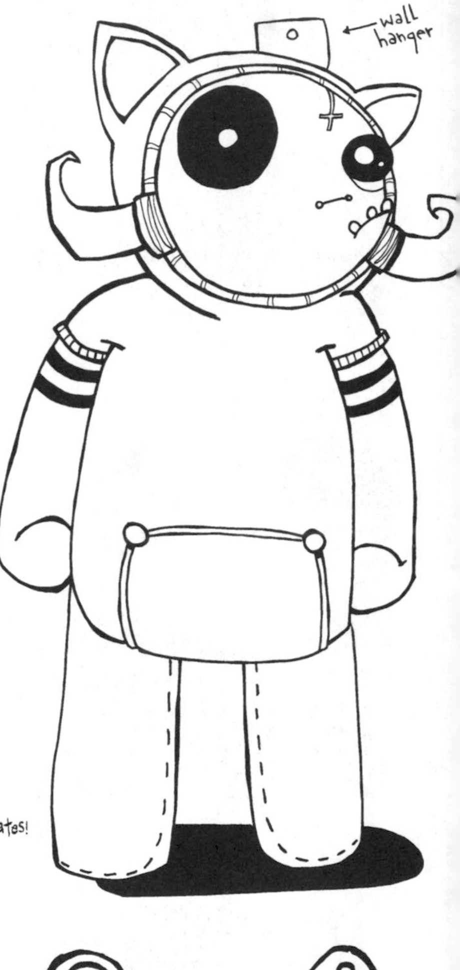
wall hanger

Directions

1. Photocopy page at 200% (hell, make it 400%!)
2. Cut out evil Aggie and pin her to the wall.
3. Cut out tails.
4. Blindfold players whom you've lured into participating in your mischievous Pagan "game."
5. Find sharp pins with rusty points.
6. Lure your victims, er, *friends,* into *a false sense of security before hastily blindfolding them.*
7. *Choose a rusty pin and tail of your choice, and violently spin them into disoriented confusion. (careful not to induce vomiting, that comes later.)*
8. *Run out of their way and laugh as they commence in ritual demon ass poking.*

Family fun for birthdays, bar mitzvahs, church gatherings and first dates!

Tail Gallery

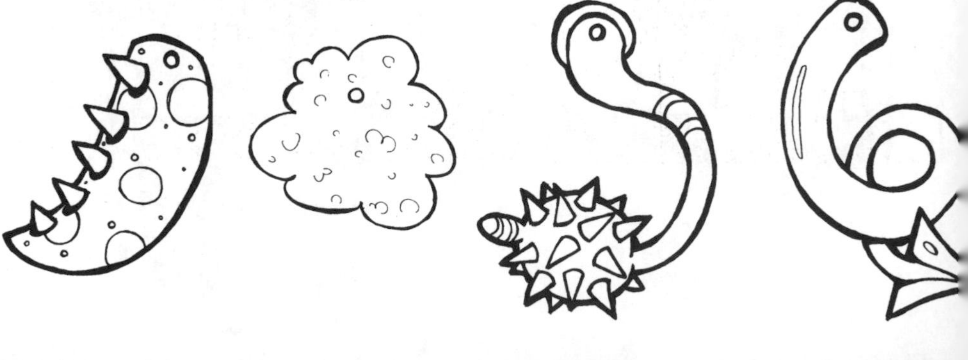

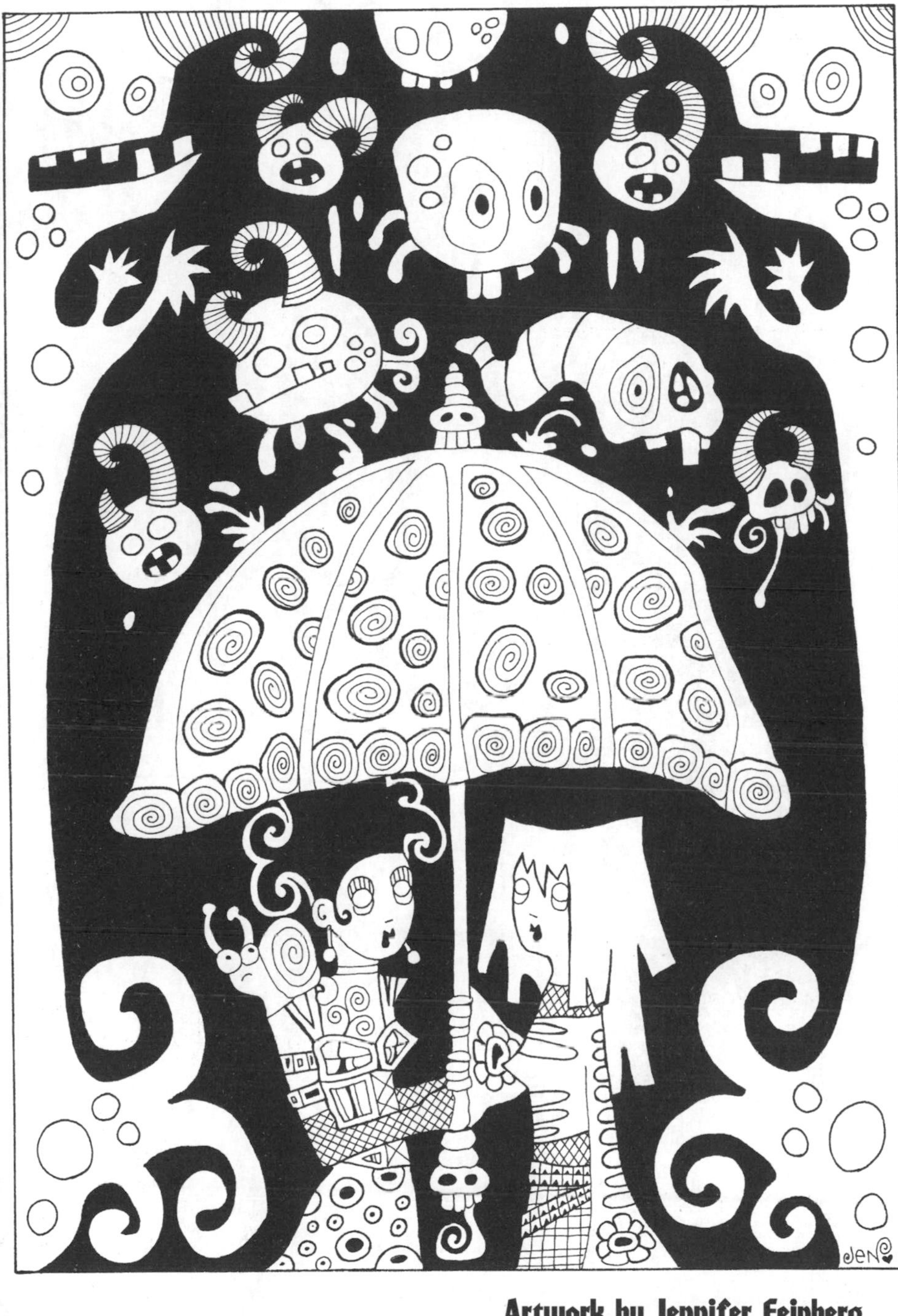
JEN

Artwork by Jennifer Feinberg
www.chi-jen.com

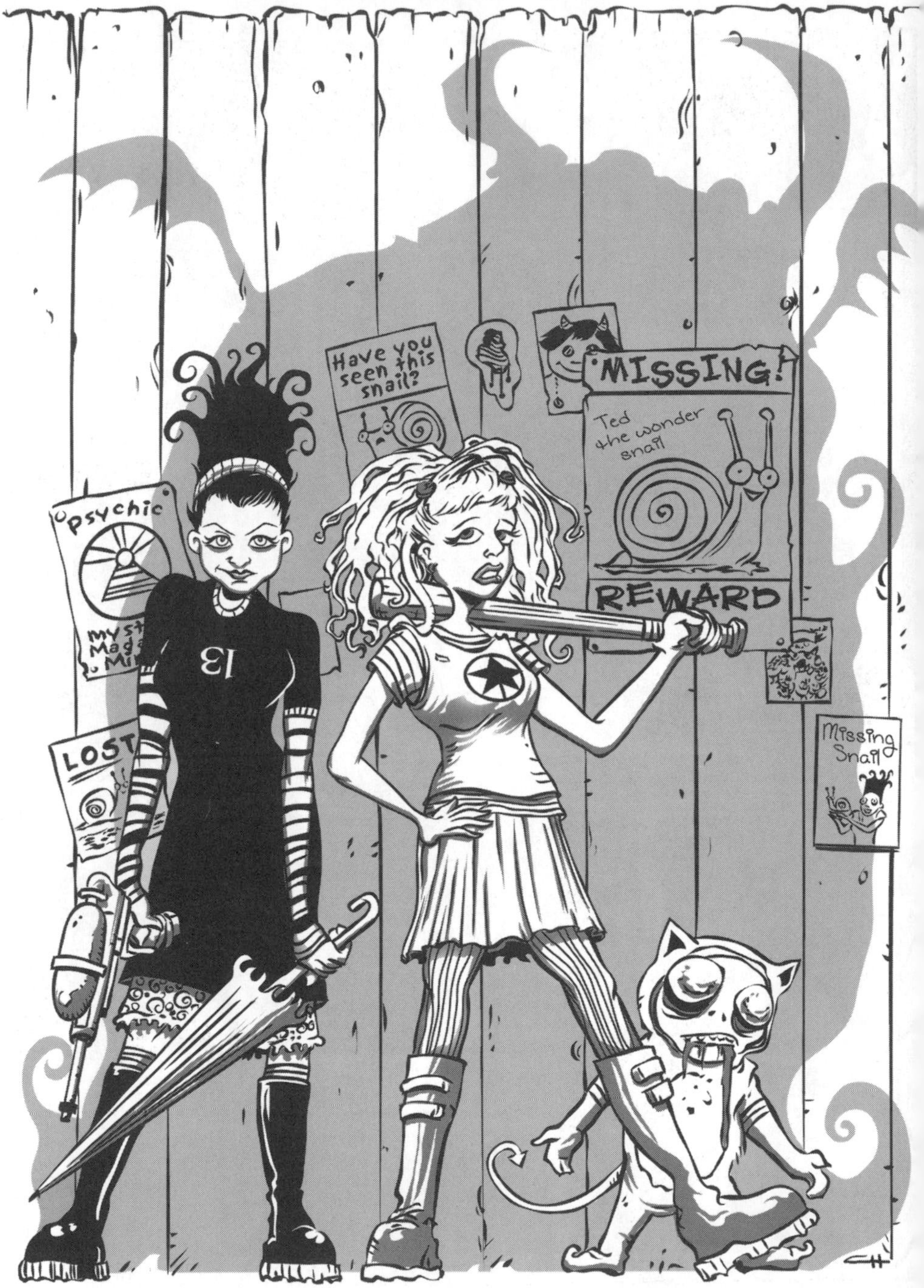

Have you seen this snail?
MISSING!
Ted the wonder snail
REWARD
Psychic
LOST
Missing Snail
13

Artwork by Christopher
www.invinciblestudios.com

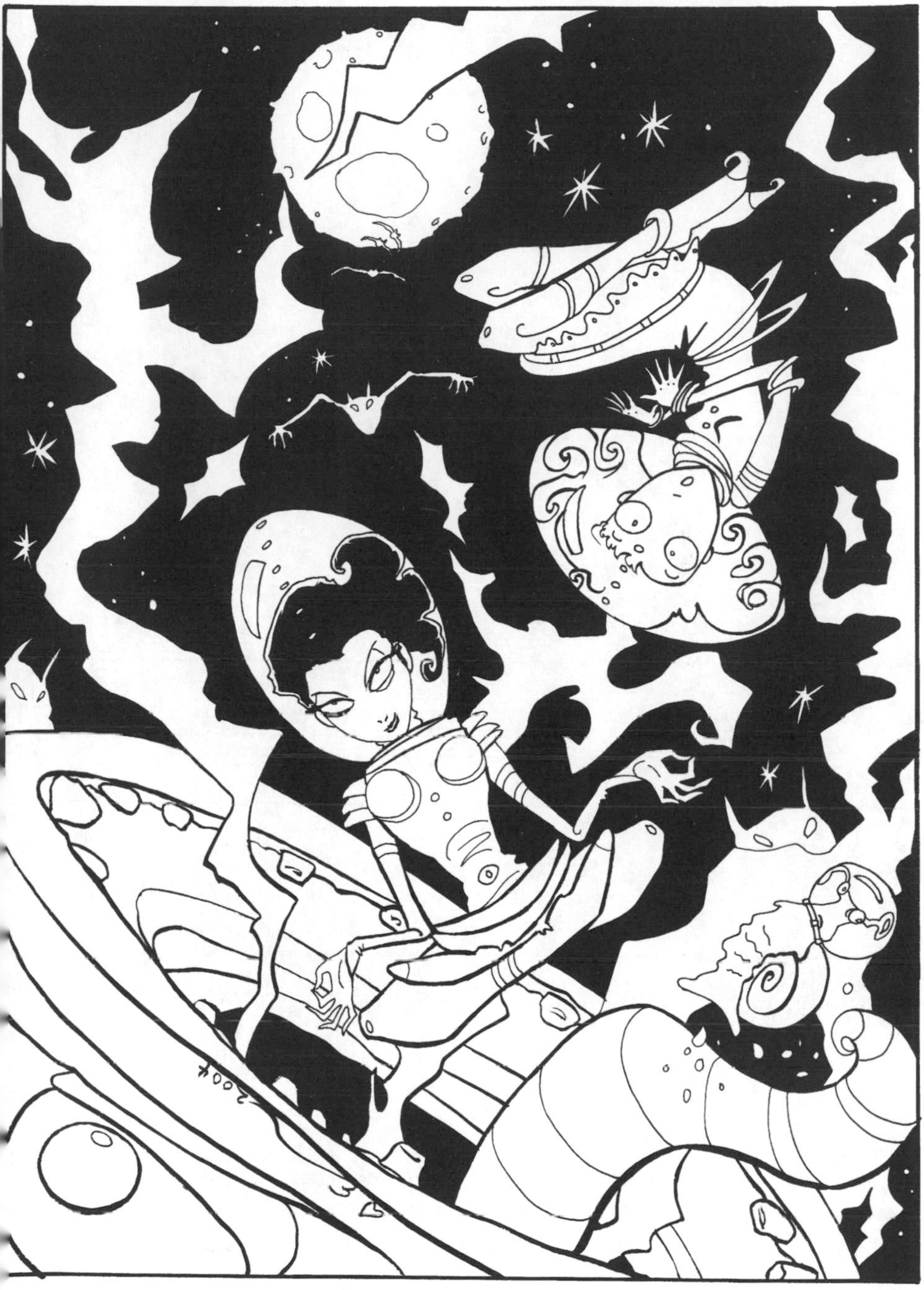

Artwork by Elizabeth Watasin
www.a-girlstudio.com

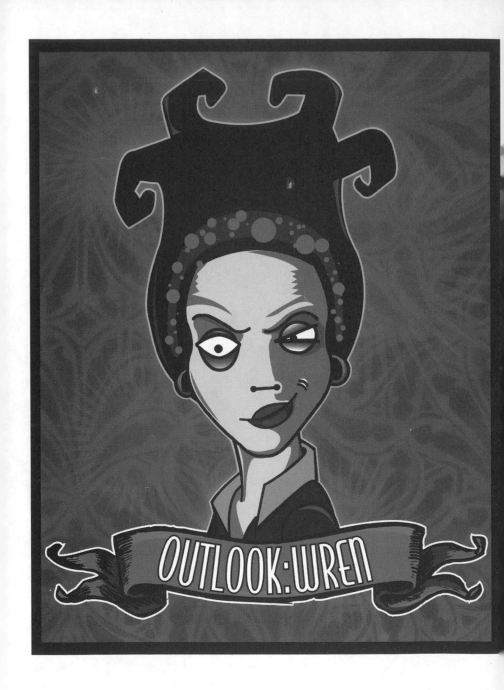

OUTLOOK:WREN

Artwork by Logan Hicks
www.workhorsevisuals.com

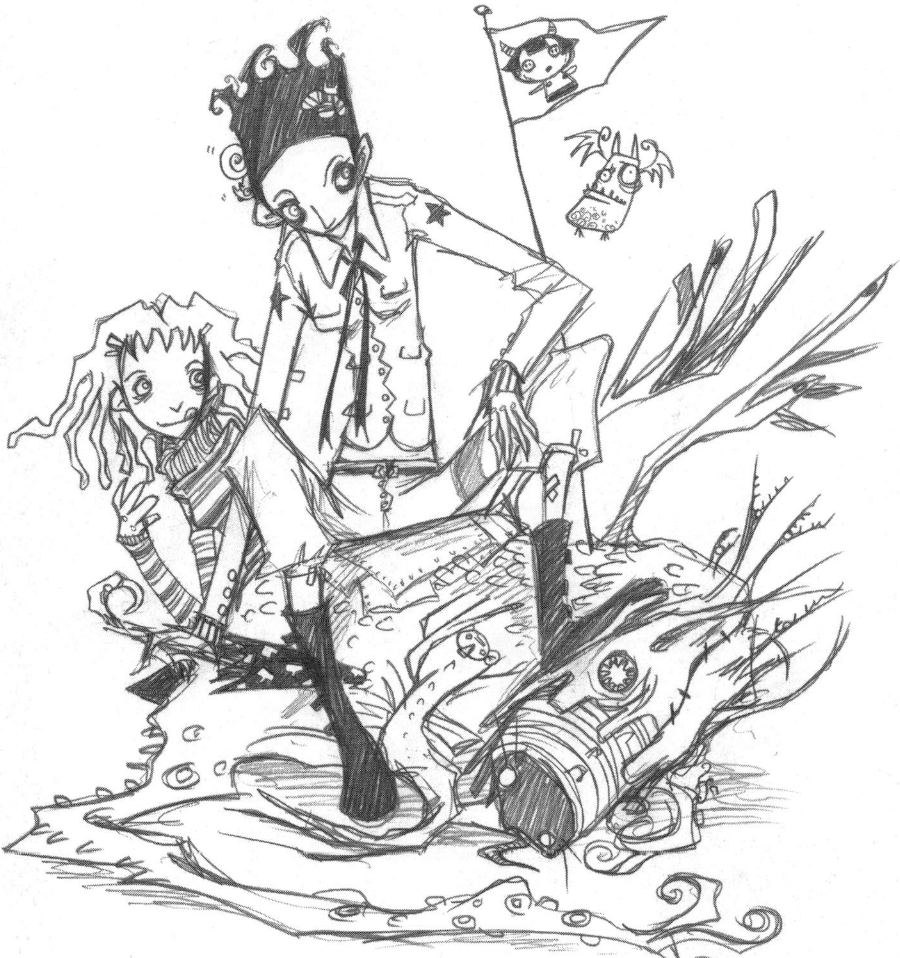

Artwork by FSc
www.fscwasteland.com

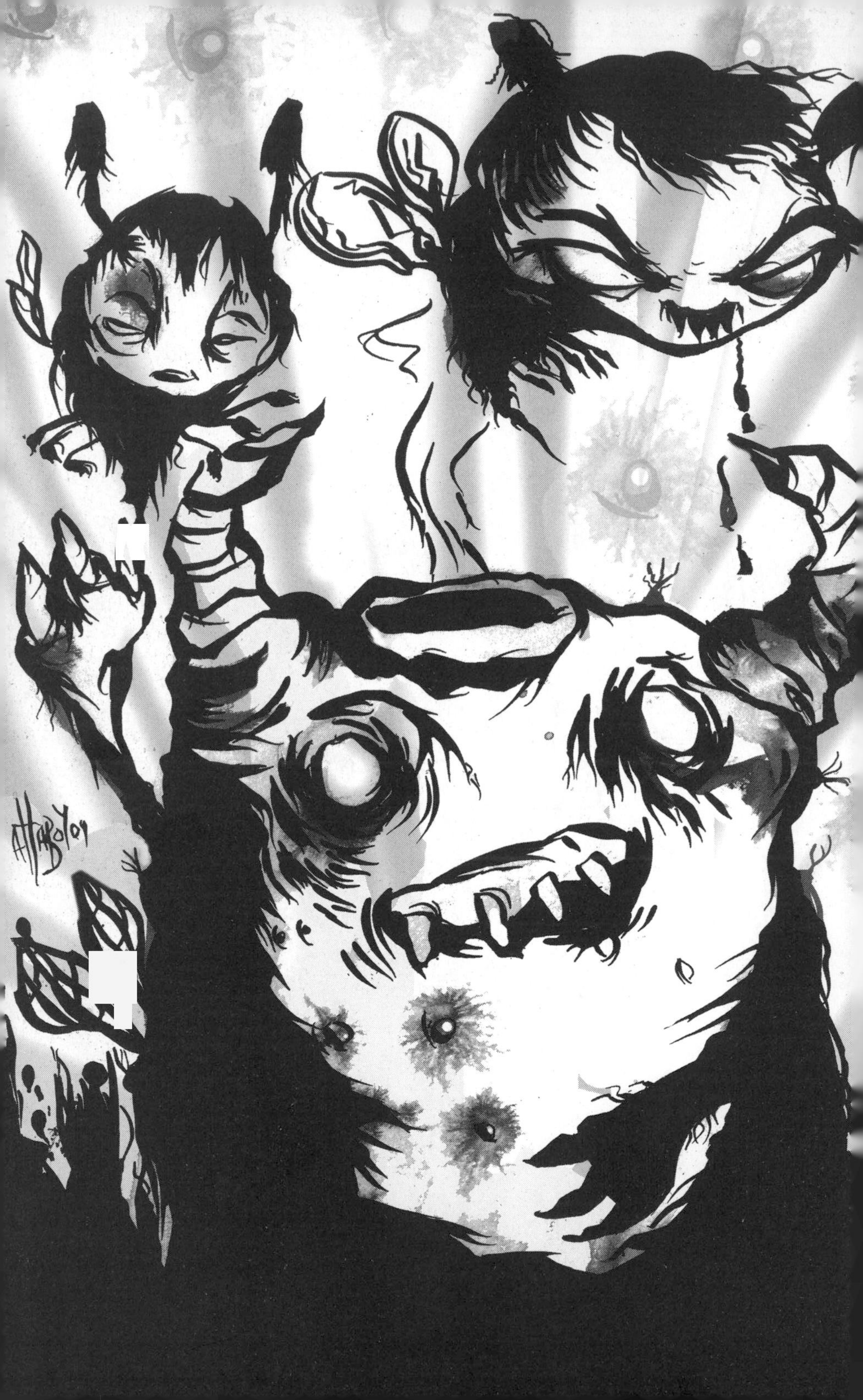